Working Towards Independence
A Practical Guide to Teaching People with Learning Disabilities

Janet Carr and Suzanne Collins

Jessica Kingsley Publishers
London and Philadelphia

First published in the United Kingdom in 1992 by
Jessica Kingsley Publishers Ltd
116 Pentonville Road
London N1 9JB

Copyright © Janet Carr and Suzanne Collins 1992

Second impression 1998

British Library Cataloguing in Publication Data
Carr, Janet
    Working Towards Independence: Practical
    Guide to Teaching People with Learning
    Disabilities
    I. Title II. Collins, Suzanne
    371.9

ISBN 1 85302 140 7

Printed in Great Britain by
Athenæum Press Ltd, Gateshead, Tyne & Wear

Contents

Negative reinforcement, 67. Reinforcement schedules, 67. Fading the reinforcer, 68. Summary, 69. Exercises, 70.

To Joan Bicknell, in admiration and affection

Acknowledgements

We acknowledge with gratitude and admiration the sterling work of the following, who are directly responsible for carrying out many of the programmes described in this book:

Students, residents and workers in all the Wandsworth Social Services residential establishments; residents, students and staff of the Gardiner Hill Unit and at the Bell; students and staff at Atheldene Social Education Centre, Tooting and at Cranstock, Fairways, Fernleigh and Lockwood Adult Training Centres, Surrey; residents and staff at Sendhurst Grange, Surrey and at St Mary's and Maryfield Convents, Roehampton; staff and pupils at St Ann's School, Morden, Surrey.

Michael Andrews, Hilary Davidson, Thomas and Laraine Delgado, Mary, Nora and Patricia Dickinson, Jonathan, Muriel and Don Kilby, Pauline Murphy, Christopher, Mandy, Maureen and Tony Pitman, Paul and Gwen Roberts, Irene Robson, Roslyn Hope and psychologists at Lee Hospital Bromsquare.

We are deeply grateful also to Marina Lewis, Carolyn Wilson-Croome and Mandy Bosworth who contributed substantially to the chapter on Home Management; and to Glyn Murphy and Paul Williams who generously read and commented on the preliminary manuscript.

We are conscious of the degree to which we and the book have benefited from all the help we have received. Nevertheless any errors or misconceptions that remain in the book are the responsibility of ourselves alone.

Part I

General Principles

CHAPTER 1

Introduction

Most of us know one or two people who have a learning disability, if only by sight. Many of us have relatives, or have a friend who has a relative, who has a learning disability. In the past we would have been less likely to be aware of such people than we are now because they would not have been around. 'Mental defectives', the 'subnormal', the 'mentally retarded', the 'feeble-minded', 'imbeciles', 'mentally handicapped' and 'idiots' (all terms used over the last 50 years or so) were seldom seen in the ordinary community because they lived in large institutions, usually in country settings well removed from the majority of the population.

These institutions were called hospitals, and it was generally assumed that, in them, these afflicted people would get the specialist care and treatment that they needed (and, incidentally, be kept well out of the way of everyone else).

The people in these hospitals were, however, with a few exceptions, not ill. They needed very little hospital treatment. What they needed, and still need, is special and extra help with what is their major problem – a difficulty in learning. For this they do not need to live in hospitals at the back of beyond; and they do not need to be treated by doctors and nurses. Increasingly, we acknowledge the right of people with learning disabilities to live in the same areas and in the same community as other people, and that their major needs are not medical but social and, especially, educational. With particular difficulties in learning, ordinary teaching methods may not be adequate; they may need special methods of teaching if they are to learn successfully. This book is about one such special method, the behavioural approach.

What is the behavioural approach?

When we use the behavioural approach we begin by making a careful study of the person concerned. We spend time watching him or her, watching precisely what he does, and how he does it. If he cannot do a task, we look at whether he can do any part of it. We try to sort out which, of the things that he at present has difficulty with, is the most important for him to learn first. We do not consider what most people with learning disabilities do or need. We are concerned with this individual, now.

While we are studying the person in this way we try to note the things he seems to like or enjoy; foods, drinks, activities, sounds, events, interactions with other people. We note as many of these as we can, especially those he seems particularly fond of. Again, we are not concerned with what we, or most people, like, only what this person likes.

Following this period of observation we are in a better position to set out to teach this person. We know what he needs to learn, and we know this not in some vague, general way ('better table manners' or 'shopping skills'), but much more specifically ('to cut meat using a knife and fork', or 'to identify silver coins correctly').

We know, too, the things he enjoys, so that we can use these to encourage his learning: we will make sure that every time he does the task (or some part of it) that we want him to learn, he will get one of the things he enjoys, and this will make it more likely that he will want to attempt the task another time and that, as a result, his learning will progress.

Other aspects of the behavioural approach include ways of sorting out the particular circumstances which make it more likely that the behaviour will occur, including looking carefully at the person's home environment – home, hostel, day service, hospital: special ways to help the person perform tasks; ways of analysing the task so that it is easier to learn; ways of ensuring that, once the person has learnt the task, he can make use of his new skill as and when it will be most useful to him; and ways of helping him get over difficult or problem behaviour. These are all useful aspects of the behavioural approach. They all depend, as does the whole approach, on the analysis of, first, the behaviour; second, what facilitates or triggers the behaviour; and third, what encourages this particular person to perform that behaviour. These form the essential basis of the behavioural approach. Without them it does not exist; with them, people with learning disabilities can make real strides in learning.

Nevertheless, behavioural methods are not only for people with learning disabilities. They are widely used for both children and adults who do not have learning disabilities, to help them get over phobias and fears of all sorts – of dental treatment, of heights or crowds – to deal with handwriting problems, to organise the carrying-out of household chores. In their time both the authors of this book have set up behavioural programmes to help with exam preparation, one for herself and the other for a member of the family.

In all these cases the behavioural methods used were similar to those we describe in this book; anybody, of any ability level, can benefit from them.

What about ethics?

Not everyone is enthusiastic about behavioural methods. Some readers of this book may have heard negative things about such methods – for example, that they lead to heartless, mechanistic treatment of the vulnerable people to whom they are applied. You may feel that the very name 'behaviour modification' (the name by which behavioural approaches are often known), implying as it does that its practitioners are out to force on unwilling victims an alteration of their way of life, invites rejection of the entire concept on moral and ethical grounds. We think these are genuine concerns, which deserve to be thought about very carefully, but we hope to show that they are essentially mistaken.

Let us start with the idea of enforced behaviour change. Behaviour modification is not the only approach which sets out to alter – to develop and expand – people's behaviours. People are doing this all the time in many different ways. Teachers teach children what they, the teachers, think the children ought to learn, and they also try to guide their pupils' behaviour into positive, socially acceptable ways. Parents 'bring up' their children – they not only feed and clothe and nurture and love them, they also try to influence them to grow up into well-adjusted, reasonably honest and truthful adults. Our friends try to influence us – 'I don't think you should buy that outfit, it doesn't suit you, let's go and look at some others' – 'I've cut down on smoking, why don't you try it?'. All around us there are influences working on us – advertisements on hoardings, in newspapers, on television – all trying to steer our behaviour in certain ways. Some medical and psychiatric treatments, psychotherapy, and drug treatments, aim specifically to change people's feelings and behaviour.

So behaviour modification is not alone in this field. Nevertheless, there is a feeling that behaviour modification is more sinister and alarming, that it is more powerful and more controlling, than are the other approaches. There seem to be a number of possible reasons for this. Paradoxically it may stem partly from the very success of the behavioural approach – it does quite often bring about change in a person's behaviour. Another factor may be the very clearly defined goals which are set up in the course of behavioural work and which make it easy to see whether the goals have or have not been attained; more hazy goals (such as 'we want this person to achieve his potential') make it less obvious whether the goal has been (or indeed ever will be) attained, and this too is seen as less regimented and controlling (even if it may at the same time be less helpful to the person). Again, the precise and careful teaching methods used in behavioural work, and the giving of immediate rewards for appropriate behaviours, may be seen, despite the fact that they help the person to learn, as manipulative and inhumane.

There are three aspects of the behavioural approach that seem particularly to worry people: reinforcement; the setting of goals; and the use of aversive techniques. We will look briefly here at each of these, although a more detailed discussion of the topics will be found in later chapters.

Reinforcement

To some people, the whole idea of reinforcement, of giving a reward when someone does what we want, seems immoral, as something close to bribery, or at least as an unwarranted reward for what should have been done anyway. The observation that the society in which we live is reward-based may be an obvious one, but one that cannot, we feel, be denied. Right or wrong, much of our behaviour is driven by the prospect of rewards to come. If we accept that we ourselves work for rewards (most of us would think twice about doing our current jobs if we were not being paid to do them), should we expect people with learning disabilities to perform and to be good just for the sake of it? Their need for reward is no less than ours.

They may, however, be less able to benefit from some rewards which non-learning disabled people enjoy. First, they may not easily link an action with a reward if the two are significantly separated in time. Ordinarily, a person may be willing to do a task on Tuesday, knowing that he will not receive any reward until the following Monday. His awareness that reward *will* follow, his lively expectation of receiving it, makes him willing to carry out the task. In many cases the anticipated reward can be delayed much further, for months or even years (as in the case of writing this book, for example).

For a person with a learning disability who cannot look ahead so far, delayed rewards may not be rewards at all. Where reward does not follow quickly, for whatever reason, the person feels he has failed. Many people with learning disabilities find their efforts are met so often with failure that they come to expect failure. This can lead to a person's becoming unwilling even to attempt tasks, with the result that he is described as 'lazy'. We can help this person's learning by arranging the reward so that it follows the behaviour immediately, so that he not only gains the reward, but also the awareness of success.

Second, there are some kinds of reward that many people experience that may not be so readily available to those with learning disabilities. Often the reward we get for our actions is a quite subtle one; we may want to please another person, or prove to ourselves that we can carry out a task or solve a problem, or we may want to obtain for ourselves a feeling of self-satisfaction at having done something we think of as good. These are very real, if rather intangible, rewards for us; it seems probable that they do not always function as rewards for people with learning disabilities. So when we ask them to do tasks, assuming that they will obtain the same kind of reward that we would in the same circumstances, we may be asking them to do it, in effect, for no reward at all. Since people seldom work for no reward at all it should not surprise us if that person does not throw himself heart and soul into the task. If we think he needs to learn the task then, simply to give him the same chance as we would have in his place, we need to arrange for him to be given something *he* sees as rewarding following his efforts. This cannot, we think, be seen as bribery. We are simply removing from him an unreasonable disadvantage.

Using reinforcement does not stop us trying at the same time to improve a person's general quality of life. Indeed, the use of reinforcement, if it enables the person to learn new skills that he or she otherwise could not learn, may open up whole new areas of experience and pleasure for him or her. Desmond was initially reluctant to take part in strenuous physical activities, but was persuaded to do so by the use of judicious reinforcement and became quite adept at balancing, climbing, and leaping. When his skills were sufficiently advanced he was taken on a week's Outward Bound course and had the time of his life. Without the reinforcers at the beginning he would not have reached the standard that enabled him to be accepted for the course he enjoyed so much.

Perhaps we should point out here that the reinforcers we use are always extras; new, pleasurable things which are added in to the person's life. In the past people aimed at strengthening the power of reinforcers by restricting ordinary access to them; for example, restricting lunch so that food reinforcers could be used in the afternoons. Such methods are never used now. We could not advocate the denial of an individual's rights in this way and, almost always, we can find alternative reinforcers to use.

Extrinsic reinforcers as we have described them are as a rule used in order to get the person over an obstacle to learning which is in itself stopping him from making greater strides to full independence. We may use them for only a short time and will fade them out when they become unnecessary or other, more natural ones take over (see Chapter 4, pp.68–69), but they can be crucially important in helping the person on to the next stage of development. We think that those who object to using reinforcers place unnecessary limitations on the possibility of a full and rewarding life for many people with learning disabilities.

Goal setting

Goals 'should be adopted...to foster the development of the client (not for) the convenience of staff, parents or guardians' (Roos 1977). In the past people have objected that workers using behavioural methods have set goals quite opposite to this definition, goals which aimed to stifle and suppress people with learning disabilities in order to make them more compliant and thus less trouble to the people looking after them. Examples of this kind of practice were brought out into the open and received, quite rightly, a great deal of bad publicity. This had two results: the general public got the fixed idea that such repressive goals were the rule where behavioural interventions were concerned, and behaviourists as a group were brought face to face with these practices and rejected them.

It is now clearly recognised that goals set for people with learning disabilities should involve improving the quality of life of the person concerned. They should essentially be concerned with skills learning, with opening avenues of interest, experience and enjoyment, with enlarging repertoires of ability and widening horizons. Equally essentially, they should not be concerned with simply stamping out behaviours in order to give other people a quiet life. In some cases the interests of the person with a learning disability and those of other people may interact: if the person behaves in ways which are unpleasant or dangerous to others, not only is this unpleasant for those others but the person herself may be avoided and disliked and may lose out socially and educationally. Other people – parents, brothers and sisters, other people with learning disabilities, staff – have rights too, and the rights of all these people need to be balanced. Nevertheless, when we set out goals for a particular client we need to be quite clear that the benefit of the client herself is of first importance.

One of the difficulties of work with people with learning disabilities is reaching an agreement with them on a course of treatment. In many kinds of treatment given in the health service the patient understands pretty well what his treatment involves, and he either agrees to and accepts it or he does not agree and refuses it. People who are prescribed drugs do not by any means always take them. This may annoy the doctors, who feel that the prescriptions are given out in the patient's own interest, but at least the patient has some freedom of choice. In the case of people with learning disabilities it can, because of communication problems, be more difficult to ensure that they understand and agree to any treatment proposed. In the past this was not considered a problem and treatment was put in hand based on the decision of the doctor or psychologist, it being assumed that these professionals knew what was best for the patient. This is now changing, and it is becoming a matter of good practice to involve the person as far as possible in discussion of the goals and aims of the treatment. The difficulty still arises when, because of limited language, the person cannot enter into a discussion and it is not clear how far he or she understands what is said to him or her. In this case it is recognised that the person should be represented in these discussions by another person, a third party who will act in his or her interest, and who will take decisions *as if* they affected the third party him or herself.

This third party can be a relative, or a citizen advocate may be appointed, a volunteer who is attached to the particular person, who gets to know him well, and is then able to speak for him, especially where human rights are concerned. It is important to realise that the advocate will not only protect the person from inappropriate treatments but will also ensure that the person has access to those treatments and opportunities for learning that will help him. So the advocate will be involved in deciding on both the ends – the goals to be chosen, and the means – the kind of intervention to be used. (This representation does not extend to giving legally valid consent for treatment, however beneficial this may promise to be. Nobody, not even a parent or guardian, can give such consent to treatment on behalf of another adult).

The use of aversive techniques

This is the area in which we think that those who object to behavioural methods have the strongest case. In the past, procedures have been undertaken in the name of behavioural methods which were quite horrific. In some cases their use led to what appeared to be a significant improvement in the quality of the person's life; perhaps the use of electric shock in the treatment of self-injury is the best-known example. In some of the most famous cases, people who had seriously injured themselves were treated by electric shock and as a result stopped their self-injurious behaviour and blossomed as people (Lovaas & Simmons 1969). Since some self-injury can be life-threatening the use of electric shock could be justified in its treatment, but the dramatic effects shown then led to shock treatment being used for a number of other, much more trivial behaviour problems. Eventually, the use of this and other punishment procedures resulted in a number of scandals and legal proceedings, the use of punishment declined dramatically and electric shock is, as far as we know, never now used in this way in this country.

Instead, the aim is to tackle problem behaviours using the Least Restrictive Alternative approach (de Kock et al 1984). Positive interventions are thoroughly explored first (see Chapter 7); if these fail then methods involving the manipulation of reinforcement will be tried (see Chapter 7); and only if these also fail, and only if the problem behaviour is of sufficient gravity to warrant it, will aversive techniques be considered. The least restrictive techniques will be tried first – for example a water mist spray, such as those used for spraying indoor plants, was used successfully to stop a person's self-injury (Dorsey et al 1980). Whichever technique is considered, it must be explicitly defined. For example, Time Out, which has come to have negative overtones because it has been associated with shutting a person in a room, has no necessary connection with seclusion. The full title is 'Time out from positive reinforcement'; any pleasurable situation the person is enjoying is briefly interrupted when the problem behaviour occurs (see Chapter 7 for a fuller discussion of Time Out). This can mean something as simple as removing a person's plate of food for ten seconds every time she spits on the plate. Time Out is not synonymous with seclusion, and indeed in some cases seclusion is very far from being Time Out.

If aversive methods, and especially those which involve inflicting even mild levels of pain or discomfort on the person, are to be used they should be so only if informed and continuing consent is given, while if such procedures are to be used in any kind of institution – hospital, hostel, day centre and so on – they should also be overseen by an ethics committee, or in the community by a multi-disciplinary team, which is able to monitor their structure and progress. Those who are to use such methods need training and, especially for relatively junior workers who may be expected to implement the methods on a day-to-day basis, supervision by senior workers. Finally, such methods should be regularly and frequently reviewed to ensure that they are having a positive effect.

Behavioural interventions do carry dangers, and are open to misuse and abuse. The same is true of very nearly every effective type of therapy, from surgery to drugs. That they can be misused is not a reason for abandoning them altogether, when the benefits they can bring are great.

The constructional approach

Theories about how to teach people have been strongly influenced by an idea developed in America by Goldiamond (1974). This idea, the constructional approach, in itself guards against some possible abuses in using behavioural methods , since it states that the main objective of any intervention is to construct new repertoires of behaviour or extend existing ones, rather than simply to get rid of behaviours.

For example, we were asked to see Gita, a young woman with both physical disabilities and learning difficulties, because she spent much of her time with her hand thrust into her mouth. This had been going on for some years and had caused her teeth to become uneven and meant that she dribbled a lot and ruined her clothes. The 'pathological approach' (often seen as the opposite to the constructional approach) would have suggested a solution such as restraining Gita, putting her hands down, using arm restraints etc. The constructional approach we took involved looking at how Gita spent her time and extending those activities which she enjoyed and which enlarged her skills, on the basis that if she were engaged in new activities which she enjoyed she would be less likely to be putting her hands in her mouth. Some of these activities were things involving her hands, such as touching an electronic plate which switched on music on her Walkman, but other skills, abilities and pastimes, not only those involving her hands, were included too.

The constructional approach accords with notions of human rights as it aims to enlarge rather than reduce the number of alternatives available to a person. Hence, it is the approach which we use whenever we can. In Chapter 7, where we discuss a series of interventions which aim, basically, to eliminate problem behaviours, we suggest always starting by trying to construct a positive programme of skill development, and *only* if this fails to use methods designed to eliminate the behaviours. Nevertheless, it is recognised that there are some situations, for example severe aggression or self-injury, where a rapid solution is needed and where the 'pathological approach' may be more appropriate (Goldiamond 1974).

What about normalisation?

Since the 1970s, the concept of normalisation (Tyne 1981) has had a profound influence on those working in the field of learning disabilities.

Briefly, it puts forward the principle that people with learning disabilities should have the same opportunities, using the same means, for the same kinds of life-style and experience as are open to anyone else. So the adult person with a learning disability should be able to use all the ordinary ways taken by ordinary people to acquire jobs, homes, material possessions, personal relationships, education, and so on. Further, where people cannot, because of their learning disability, achieve these socially-valued goals, they should have specialist support and help to attain them; but this support and help should not demean or devalue them as people and the goals aimed for should not be diminished or modified just because the people concerned have learning disabilities.

For example, as a first step towards getting a job, Emerson had the opportunity to spend six months at a workshop in order to build up his work skills. Unfortunately, he found it difficult to get up in the morning and was not arriving at the workshop on time. Rather than say that Emerson was not suitable for work training because of his bad time-keeping and leave it at that, an approach guided by the principles of normalisation indicated that, first, having a job is an important aspect of adult life and is therefore worth pursuing; and second, since what was holding him back was his poor time-keeping he should be given special teaching to help him to reshape his early morning routine so that he would arrive at the training workshop on time. (Emerson's programme is discussed in greater detail in Chapter 13.)

Ideas about normalisation have made us more aware that the physical setting in which services are offered should be as much as possible like those for most people – workshops should be on industrial estates rather than in Day Centres, and homes in houses rather than in hospitals. We have also been made to think about how activities are provided and time-tabled; is this how things would be organised for me or any other ordinary member of the public? Would I be willing to travel on this sort of transport or live in these sorts of conditions? We have become more critical about the ways in which we behave and talk to and talk about people with learning disabilities. Staff who work with people who have learning disabilities are tremendously important, not just in taking part in programming and organisational decisions, but also in setting atmospheres, and in using language which describes the service and the people who use it in respectful and age-appropriate ways.

Normalisation principles, then, give us a sensitive guide to what services and facilities should be available to people with learning disabilities – that these should be the same, or as nearly as possible the same, as those available for anyone else. This does not imply that we know exactly what is needed in every case, but rather that for each person there should be a range of ordinary and socially-valued possibilities. This view has, in turn, influenced us when making decisions about goals and interventions for people who have learning disabilities.

Is normalisation compatible with the behavioural approach?

Normalisation, essentially, does *not* mean just turning people out of hospitals, and dumping them into the community without the special support they require; nor does it mean pretending that their needs are exactly the same as those of 'Mr, Mrs or Miss Average'. What it does is to challenge us to find ways to provide the help which people with learning disabilities need, in ordinary ways and places and with procedures which do not stigmatise or undervalue the people concerned.

Both normalisation and behavioural approaches avoid blaming the person for his or her circumstances. Behavioural approaches tend to do this at the level of detailed interpersonal interactions while normalisation looks at ways in which we can have (inadvertently) damaged the status, competence and quality of life for people through social practices, and especially patterns of service provision. Both these approaches recognise the importance of giving help to people to achieve competence and to overcome their basic disabilities. Within normalisation there is the strong idea that the most up-to-date technologies for teaching should be used to help people and it seems clear that the behavioural approach is one such 'strong' technology.

This is where people who espouse normalisation often part company with the behavioural approach. Behavioural methods are not ordinary, they say – how can you see it as ordinary if a person is given a Smartie each time he puts a piece of cutlery on a dining table? Where in the ordinary world do you see a star chart in an adult's bedroom? These methods treat people with learning disabilities as less than human and are therefore unacceptable.

There is some truth in this. Certainly it would be unusual to see a non-disabled person being given Smarties (for one reason, not that many are enamoured of Smarties) but we have run programmes with non-disabled adult people and used whatever they particularly fancied as reinforcers. In fact, we seldom use Smarties and other sweets as reinforcers; we find adults prefer other things, and a cup of tea (which would not be out of keeping in a dining-room setting) is one of the most frequently chosen.

Charts have been used in programmes for people of all ability levels and, if it seems more appropriate, we can always conceal such a chart in a folder or inside a cupboard door.

We thus try to ensure that the programmes respect the dignity and integrity of the person they are intended to help. This is important, and on any occasion when methods appear to conflict with normalisation, they would not be adopted without careful consideration and only when we believed that short-term disadvantages were outweighed by the likelihood of longer-term achievements. If we look back at p.22, we see that normalisation rests on the principle that, where people cannot achieve their goals, they should have 'specialist support and help'; this the behavioural approach can help to provide. If the normalisation principle determines the goals we should be aspiring to for people with learning disabilities, the behavioural approach can help them to attain these.

Normalisation thus provides a very helpful context for behavioural approaches. It broadens our perception of what goals we can and should pursue and helps us to go beyond goals which are concerned only with direct development of new skills or the avoidance of problem behaviours. Normalisation is itself an ideology based ultimately on moral and ethical issues of equality and justice. As such, it is made up of a detailed set of guidelines which can help to avoid the abuses of and objections to behavioural methods which we have mentioned earlier in this chapter.

Who can use the behavioural approach?

In the past, the behavioural approach was thought of as a highly technical affair that could be put into practice only by highly trained specialists who worked in special centres and who alone had the expertise to carry out the programmes with sufficient rigour for them to be effective. Certainly, the specialists produced some interesting results. Other facts began, however, to emerge. First, there were not enough experts to go round the number of people with learning disabilities who needed help. Second, people could perform the skills they learnt within the special centre under the eye of the expert, but these skills often deserted them when they returned to their more usual surroundings, with their own families or teachers. So a move was made towards teaching the skills in the person's usual surroundings, to transferring the teaching skills from the 'experts' to those who had much more to do with the person – the families, teachers, care staff and so on. These other people were well able to learn behavioural methods, and to use them to teach people with learning disabilities. As more people have heard about these methods and how useful they are in helping to deal with the problems that people with learning disabilities encounter, the more the demand has grown for teaching in the methods.

This is not to say that those working with people with learning disabilities have gone overboard about behavioural methods. They do not usually need any special methods, but use much the same methods as they would use with anyone else, perhaps taking them rather more slowly, perhaps repeating important points, and progress is made. If, however, progress slows down or problems persist, extra help may be needed. Then behavioural methods can be brought in, to help get over the particular difficulty. Once this has been done things can go back to normal and the behavioural methods can be put aside.

The fact that they are used does not mean that they are a life sentence, to be used for ever. Sometimes, it is true, people find that one or two of the methods can be kept going without too much strain, almost as second nature, reinforcing small pieces of appropriate behaviours for example, or teaching parts of a task rather than all of it at once. But the systematic, concentrated approach will be used only as long as it is needed.

How much time will it take?

How long we need to spend on a programme depends partly on the kind of programme and partly on how much time we have to spend. If, on the one hand, we want to help the person to learn a skill, such as cleaning fingernails or knowing the difference between a 10p and a 20p piece, we can decide at what time of day we will do it, and how long we will do it for. If on the other hand we are working on a programme to lessen a behaviour and this means that we have to react to the behaviour (supposing for example we have decided that whenever Tania pokes her eyes we will hold her hands down) then we have to do that whenever the behaviour occurs. It is difficult to say in advance how much time that will take.

It is difficult, too, to say how long it will take to teach a particular skill or to deal with a problem behaviour. One very difficult behaviour (aggression and violence) was virtually gone within ten weeks, whereas another, apparently minor, problem we have worked on (late attendance at the Day Centre) is almost unchanged despite two years of intensive efforts. Similarly, we cannot predict with any confidence how long it will take to teach a particular skill, although, interestingly enough, once we have drawn up a specific programme, with specific reinforcers (see Chapter 4) and have begun to have even quite brief teaching sessions it has often surprised us how quickly the person has learnt: 'I was amazed at how quickly she cottoned on'.

How much can we hope to achieve?

We believe behaviour modification to be a powerful, effective tool for the teacher, and especially useful for teaching people for whom other ordinary teaching methods have been unsuccessful. Nevertheless, it is not all-powerful; it is not magic. We cannot say that it will cause all problems to melt away, nor that it will always work. The examples we quote in this book are mainly from programmes which have worked because we think these should be the most helpful, but we have quoted some that have failed, and you can be sure that there are a good many others we could have described. If behaviour modification is not magic we most certainly are not magicians. Nevertheless, with our emphasis on individual observation and individual programmes we tend to meet failure, not with 'It's no good, she can't do it', but with 'Something in the programme isn't right. Let's go back and look at the behaviour again, and see whether there is something in the programme we could change to give it a better chance of success'. Putting the responsibility for success on the programme, not on the strengths and weaknesses of the person is, we think, one of the cardinal virtues of the behavioural approach. If one thing doesn't work, we think again and try another. If we see that we have been too ambitious, we try for something more attainable but still valuable – if the person is unlikely to be able to learn to drive a car we will at least try to teach him how to get about by public transport.

Asking for help from outside

Trying to rethink a programme is hard work. Talking it over with somebody else can often give it a boost. If you are having difficulties it could be worthwhile asking for outside help, somebody from your local Community Team for People with Learning Disabilities, or your local psychological service. They may have ideas that have not occurred to you, while your ideas, and the experience you have had already, will be invaluable to them.

Nevertheless, we know that not all our programmes will succeed. We do not give up too easily and, if a programme fails to work, we look first at the reasons for this and what else we could try (see Chapter 16 for some suggestions on how to go about this). In some cases, however, we seem never to find the right answer: we have to accept the situation as it is and soldier on, giving as much support as we can to those in direct contact with the person and remaining always on the alert for any new approach that may offer new hope of a better solution.

Settings described in this book

In the examples we give in this book, we describe the places in which the people are living and where they work, and we realise that in many cases these are not ideal. We are describing things which have actually happened, so if we say that someone was living in a hostel and spending his days in a social education centre, that was how it was. It does not mean that we think that this is how it should be for everybody, nor that we think that we should use the training methods we describe to fit people into these settings; it is just that it is how things are at the moment for most people with learning disabilities. Many of the behaviours and problems previously associated with learning disabilities can be eliminated by environmental changes. Much of our work, in contrast with that of 10–15 years ago, is now concerned with changing institutions and with finding ways of teaching people, both those who live at home and those who have been in institutions, how they can extend the range and variety of their skills so that they can cope more independently.

This more 'political' side of our work with people with learning disabilities seems to us to be compatible with the skills-teaching approach we outline in this book. Problem behaviour is closely connected with general deprivation and lack of skills. To concentrate on both environmental change, and the development of skills, is a constructive approach which we feel in the end will pay dividends for everyone concerned.

What you will find in this book

The book falls into two sections. In Part I we describe the behavioural approach in general. Part II is concerned with ways of teaching some of the skills that adults with learning disabilities may need to learn and of tackling some particular problem behaviours. The last chapter looks at problems that may come up in this kind of work and offers some suggestions on how to deal with them.

What you won't find in this book

There are some topics we have not been able to cover in this book, usually because we ourselves have little or no experience of work in that area. One of these is language. Where adults' language skills are concerned, the work is usually the province of speech therapists and we have not been much involved with it. Neither have we dealt with recreational pursuits, nor with the major issue of sex. We realise that these are serious omissions, but, partly because they are such large topics, their inclusion would make this an unwieldy book. (In the case of sex the first intervention approach might not in any case be a behavioural one.) We have given at the end of the book some references to relevant books and articles to help those whose problems lie in these areas.

Most of the examples we give in the book are of work that we or our colleagues have done. In some cases, however, we have read of work by other people that seems particularly useful or apt; we have described these briefly and given the full reference so that anyone who would like to can read these in the original.

Finally, two points on our use of words. First, as we pointed out at the beginning, many different terms have been used to identify the people we are talking about, and when we started on the book the term 'People with mental handicaps' was the one used. Things have changed, and now 'People with learning disabilities' is the one preferred in the United Kingdom, and so that is the one used in the book.* Second, where we talk about 'a person' rather than about some particular individual we have tried to use 'he' and 'she' impartially. Learning disabilities affect both sexes; we do not want to imply that it is either exclusively or predominantly a masculine or feminine condition, nor that the work we do ignores the needs of either women or men.

Exercises

At the end of each chapter we have included exercises which are meant to provide a chance to think about ways of tackling different problems, using the ideas and methods described in the chapter.

At the end of the book we have given our answers to some of the questions, so that your answers can be compared with ours. You shouldn't worry too much if yours are not the same as ours; there are often many different ways of tackling these problems, but we thought that we should at least show that we have thought about them too.

---

* If any reader feels that another form of words would be better, we would be happy to hear from them.

CHAPTER 2

Looking at Behaviour

When we use behavioural methods, everything we do starts with observation of the person we want to work with. We try to make no assumptions about what he does or what makes him tick. Even if we know him quite well, we will begin by watching him carefully to see what, exactly, he does; when he does it; where; who with; how often. Everything we do depends on this; without this we may be trying to work from false impressions. Something the person does may loom large in our minds because it is important (the 'He does it all the time' effect) although it may actually occur quite rarely; our idea of what he does, and when and where, may be quite hazy, missing a lot of detail; we may see mainly what we want to see. If the person is someone we are fond of, we may overlook a good deal of tiresomeness; if he is someone we do not care for, we may simply ignore reasonable behaviours. Furthermore, if we can gain a clear, accurate picture of exactly what the person is doing *now* we can compare this with what he does once we have begun our programme and can see whether or not this is working.

What to observe

When we make our observations, we look very specifically at what the person *does*: his movements, actions, words, facial expressions and so on. These are the stuff of our observations. We try hard *not* to include what we think of as his or her ideas, moods, feelings, or wishes, unless he tells us of these himself. We say 'He became red in the face, used swear words and slammed the door'; not 'He was angry'.

In everyday life we often say things like, 'He was angry', 'She was lonely'. These expressions are a shorthand which gives us a general idea of what the person did, and most of us understand the shorthand pretty well – up to a point. The snag is that our interpretation of the shorthand may be, first, wrong: what we think the person was feeling may not be what he was feeling at all, so that when we say 'that boy is sad' the boy may simply be deep in thought. Second, our interpretation of the shorthand may differ from somebody else's. To see what we mean by this, let's look at an example.

As an exercise in observation, somebody wrote down what she saw in a dentist's waiting room. It went like this:

> Mrs Jones arrived at the reception desk. She gave her name and the receptionist showed her to the waiting room. She was flustered and breathing rather heavily, and she sat down and leafed through the pages of an old magazine, obviously very anxious. She put the magazine down and started to bite her fingernails. Going to the dentist really worried her.

We can reorganise this description into two columns, under the headings 'Description' and 'Interpretation'.

Description	*Interpretation*
Mrs Jones arrived at the reception desk.	
She gave her name.	
Receptionist showed her to the waiting room.	
She was breathing heavily.	She was flustered.
She sat down.	
She leafed through the pages of a magazine.	Looking obviously very anxious.
She put the magazine down.	
She started to bite her nails.	Going to the dentist really worried her.

Some of the things which were written down that morning were straight-forward descriptions of what Mrs Jones did, but some of them were interpretations, what the person thought that Mrs Jones' behaviour meant. The column on the left shows the descriptions, while the interpretations are on the right hand side. Two interpretations indicate that Mrs Jones seemed anxious, and that she seemed worried. Supposing we asked our observer to write down the things that Mrs Jones did that made her seem worried; in this case, the list would consist of:

- Breathing rather heavily;
- Leafing quickly through the pages of a magazine;

- Biting her fingernails.

'Worried' and 'anxious' are rather 'fuzzy' words and may mean different things to different people, and we cannot be sure whether any of these three really do mean that Mrs Jones is either worried or anxious. In this case it was possible to talk to Mrs Jones, and she said that yes, she does bite her nails if she is worried, but that she was breathing heavily because she had been running, and she only flicked through the magazine because she had read it before. Two of the things which we thought showed that she was worried were quite misleading. We are on safer ground if, when we are making our observations, we note what the person actually says and does, and steer clear of interpretations. We try to describe the behaviour we are observing in clear, concrete terms – 'He hit out with his fist, kicked at the dog and screamed'; we try to avoid 'fuzzies' – 'He was aggressive'.

In fact, 'aggression' is a well known 'fuzzy'. An instructor in a Social Education Centre (SEC) asked for help with Stephen, who, he said, was 'often aggressive': Stephen is a young man in his late teens who has attended the SEC since he left school, and is very good friends with the instructor. He has little speech and, to attract attention, he will often pull someone's clothing; if the person does not respond at once, he pulls harder and sometimes even tears the clothes or hits the person. If this leads to a scuffle, other people may try to help, but this often makes matters worse, with Stephen, and sometimes other people also being hurt.

Tugging at people's clothes hardly seems like aggression, but as this behaviour sometimes preceded an incident which turned out to be quite dangerous, we decided to observe and to count how often Stephen (1) tugged other people's clothes; (2) tore clothes and pulled off buttons; and (3) hit other people.

Once the instructors started to observe and record Stephen's behaviour they realised, first, that he tugged at people very frequently and on most occasions this did not lead to a fight, or to clothes being torn. Second, tearing clothes and pulling off buttons did not seem to be deliberate, but appeared to happened accidentally. Third, if people who did not know him very well tried to intervene, the situation almost always deteriorated. However, these acutely difficult incidents occurred very infrequently – less than once a month. So these observations were useful in making the behaviour and the surrounding events clearer, while they also put the problem into better perspective. This highlights the advantages of making observations. Violence or extreme behaviour of any kind often colours our general impressions of people. Actually observing and recording a person's behaviour can give us a better perspective on how severe the problem really is.

What else goes on?

As well as looking at what the person does, we need to look at what else is going on at the same time. Where does the behaviour happen – does it happen more in one place than in another? Who does it happen with – more with certain people than others? When – at any particular time of the day, or day of the week? Any of these antecedent events, things which are going on before and when the behaviour happens, can make a difference to it, and knowing about them can give us clues as to what we should do about it. They are of two main types; setting conditions and triggers. Setting conditions are the main features of the environment which are present when a behaviour occurs – for example, the setting for hailing a bus is queuing on the pavement beside a bus stop; the trigger is the immediate cause of the behaviour – in the case of hailing a bus, catching sight of it coming round the corner.

Another important question concerns the consequences of behaviour. What happens afterwards and, especially, how do people react to it? The consequences, together with the antecedents and the behaviours, make up what has been called the ABC of behaviour. It was not called this to fool ourselves that it was easy, but to remind ourselves that, when we begin to look at a problem, these are the areas in which we need to have a great deal of detailed knowledge. We have thus broken our analysis down into detailed areas so that we can begin to see how settings, triggers, behaviours and consequences are related to each other. We are then on the road to tackling and, maybe, solving the problem.

Recording our observations

Once we have decided to make observations, it can be helpful not just to try to keep them in our heads, but to write them down. Busy people carry an enormous amount of information in their heads and some things will get crowded out. It is easy enough to forget whether Sue said 'thank you' five times or seven, or whether Zoë's bed was wet on Thursday as well as Monday, Friday and Saturday, or whether that was last week. If we write down our observations, we have a permanent record of what happened. Later on, we can look back to see whether things have changed or remained the same – this would be quite difficult if we had to rely on memory.

Different ways of recording

(1) Continuous recording. We settle ourselves down with a pad of paper and a pencil and we try to write down everything that happens. This can be quite a good way to start, to get an idea of what is going on. Harry's uncle knew that Harry was not able to dress himself completely and independently, but he did not really know how much Harry could and couldn't do on his own. He started, then, by watching Harry in the morning from the time he got out of bed until he left the house, and he wrote down as much as he could of what he did. He found that Harry could put on his underclothes, his socks, jumper and trousers, but needed help with buttons, zips and laces. He also found that Harry could wash his hands well but needed help with his face and neck, and that he could brush his teeth and hair, but could not unscrew the toothpaste tube or squeeze the toothpaste out accurately onto the brush. By keeping this kind of a record, Harry's uncle was able to learn a good deal about what Harry was doing in the mornings.

It was, however, quite a time-consuming and difficult procedure. Harry's uncle found that each time he stopped to write something down he missed what Harry was doing at that particular moment, while he also found that, because so much was going on, there were a good many things that he had no time to write down, and it worried him that some of the things he did not write down might have been just as important as those he did. Later on, then, when he had got a better idea of the overall situation, he went on to use one of the other methods to record more specific parts of Harry's routine.

(2) Event recording. When we use event recording, we select one, or two, or even more, kinds of behaviour, and record them every time they occur. For example, we might record every time someone brushed her teeth, or used the toilet, or went out of the house. If the event we have chosen occurs very frequently, so that much of the day would be taken up in recording it, we may choose to record it over only a particular period of the day. Jennifer's sister was trying to help her stop biting her nails. As they were both at work during the day, they chose the period after their evening meal together to count the number of times her nails went into her mouth. They had already found that this period in the evening, between supper and bedtime, was a time during which Jennifer did a good deal of nail-biting, so, in order to have some time in the evening to relax, they recorded the nail-biting only in the first hour after their evening meal.

If, on the other hand, the behaviour happens quite infrequently, it may be possible to record every time that it happens, throughout the day, without putting too much stress on the person doing the observations.

Most people using event recording jot down their observations on a piece of paper. They write down the kind of behaviour they want to record, and then they have only to put a tick, or a cross, to show that the behaviour has occurred. This saves a lot of writing. It is particularly helpful if they want to record more than one behaviour at a time, in which case they will write down each of these behaviours and put the tick or cross against each as it occurs. So, if Jennifer's sister had wanted to record not only her nail-biting but also another habit, of cleaning one fingernail with another, she would have made a record sheet something like this:

Nail-biting ✓ ✓ ✓ ✓ ✓ ✓ ✓ ✓
Nail-cleaning ✓ ✓ ✓

If only one behaviour is being recorded, a device such as a golf tally (used by golfers to record the number of strokes they have taken) or a knitting counter can be convenient. Each time the behaviour occurs, we move the counter up another notch.

(3) **Duration recording**. When we use duration recording, we record how long a particular piece of behaviour goes on for.

Some kinds of behaviour are not easy to count because they do not have discrete beginnings and ends. For example, if we try to record somebody smiling, or working in the garden, it would be quite difficult to say when one smile began and ended, and although we could record when somebody first started and then stopped working in the garden, it might not tell us very much about the amount of work he had done. For these sorts of behaviours, it can be more informative if we record not just that they happened, but how long they lasted. For example, Hugh and Sadiq both had sleep difficulties, although their problems were quite different. Hugh slept a great deal, in fact the worry was that he was sleeping far too much. Sadiq was just the opposite; he was driving his family to distraction by staying awake for most of the night. If we had been using an event recording method there would have been very little difference between them; in one 24-hour period, they both went to sleep twice. Using duration recording, however, we found that Hugh actually slept for 15 hours of the 24, while Sadiq slept for only three, and that made each problem very much clearer.

A cumulative stop-watch (one which can be started and stopped and then re-started to continue where it left off the last time) is very useful when carrying out duration recording. An instructor in a workshop wanted to record how long James spent actually working each morning. The instructor had a cumulative stop-watch and so, every time James began to work, he set the watch going; when James left off work to chat, he stopped it, then restarted it when James began his work again, stopped it when James was off to the toilet, restarted it when he returned to work, and stopped it again when James went to have his coffee. By lunchtime each day, the instructor had a total of how much time James had actually spent working that morning.

This makes duration recording very easy, but it is quite possible to make duration recordings using an ordinary watch or a clock, especially if these have a minute hand. This does also involve having a pencil and piece of paper to jot down the times at which the behaviours start and stop.

(4) Partial interval recording.* Using this method, we divide up the period which we have set aside for our observations into intervals. These intervals can be of any length we choose – five minutes, ten minutes, half-an-hour, a day, a week – what we choose is up to us. At the end of each interval we record whether or not the behaviour we are interested in has occurred. It does not matter whether this behaviour has happened one or 20 times in the interval, we simply have to record 'yes it has', or 'no it has not' happened.

This is quite a simple form of record-keeping, and makes it easy to record more than one piece of behaviour at a time. Robert was trying to give up smoking. Before he set about it he thought he would see whether he smoked at certain times of the day, rather than at others, and also how this related to his cups of coffee. He decided to use partial interval recording, and a section of his record sheet looked like this:

	09.45 -10.00	10.00 -10.15	10.15 -10.30	10.30 -10.45	10.45 -11.00	11.00 -11.15	11.15 -11.30	11.30 -11.45	11.45 -12.00
Cigarettes	✓	x	✓	x	✓	x	x	✓	x
Coffee	x	x	✓	x	x	x	x	✓	x

---

* There is also whole interval sampling. We have never found it an appropriate method to use.

He found that he always had a cigarette in intervals when he drank coffee; however, he had cigarettes at other times as well, and these times seemed to be quite evenly spaced over the morning.

When we use partial interval recording, we have to keep alert to the passing of time so that we do not let several intervals go past without any recording being made, especially if not very much is happening. It makes it easier if we set a kitchen timer, or an alarm clock, to go off at the end of each interval, and reset it again each time it goes off. Partial interval recording is quite easy to manage if the behaviour is occurring quite frequently, or if it occurs at the beginning of the interval; we can then mark it off and relax until the next interval begins. However, if the behaviour is occurring very infrequently, or does not occur at all, we may have to remain alert right to the end of the interval, then record that it has not happened, and then begin again with the next interval. So this kind of recording can get to be rather hard work.

(5) Momentary time sampling. Here we again divide the selected time period up into intervals. This time, however, we observe whether or not the behaviour is happening at only one point in the interval, usually at the end of it. So Robert would record whether he had been smoking, or having a cup of coffee, during the few seconds before 10.00am, 10.15am, and so on.

We have used time sampling to record the work performance of a group of 18 people with profound learning and physical disabilities, who work in a large room from 10.00am to 12.00 midday. Some of the people have staff working with them, and some work alone. Each hour is divided into ten-minute intervals, and in the last 15 seconds of each interval, an observer looks up and checks whether each of the people in the group is working, and records this on a sheet (see below). At the same time she can record which people have staff working with them and which are working alone. Even for quite large numbers (in this case 18 people) and relatively short intervals, this method makes record-keeping quite straightforward. The observer has each person's name written down, and observes and records the behaviour of each one in the same order each time.

	Joe	Ellie	Tess	Paul	Chris	Tim	Alice	Jean	Mark	Ali
10.00	x	x	x	x	x	x	x	x	x	x
10.10	✓ 0	✓	✓	✓	✓	x	✓	✓	✓	x
10.20	✓	✓ 0	✓	✓	✓	x	✓	✓	✓	x
10.30										

(and so on)

Key: ✓ = Working;   x = Not working;   0 = Member of staff present

Besides being quite manageable, time sampling has the advantage that, if two people were making records at the same time, and were accurate about the observation time, it is very likely that they would record the same event. This means that it is the most efficient way of ensuring the reliability of two people's records – that is, the extent to which two people observing a behaviour agree on the behaviour that they record (reliability is discussed further on page 42). Using any of the other methods we have described, we can be less certain that two observers would record the same behaviour.

(6) Other measurement methods. Sometimes it is possible to make records which do not depend so much on observations of the person we are interested in, as on certain physical measurements. For example, for somebody who wants to lose (or gain) weight, a useful measure would be their actual weight, which can be recorded at certain fixed times. Another kind of measurement that we can make is of the *results* of somebody's activity. For example, if someone is doing mathematical calculations, or making Christmas cards, we can count the number of sums they complete, or the Christmas cards they produce. This is a record of 'permanent products'. Albert worked assembling exhaust clamps. A simple way of recording how much work he was doing every day was to count how many clamps were completed at the end of each day. We could then see how much skill he was acquiring by seeing how many more of the clamps he was able to produce as time went on.

Baselines

The record of the observations we take of what the person can do before we start to help him learn is called a baseline. So, before we start to teach the person to put on some garments or to give up smoking, we record how many garments he can put on and how well; or how much he is smoking, and when and where, at present. This is an extremely important stage in any teaching programme because, unless we know what the person does before we start our teaching, we have no way of knowing whether our intervention is actually working. Once we have a baseline, we can then take further records when our teaching has been in progress for some time and compare how much the person can do now with what he was able to do before.

A record may show that a behaviour is happening more often, or less often, over time; or it may show that, although the behaviour varies a bit, there is no consistent trend either up or down. Examples of these three kinds of record are shown below.

When baseline records are being taken, the most satisfactory for most purposes is a stable baseline, showing that, before we begin our intervention, the behaviour was fairly regular, neither increasing nor decreasing. Ascending or descending baselines suggest that, even if we are doing nothing deliberately about it, something is happening to alter the rate of the behaviour. In particular, if we are recording a negative behaviour, which we would like to reduce, and we get a descending baseline, then something is already reducing the behaviour; so there may be no need for us to do anything further about it. In fact it is not uncommon for negative behaviours to decline when baselines are taken, although it is not always clear why this should be so.

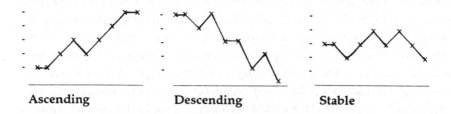

Ascending   Descending   Stable

Kay was a 'misery', often having long bouts of crying which, besides being distressing for her, upset everyone around her. Tina decided to try to help her, and began by taking a baseline. In the two weeks' baseline period Kay had only one period of crying which lasted about five minutes. When we tried to think why this should be, Tina suggested that Kay might have been getting, because of the baseline, more attention when she was not crying: she had noticed that, when she popped her head into the room to see how Kay was, Kay would look at her and smile, and Tina would smile back. You can see that this means that the observation of Kay's behaviour did not provide a true baseline, in that it involved a slight change in Tina's behaviour towards Kay, whereas, in a true baseline, the behaviour is treated exactly as it has always been. In practice it can sometimes be impossible to treat the behaviour exactly as it has been, if only, as in Tina's case because it must be observed and recorded. However, with so happy an outcome, even the most dedicated scientist among us can hardly repine.

Similarly, if we want to build up a skill, such as table-laying or good time-keeping, and if the baseline shows the skill already increasing, this is not the moment to embark on special teaching – the person may develop the skill quite satisfactorily without it. In either case, if we started on a programme to decrease a negative behaviour when the baseline was descending, or to increase one where the baseline was ascending, we would not know whether any successful outcome was due to the programme or to some other factor that was in operation before the programme started. So, in either case, the most useful thing to do is nothing, apart from continuing the baseline record. Then, if after a while the behaviour levels out, we start our programme: if it shows the behaviour reduced (or developed) to the point where everyone is happy with it, we just smile.

Making sure the effect was the programme's

We may think it important to know whether the programme we have been using was really responsible for any change in the behaviour that we see. Our programme is, after all, not the only thing happening to the person. Other things in his life may change – the weather, or his health, may get better or worse, he may lose a friend or gain one, routines at home or at work may be altered. Any of these may be responsible for a change in the person's behaviour, and the fact that our programme started at the same time may be just coincidence.

It may seem obvious that our programme has brought about change. We take a baseline; then we start the programme. At this point the behaviour changes.

A   B

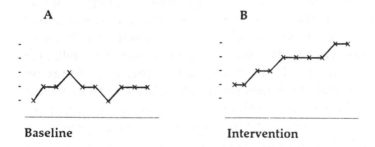

Baseline   Intervention

This is called an AB design, where A is the baseline and B the programme or intervention. While this looks pretty convincing, some people have felt that, with this kind of record, there was a possibility that something else might have happened, simultaneously with the start of the programme, which could in fact have caused the change. So, for a time, it was fashionable to use ABAB designs, in which first the baseline was followed by the intervention; then, when a change had taken place, the programme was stopped for a time and a further baseline was taken. Finally, the programme was reinstated until the behaviour reached a satisfactory state. So the records looked something like this:

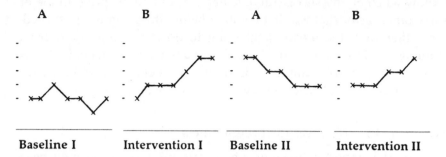

A	B	A	B
Baseline I	Intervention I	Baseline II	Intervention II

Since the behaviour changed whenever the programme was in or out of use, it seemed sufficiently certain that the programme *was* responsible for the change.

This gave the interventionists confidence that they were working along the right lines. There are however some serious drawbacks to ABAB designs, of which the main one is the unwillingness of practically all right-minded people to discontinue a successful programme and to see success jeopardised. Fortunately there are a couple of other things we can do, if we want to ensure that it is the intervention, and not some other serendipitous coincidental happening, that is responsible for the change.

The first is to use what is called a multiple baseline design. We take several baselines – say, three – at once. These can be baselines across settings, or subjects, or activities/problems. So, if we wanted to work on messy eating habits, we could take baselines for Harold's food-spilling at home, in his day centre, and in the Wimpy bar he goes to on Saturdays (across settings); we could take them for Harold, Clark and Hugh (across subjects); or we could take them for Harold's food-spilling, food-grabbing, and gobbling (across problems). We would then start the programme in one condition, while continuing to take baselines on the other two; later we extend the programmes to the second condition; and later again to the third. If we find that the behaviour changes each time the intervention is put into operation, we can feel pretty sure that it, and not something else, has produced the change.

Alternatively, we may be able to use a 'matching to criterion' design. After taking a baseline, we begin the intervention, requiring (say) a fairly low level of behaviour from the person. Gradually, as he makes progress, we require increasingly better levels of behaviour. If, each time we raise the

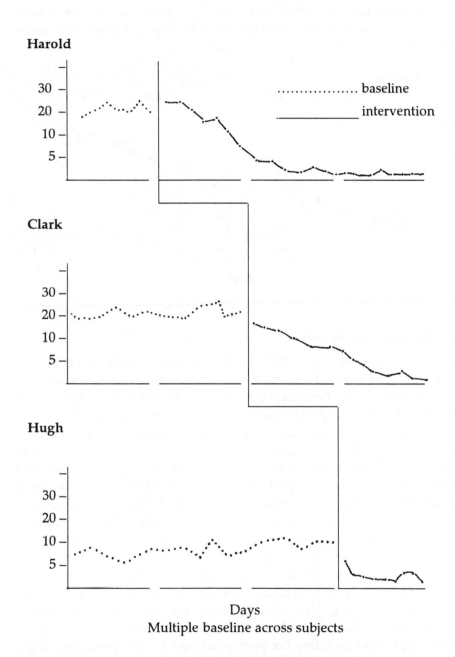

Days

Multiple baseline across subjects

criterion, he increases the level of his behaviour, it seems likely that it is the programme that is affecting his behaviour. An example of this was a programme to help Simon to get up in the mornings. At first he was reinforced for getting up by 7.45am, then by 7.40am, then 7.35am, finally by 7.30am. Each time he was reinforced for getting up earlier, he was able to do so.

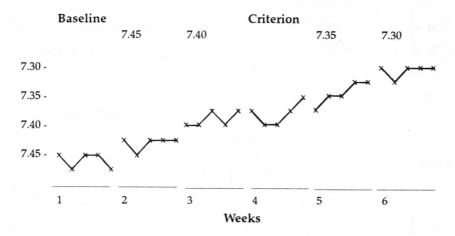

The reliability of records

We have already mentioned that momentary time sampling is a good way of ensuring that records are reliable. We particularly need to know that records are reliable, because we need to know that any changes in the records are due to real changes in what the person is doing, and are not due to mistakes made by the observer. Although the observer may have every intention of recording only what happens, many things can contribute towards mistakes – she may be tired or upset, she may have many other things on her mind; if she particularly likes or dislikes the person she is observing, her observations may be biased. In particular, it has been found that if the observer knows that no checks will be made on her observations, she is more likely to be careless. If two observers are recording the behaviour at the same time, these slips are likely to show up as disagreements between the records. On the other hand, if two observers, using time sampling, finish up with records which are substantially in agreement, we can be reasonably sure that what they have recorded is what happened.

One factor which can make for disagreements between the records of two people (and therefore for poor reliability) is poor definition of the behaviour in question. For example, if the observers agree to record the number of handshakes that take place, one observer may be counting a handshake as an up-and-down shake of the hands, while another may count each 'up' and each 'down' as a handshake, while a third may count it as a handshake from the time the hands meet until they part. Discussion in advance solves many of these problems, while practice in carrying out the observations, followed by redefinition of the behaviour if necessary, can bring much closer agreements between observers.

When two observers have taken records of the same behaviour over the same time period, the reliability of their records is worked out by counting how often they agreed on whether or not the behaviour occurred, and how often they disagreed. Further, we may count separately the agreements and disagreements on when the behaviour *did* occur and when it didn't (because if, for example, a behaviour occurs only very infrequently, there is a good chance that the two records would agree highly even if one observer simply recorded that it never happened at all). In each case, the number of agreements is divided by the number of agreements plus the number of disagreements, and the result multiplied by 100 to express it as a percentage. So, suppose the two observers agreed on the occurrence of the behaviour twenty times, and disagreed on the occurrence twice: and they agreed on the non-occurrence twelve times and disagreed on the non-occurrence six times. Overall, they agreed 32 times and disagreed eight times. So the overall reliability is:

$$\frac{32}{8+32} \times 100 = \frac{32}{40} \times 100 = 80\%$$

Reliability is usually thought to be acceptable at 80% and above, so that looks pretty good. However, if we look at the occurrences and non-occurrences of the behaviour separately, we can see that, although the occurrences yield a respectable 91% – that is,

$$\frac{20}{20+2} \times 100 = \frac{20}{22} \times 100 = 90.9\% \text{ or } 91\%$$

the non-occurrence reliability is only 67%:

$$\frac{12}{12+6} \times 100 = \frac{12}{18} \times 100 = 66.66\%, \text{ or } 67\%$$

So these two observers would want to do some work on improving either their observations or their definition of non-occurrence.

Probably many parents and other workers will find it hard enough to do observations at all, without going to the extra work of getting someone else to do it as well, so for them the previous section may be redundant. For those who do want to try it, it is quite acceptable to have two observers on only a proportion of the sessions, say one in seven or eight, especially if these are not done all at the same time but are scattered through the baseline and the treatment sessions; and it can be quite satisfying to see how much agreement the two observers can achieve in their records.*

---

* For those who would like to find out more, there are more sophisticated statistical techniques for assessing the significance of occurrence/non-occurrence agreement – see Hartmann, 1977.

Finally, it should be remembered that some differences between observers may be legitimate. For example, someone may well smoke more at work than at home, or dress themselves better for their mother than for a nurse. Differences such as these, observed in different situations, can be real differences and reflect something we are probably aware of in ourselves – that we often behave differently in different environments. These are the kind of differences which contribute much to our analysis of the factors affecting a behaviour and which give us possible leads to the way we approach it.

Summary

1. Careful observation of the individual is the essential basis of behavioural work.
2. We observe and describe people's *behaviour*, what we see them do, not what we think are their thoughts and feelings.
3. We try to use clear, specific words, not vague, general ones ('fuzzies').
4. Observing and counting behaviours helps to put them into perspective.
5. We need to look at the ABC of behavioural work:

   Antecedents
   Behaviour
   Consequences
6. Observations need to be recorded.
7. Continuous recording involves writing down as much as possible of what is going on.
8. Event recording involves selecting one or more specific behaviours and recording how often they occur.
9. Using duration recording we record the length of time a behaviour lasts.
10. In partial interval recording, we divide the observation period into shorter intervals, and record whether or not the behaviour occurred at all in each interval.
11. Using momentary time-sampling, we also divide the observation period into shorter intervals and record whether or not the behaviour was occurring at one brief point in the interval (such as the last two or three seconds).

12. We may also record physical measurements (height, weight); and 'permanent products' – the result of a person's activity.

13. A baseline is a record of a person's behaviour before we begin to try to change it.

14. Reliability is shown by the degree to which two observers agree in their records of the same behaviour.

15. A stable baseline is the most appropriate starting point for any kind of intervention.

16. If we want to be sure that it is our intervention that has changed the behaviour, and not something else that happens to have coincided with the intervention, we can use a reversal, or a multiple baseline, or matching-to-criterion design.

Exercises

1. Which of the following are observation and which are interpretations?
   - a. He is attention-seeking.
   - b. He slapped me on the back.
   - c. She needs to socialise more.
   - d. Sally is not achieving her potential.
   - e. She drank her tea.
   - f. He was upset at missing the party.
   - g. He hit the ball.
   - h. He is careless about personal hygiene.

2. Why should we observe behaviour before we start a treatment programme? (Up to three reasons).

3. How will it help us if we record our observations?

4. Which recording method would be suitable to record?
   - a. Talking to peers.
   - b. Door slamming.
   - c. Saving money for a holiday.
   - d. Working on a task.

5. An ascending baseline would/would not be acceptable where the intervention seeks to:
   - a. Deal with swearing.
   - b. Teach the names of foods.
   - c. Teach dressing skills.
   - d. Work on toileting accidents.

CHAPTER 3

Assessment and Goal Planning

The way we set about using behavioural methods usually follows a certain pattern.

Observation
Assessment
Applied behavioural analysis
Intervention
Evaluation

Each stage is important and cannot be omitted; each contains information vital for the others.

During the first two stages, observation and assessment, we collect our data. In the third, applied behavioural analysis, we look at our data and decide what they mean. Then we go on to the fourth, intervention (or treatment), and finally, at the fifth stage, evaluation, we look at how successful the intervention has been. If it has not been successful, we may need to go back to one or other of the previous stages. Our observations and assessments may not have been accurate, or we may not have had enough of them. Our interpretation of the data may have been rash. Or we may have chosen the wrong intervention. Observation has been discussed in the last chapter.

What is assessment?

By assessment, we mean finding out exactly what the person's abilities are, in many different spheres, at the moment. So we might want to look, for example, at the person's cognitive (thinking) abilities, her ability to use and understand language, general knowledge, sight and hearing and how well she uses these. We might also want to know about her self-help skills, ability to perform domestic tasks, to budget, shop or go on buses. All this information helps to give us a full picture of not only the things that the person cannot do (her deficits) but also the things she can do (her skills and assets). In general, we want to base our interventions on the skills which people already have.

Assessment, then, is the process by which we gather information about a person so that we arrive at a clear picture of that person's present state of functioning. This helps us to pinpoint areas where the person may need to improve in order, say, to lead a more independent life.

Applied behavioural analysis

Some of the assessments we are going to talk about come ready made (see Appendix 2b, *Assessment Materials*), or we ourselves prepare the items in them in advance. They give us guidelines about areas of interest: just how good is Jonathan at dressing himself and what extra skills would he need to learn to be able to do this completely independently? The approach we are adopting throughout the whole of this book is based on a particular group of psychological theories about how people learn, and it is one system of analysing and interpreting behaviour in ordinary situations. The observation and assessment stages are when information is collected. Often we need to know about more than simply the behaviour itself. We need to know about the antecedents (the setting and the triggers) that set the behaviour going, and about the consequences (what happened afterwards as a result of the behaviour). Later, we may want to change some part of this – to alter either the setting conditions or the trigger, or to alter the consequences – and then see how this affects the behaviour. This process is called Applied Behavioural Analysis.

We take detailed observations using a form something like this:

Antecedents			
Settings	*Triggers*	*Behaviour*	*Consequences*
....	....	....	....
....	....	....	....
....	....	....	....

Organising our observations in this way enables us to make interpretations about why some things are happening. When we are doing this we would also take into account what the person has learnt in the past and how this affects their present behaviour. Perhaps this can be made clearer with an example.

At home

| | Antecedents | Behaviour | Consequences |
Settings	Triggers		
At home in bedroom	7.45am M wakes J with cup of tea	J drinks tea	7.45am M collects empty cup
	7.50am M tells J to get up and choose his clothes and then goes out	J gets up, takes off his pyjamas and puts on his underclothes	7.55am M sees he is ready to wash
	7.56am M calls from the bathroom that the water is hot and puts towel to heat on the radiator	J goes to the bathroom, washes and dries himself, then goes back to his bedroom and dresses himself	8.15 M calls from the kitchen that the breakfast is ready
in kitchen	8.15am M puts plate of cereal on table	J pours milk, eats cereal and drinks tea	8.17am M sits down at table, drinks tea and eats toast

etc, etc

The observations at the hostel looked more like this:

Settings	Triggers	Behaviour	Consequences
At hostel in bedroom	7.15am Bell rings throughout building, staff pops head into room and calls 'time to get up'	J stays in bed	7.30am Staff come back and say 'get up' again
in bedroom	7.45am Staff walk right up to bed and help J out saying 'come on J, time to get dressed'	J gets out of bed	Staff walk out
in bedroom	8.00am Staff come back in and start getting J's clothes organised	J sits on bed	Staff start to try to help him dress

etc, etc

Jonathan used to go to a social services hostel for rota care one week in twelve. When he was there, he did not seem able to dress himself very well, despite the fact that his mother had said he could do so.

We resisted the temptation to make vague generalised statements such as 'His mother must have been exaggerating' or 'The hostel are not doing it right' and looked at exactly what was happening in the two different situations. We observed Jonathan both at home and in the hostel (see page 48).

As can be seen from these two scenarios, no-one is doing anything wrong, it is merely that the antecedents and consequences are different in the two environments. Jonathan's mother constantly sets the scene for each next action that he needs to take, whereas in the hostel the staff expect him to carry out whole chains of action following brief initial instructions. It is not surprising that the skill that Jonathan is able to display at home has not become apparent in the hostel.

If we were being asked to help on this occasion, we would need to discuss this with all the people involved – Jonathan, his mother, the hostel staff – and see how they felt about it. Then, we might make suggestions at both ends; for example, we might ask the hostel to increase their interaction with Jonathan and to shadow the pattern of the routine as developed by his mother. We might also suggest that his mother cut down on the amount of material and verbal cues she gave Jonathan until the two routines hit the same level and he is able to dress independently in both places. By carrying out our applied behavioural analysis in this case, we had uncovered a problem of generalisation (dealt with further in Chapter 6), so we might want to institute more training to make sure that Jonathan can dress himself wherever he is. Applied behaviour analysis can reveal not only problems of generalisation, as we have described here, but also the skills a person lacks, inappropriate behaviour being reinforced or appropriate behaviour being ignored, and many environmental conditions which, once we spot their significance, can be changed quite easily. All this can make a great deal of difference to how people behave and how quickly they learn new skills.

Assessment of intelligence

The assessment of intelligence, which can only be done by a qualified psychologist, has in recent years rather lost favour where people with learning disabilities are concerned. Intelligence tests are best at predicting how well people will do in school work, which is not usually of first interest for people with learning disabilities. In addition, intelligence tests tell us little about a person's social abilities – how well he will get on with other people – and little about the kind of teaching the person needs. Moreover, an IQ or 'mental age' can label a person as being more disabled than she actually is. Saying that someone has a mental age of five means that when doing certain tasks (mostly table-top things such as formboards and jigsaws) she can do as well as an average five-year-old. It does not mean that she is like a five-year-old in every way. For example, James, who from his results on a particular test could be described as having a mental age of five, is 37 years old, has 37 years of social experience, can travel on buses alone, enjoys going to the cinema and has a girlfriend. None of this is like a five-year-old. Only by doing a more wide-ranging assessment would we find out what skills James had and what was his motivation and enthusiasm for learning more.

Despite these large reservations, IQ tests can provide information which will inform our judgements in other spheres. For example, there is some evidence to suggest that people with very low IQs (25 or less) will have particular difficulty in learning new skills. On the other hand, we have sometimes tested a person's IQ and then been able to tell his parents or day centre staff that he was much brighter than they had thought and that they could have higher expectations of him.

Similarly, it can happen that someone is thought to be learning disabled and is being catered for by services designed for learning disabled people, whom tests show to have intelligence which is within the normal range. When this happens, these people are reorientated to services which are more appropriate for them. Despite their drawbacks, intelligence tests, used not as a routine but only where they are seen as necessary, have a useful place in our assessment methods.

Rating scales

We include under this heading many standard assessments used to assess a person's adaptive behaviour, those skills necessary to the individual if she is to have an independent life. In the appendices we have included a list of some rating scales which we commonly use.

The advantage of using ready-made rating scales is that they provide a structure for information-gathering, thus making it less likely that whole areas of activity are omitted just because we forgot about them during the time we were asking the questions. They provide a permanent record of information which we can refer back to, and they ensure that information

Typical self-help scale

Toilet Training

(a) *Degree of training*
  0 – not toilet trained
  1 – uses toilet when placed on it
  2 – indicates need to go to toilet
  3 – goes to toilet when told
  4 – goes to toilet by self –
    occasional accidents
  5 – goes to toilet by self – no
    accidents during day

(b) *Enuresis*
  0 – wets self day and night
  1 – wets bed at night – dry in
    daytime
  2 – dry day and night

(c) *Toileting*
  0 – does not wipe self
  1 – occasionally wipes self
  2 – frequently wipes self
  3 – nearly always wipes self

(d) *Flushing toilet*
  0 – never flushes toilet
  1 – sometimes flushes toilet
  2 – usually flushes toilet

(e) *Washing hands*
  0 – never washes hands
  1 – sometime washes hands
  2 – usually washes hands

Eating skills

(a) *Drinking*
  0 – cannot drink from glass or cup
  1 – drinks from glass or cup with
    help and sloppily
  2 – drinks by self, much spilling
  3 – drinks by self, uses both hands
    neatly
  4 – drinks by self – holds glass in
    one hand

(b) *Eating skills*
  0 – does not feed self
  1 – feeds self with fingers and
    hands
  2 – uses spoon only, very messy
  3 – uses spoon only, reasonably
    neat
  4 – uses spoon and fork –
    considerable spilling
  5 – uses spoon and fork neatly
  6 – uses knife, fork and spoon

Dressing

(a) *Getting dressed*
  0 – does not put on any clothing
  1 – puts on one or two items
    (pants or shirt) only
  2 – puts on most clothing, cannot
    zip or button
  4 – completely dresses self, except
    for shoe-tying
  5 – completely dresses, including
    shoe-tying

(b) *Tying shoe laces*
  0 – does not pull laces tight
  1 – pulls laces tight
  2 – makes first part of knot
  3 – ties bow – soon comes untied
  4 – ties bow – remains tied

(c) *Initiates dressing*
  0 – never tries to dress self
  1 – must be told to dress
  2 – sometimes starts dressing
    without being told
  3 – usually starts dressing by self
  4 – dresses by self at appropriate
    time

(d) *Undressing*
  0 – does not remove any clothing
  1 – takes off some clothing (shirt,
    pants, socks only)
  2 – takes off most clothing, can
    unzip or unbutton
  3 – completely undresses self

is gathered about skills and behaviours that are generally agreed to be important.

We gather the information for our rating scale from three main sources: first, from the person herself; second, from other people, such as parents, nurse, SEC instructor; and third, by direct observation. The third method we often use to verify information obtained from the first two.

An example of a typical rating scale, which we have used, but which is not available commercially, is given on p.51. Despite the fact that it looks quite straightforward, we recommend that anyone wanting to use any-thing of this kind should be trained to do so first. This is because differences in ratings should represent real differences in behaviour, rather than dif-ferences in interpretations of what the questions mean. Training in using such a rating scale is made easier by using video, where the same piece of behaviour can be rated over and over again until everyone concerned is marking it in the same way. Usually, we video a role-played interview, with one person pretending to be a parent and another being the interviewer. The group of people being trained to do the assessment then go through the video, filling out the relevant parts of the form. The first time they do this without any prior discussion. Having discussed the exercise and each individual item in detail, the group go through the video (with fresh papers) again. The meaning of each item must be clarified as well; what do we do if a reply falls between two points on the scale – do we score up, or do we score down? For example, if a person has flushed the toilet only once out of 14 possible occasions does that count as 'never' or 'sometimes'? ('Sometimes' seems to suggest rather more than this.) The video exercise is then run again and again until for any one item there is a general agreement on how to answer it (we judged this by saying that in a group of 10-13 people – the numbers we have normally trained – we wanted no more than one person to disagree on only one item).

Ideally, we then follow up how people later fill in the items in real interviews, perhaps using the original trainers' ratings as the standard. Having trained the people who are doing the assessments in this thorough way, we can then expect that differences shown on the scale over time and between different environments represent real differences in the abilities and behaviour of the person being rated.

The content of these sorts of rating scales usually includes social inde-pendence, self-help skills, domestic, work and leisure activities. The com-pleted scale shows us what skills the person lacks and so what he needs to learn; if it is repeated some time in the future it shows us what changes have taken place and how good our teaching has been. If we fill in the details separately for the different environments the person functions in, we may see differences in behaviours which may suggest how different environments help or hinder a person's skills.

Some of the difficulties in using these sorts of rating scales have already been touched upon. Items may be open to interpretation, although thorough training should take care of this; people may be rated differently in different settings, although if the forms are filled in consistently and real differences are reflected, this gives us important information. Standard rating scales do not always suit the particular purpose to which we would like to put them, items may be omitted or the steps between items may be too large. The scales may not be at the level of the people we are currently working with; the items may be too advanced or too simple. Many people have been unable to find a scale that suits their purpose, so they have made their own scale, thus adding to the number of alternatives available. Finally a rating scale *per se* does not provide a teaching programme nor strategies for working, although it should suggest goals or targets for teaching. Some more recent developments in this field (for example, the Portage and Bereweeke systems (see Appendix 2), do suggest teaching programmes too, and have been seen to be important developments in this field.

Goal setting

In the chapter on observation, we have already talked about the importance of using clear rather than fuzzy words to describe people's behaviour. When we have assessed the current level of a person's skills we will probably want to set goals, in discussion with the person concerned, to aim at in our teaching. We will try to define the goals clearly, avoiding fuzzy or ambiguous language; we will try to choose goals directly relevant to the person's needs; and we will try to choose goals in accordance with principles of normalisation. People with learning disabilities have the right to be helped, according to their needs and abilities, to achieve the same sort of goals that the rest of us value.

We begin by asking the person concerned what are his or her own wants and needs. We decide whether the goal is functional; whether the skill is likely to be used once it has been taught, and whether it will enhance the independent functioning of the person. For example, Hilda's mother wanted her to spend more time learning to read. This seemed a good goal, as it would enable Hilda to be more independent when she was out on her own, and would give her something to do in her free time. Hilda however took quite a different view of the matter. She had spent a lot of time learning to read already and knew that in order to make even small amounts of progress she had to work hard and put in lots of time and she did not feel that it was a skill which significantly added to her independence. Hilda herself felt that she wanted to learn to travel on buses alone. This would enable her to visit friends and go to clubs without having to make special arrangements with a member of her family to accompany her. In the end we all agreed with her, and we set up a programme to teach her to travel independently, and left the reading for the time being.

Table 1. Goal Selection

	Client	Environment
Needs	1. What are the person's deficits? 2. What does the person want to tackle? 3. What is the most important thing to learn first?	1. Will the learning of this skill help others in the person's life?
Resources/ assets	1. Does the person have the relevant skills to build on?	1. Do these people (staff/family/friends) have the necessary skills to teach? 2. Will others continue the training/ provide encouragement? 3. Are there the necessary equipment/ facilities?
Constraints/ possible contra- indications	1. Does the person agree? 2. Are there other skills more vital? 3. Is there a risk involved? Is it acceptable to the client?	1. Will the behaviour/ skill be maintained? 2. Is there a risk involved? Is it at an acceptable level to others? 3. Will training interfere with other people?

Sometimes, making a decision as to which is the most appropriate goal can be complex. In the exercises at the end we have included a goal-setting exercise which you can try on yourselves. It aims to help you to sort out the sorts of conditions which might facilitate or hamper the achievement of a particular goal. When choosing the goal we look at the assets and the deficits of both the individual and the environments in which she lives and works. We also think about whether the skill could be taught in its natural environment and, if not, how we would facilitate generalisation. Furthermore, we want the goal to be positive and realistic, teaching new skills and not just trying to stop behaviour. Some of these issues are summarised in Table 1.

Clarifying the goals

Having decided on the goal, the next step is to define it carefully and write it down as a clearly understandable plan of action. A clear goal shows us:

> Who (the client)
>
> Will do what (the task)
>
> Under what conditions (antecedents)
>
> To what degree of success (criteron)
>
> With what result (reinforcement)

When these elements are contained within the goal, different people who read it and want to put it into operation will not be mistaken about what is required. We can record progress and reassess the goal in a reasonable time and make any necessary adjustments. A good goal might be:

> Susan will drink a cup of tea without spilling any while sitting at the table after supper: she will do this on five out of six days. Each time she does it she will be praised and can go into the TV lounge.

Let's make sure all the elements are present.

Who	Will do what	Under what conditions	To what degree of success	With what result
Susan	Will drink a cup of tea without spilling any	While sitting at the table after supper	Five days out of six	She will be praised and can go into the TV lounge

Here are some other examples of well-written goals:

Who	Will do what	Under what conditions	To what degree of success	With what result
Fred	Will fasten his shirt buttons	When dressing in the morning	3 out of 4 mornings	And then go down to breakfast
Bina	Will use the escalator	After she has bought her ticket	Five out of six times she travels by Underground	And will give herself a piece of chocolate at the bottom

The 'With what result' column builds the reinforcer into the goal so that it is not forgotten.

There are some examples of incomplete goals which you can try your hand at, in the exercises at the end of this chapter.

Setting the goal does not in itself indicate how that goal is to be taught. Chapter 6 will give you some ideas about the sorts of methods we might use when teaching new skills. They include shaping, prompting and modelling. However, before a specific teaching method is chosen we sometimes – or perhaps almost always would – want to break the goal down into smaller sections. This we call a task analysis.

Task analysis

Task analysis (breaking a task down into small steps) is an important part of assessment, and to carry it out successfully, we need to know how much a person is able to do.

If we look back at the first clear goal, we wrote 'Susan will drink a cup of tea, without spilling any, while sitting at the table after supper'. Obviously, drinking a cup of tea is a complex piece of behaviour which may be taught more easily in smaller pieces. Let us try and write down all the steps which are involved in drinking a cup of tea.

(1) Sit down at table

(2) Extend hand to cup

(3) Grasp handle of cup

(4) Lift cup from the saucer

(5) Bring cup toward mouth

(6) Touch cup to lips at angle, depending on level of liquid

(7) Tilt cup, and head as necessary

(8) Straighten cup and head

(9) Place cup on table

Repeat (1)-(9) when required

The task analysis can be used as a sort of assessment of the task concerned. For example, we can take Susan through steps (1)-(9) and see which ones she can and cannot do. In doing so we may find that we have not included enough steps, for example between (7) and (8) we might want to include 'swallows liquid'. We can also see at which point she is most likely to spill the tea. With Susan, it was at point (9), as she had a tendency to more or less fling the cup back at the table after she had swallowed most of the tea. Ordinarily, if we watch people drinking tea, we find that they tend to sip it, lifting the cup and putting it down frequently. Both Susan and her teacher agreed that this was the style of tea-drinking which they would like to aim for and so they rearranged the task analysis in the following ways.

(1) Sit down at table

(2) Extend hand to cup

(3) Grasp handle of cup

(4) Lift cup from table

(5) Extend cup toward mouth at an angle of 45%

(6) Touch cup to lips

(7) Tilt back cup and head

(8) Sip and swallow liquid

(9) Straighten cup and head

(10) Hold onto cup handle firmly

(11) Place cup gently back on table

Repeat (2)-(11) as required.

We were then able to keep more accurate records of how Susan was doing at each stage, which teaching methods were being used and how and what reinforcers were given.

Getting our task analyses right for the individual person is a skill which we have to learn and practise. We do not think that it is really possible to have a standard task analysis, say for tea-drinking, which will do for everyone. However, if we do have some standard ones available (as is sometimes the case in day centres) they can be used as an initial assessment instrument to be adapted or enlarged to suit individual needs.

Individual Programme Plans (IPPs)

An individual programme plan is a combination of most of the things we have been talking about in this chapter, a comprehensive assembly of the assessment of and the goals drawn up for an individual and details of how these are to be achieved. As far as possible the programme is discussed with the person concerned and, with her co-operation, goals and priorities are set. A Strengths/Needs list is made, listing on the one hand all her assets and abilities and on the other her deficits and difficulties. Resources necessary for carrying out the plan are identified – who will carry out or back up the plan, where it will be carried out and what equipment will be needed for it. If it turns out that certain goals may be unattainable because one or other of these resources is lacking, the people concerned are responsible for notifying those in authority of this lack and for bringing pressure to bear to have the lack made good. Finally, as with all other programmes, individual programmes are regularly reviewed, to check progress, to see whether the goals are being achieved; and if they are not, to search out the reason for this, reframe the Plan, and set it in motion once again.

There are standard forms available for drawing up IPPs (Individual Programme Plans) which make it easy to ensure that no important point is overlooked (see a pamphlet by the Applied Research Unit, South Wales, quoted in Appendix 2). However, the setting up of IPP meetings is only one part of what needs to be done. The IPP meetings and the preparation which goes into them are only really a dig in the ribs to remind people of the work which has to be done to ensure that people with learning disabilities have the opportunity to live in normal environments and that structures are set up to teach them the skills which they will need to do this.

Summary

1. A behavioural intervention usually consists of:

- Observation
- Assessment

- Applied behavioural analysis
- Intervention
- Evaluation

2. Assessment means gathering information about a person's abilities in many different areas.

3. An applied behavioural analysis is a detailed way of looking at the context of a particular piece of behaviour.

4. The assessment of intelligence, while no longer considered to be of first importance, may sometimes be worthwhile.

5. Rating scales are used to make assessments of skills.

6. When we set goals we make judgements, in conjunction with the people concerned, about where their strengths and skills lie and which are likely to be the most productive areas in which to begin teaching.

7. Clear goals have the following elements.

- Who
- Will do what
- Under what conditions
- With what degree of success
- With what result

8. A task analysis involves breaking a goal down into the small pieces of behaviour which make it up.

9. Individual programme plans provide a structure which can be used to ensure that goals are set for the individual and that someone is responsible for following them up.

Exercises

1. Rewrite the following goals so that they do not contain any fuzzy words and give clear instructions.

  (a) Peter needs to learn to dress himself.
  (b) Carmen should have a better social life.
  (c) Susan needs to learn to feed herself.

2. Do a task analysis of:

- Washing your hands
- Putting on a jumper
- Paying for your purchases at the checkout of a supermarket

3. Goal-setting exercise

I Goals

(a) Write down a goal you yourself would like to achieve

(b) How much time will you need to work on it per day/week/month

(c) Where will it be done?

(d) Which workmates/family/friends will be involved? (Give all names)

II Assets

What skills do you already possess which could be useful in the achievement of this goal?

III Priorities

Why is it important for this goal to be achieved? Who will benefit from it?

IV Constraints

Is there anything you do which might interfere with this goal being achieved?

V Resources

(a) If you want to learn something, is there someone with the time to teach it to you?

(b) Is there someone with the skills to teach you this?

(c) Is equipment needed? If so, is it available?

(d) Will learning this task fit into the natural routine of your day?

VI Constraints

Which are likely to interfere with goal achievement – tick those which apply

(a) Friends/family/etc do not have time

(b) Friends/family/etc do not have skills

(c) Friends/family/etc do not want to do this

(d) I may not stick at it.

(e) It may involve some risk to myself

(f) The necessary equipment is not available

(g) The physical location is not available

(h) It will adversely affect other family/friends – how?

When you have completed the checklist put a star by 'stumbling blocks' – ie, items on the checklist likely to cause goal failure. Consider each of these separately and see if they can be overcome and note them down. List stumbling blocks on the left hand side, with the possible solutions on the right. Then decide whether to go ahead with the target.

CHAPTER 4

Giving Encouragement

We once asked a group to think about what motivated them to do their job and to do it as well as they could. The answers they came up with included:

- Interest in the work
- Not wanting to let colleagues down
- Money
- Hope of promotion
- Fears of the consequences of performing badly
- A lively wish to help the clients

  ...and several others

From this we saw that there were many different reasons for doing a job. In some cases, the benefit we looked for was one directed to ourselves (money, hope of promotion); in others, although the immediate benefit was to others (to be of use to clients, not let colleagues down) we saw that we ourselves would also benefit from a feeling of satisfaction at the rightness of what we were doing. In yet other cases, we aimed to avoid something unpleasant happening to us (fear of the consequences). Even at our most disinterested, there was always something in it for us.

It seems true that, whatever we do, we anticipate getting something out of it. That is why we do the things we do. We perform an action: we get something – the reinforcer; we are more likely to perform that action again in order to get the reinforcer.

Reinforcement is defined as:

> Anything which, when it follows a piece of behaviour, makes that behaviour more likely to occur in the future.

We know reinforcement as a fairly ordinary word – reinforcements for an army, reinforced concrete, reinforced glass. In each case, it implies strengthening: of the army, or the glass, or the concrete. When we use it in behavioural work it implies the strengthening of behaviour. So when we want somebody to learn to perform a particular behaviour, we need to look for what is reinforcing to that person; then we make sure that, every time he or she does the task, the reinforcer follows. Then we can expect to see the behaviour occur more readily in the future.

To look for and use reinforcers in our teaching seems to be particularly important when we are teaching a person with learning disabilities. In many of our activities, the reinforcement arises naturally out of the activity itself. Once we have learnt to read or roller-skate, we continue to go back to these activities because of the pleasure we get from them. In the learning stages, this pleasure had to be anticipated and this anticipation needed to be sufficiently strong to get us over the learning stage when all we got was boredom and bruises. For people with learning disabilities, such anticipation, the conjuring up in the imagination of future reinforcement, may be less powerful. For them, we need to find other, immediate, reinforcers for their learning so that these will pave the way for the natural reinforcers to function once the activity has been learnt. Again, people with learning disabilities may seldom have had the experience of reinforcement following their efforts. So often whatever they have tried has been met with failure that they may give up expecting it at all. As a result, they give up trying: so we call them lazy. If we can ensure that reinforcement *will* follow what they do, so that they begin to experience success, wonderful things can happen.

Kinds of reinforcers

Reinforcers fall into four main groups.

(1) Primary reinforcers. These are the things that are necessary to life – food, drink, warmth, sleep. In practice, we are concerned only with the first two: food and drink. The manipulation of warmth and sleep would not be used in our work. Even with food and drink, it is not quite fair to call them *primary*, because in our work they are never used to sustain life: the people we work with are never so hungry or thirsty that they will eat or drink *anything*. Instead, we look for their favourite foods or drinks. Where possible, we avoid sweets, as they are bad for teeth and are fattening, and often the people we work with prefer cheese or savoury foods, or yogurt. Drinks are good because they slip down easily and don't need chewing.

Cups of tea or coffee have often been found to be effective reinforcers for adults with learning disabilities.

(2) Secondary reinforcers. These are things which are not themselves of any use, but which become reinforcing because they represent other, real, reinforcers. Money is a good example. In itself it does little for us – we can't eat it or drink it or play with it – but money is a powerful reinforcer because through it we have access to all sorts of other things we want. Indeed, it is particularly powerful because it does not tie us down to any one thing; we can choose for ourselves what we will have. (In competitions offering a holiday in the Bahamas or the equivalent in cash, the cash is often chosen.) In the same way points, or stars, or tokens which can be exchanged for a whole range of items can be excellent reinforcers, especially for more adult or able people. (Using secondary reinforcers is gone into in more detail in Chapter 5.)

(3) Social reinforcers. Praise, hugs, kisses, strokes, pats – all these are ways of indicating our responsiveness to a person's behaviour. This is a popular form of reinforcement – indeed, some people will use nothing else, which is fine when it works but may land them in trouble in those cases where it does not (like Tom, see p.65). Like every other kind of reinforcer, it is only useful if it increases the behaviour; if it does not, then no matter how convenient or acceptable it is to us, we should look to something else.

We usually think of social reinforcers as involving approval, but almost any kind of social response – a glance, a turn of the head, even anger or disapproval – can in some cases act as a reinforcer. If a person very much wants attention and does not get it, even angry attention may be better than nothing (see *Reinforcing appropriate behaviours* p.66).

(4) Stimulating reinforcers. There are a number of things that can act as reinforcers which do not fit easily under the previous three headings. Many of these are activities – games and sports, outings, visits to cinemas or concerts, a drink at the pub or a meal at a restaurant (it is not just the drink or the food, it is the whole outing that is valued). With people with more severe disabilities, all sorts of happenings, such as bright lights, music and other sounds, vibration, and many different kinds of sensation, may be effective. What these seem to have in common is the stimulation and enjoyment the person derives from them.

These, then, are the four major groups of reinforcers. If we have great difficulty in finding a reinforcer for a particular person we may employ the

Premack principle. David Premack, an American psychologist, first put forward the principle that a high frequency activity – something the person does whenever he has the chance – can be used to reinforce a low frequency activity – something which (although we would like him to do it) he does very little or not at all. Derek is a man with severe disabilities and limited skills. Amongst the other things he needed to learn was recognition and matching of colours. Derek was not interested in foods or drinks or praise, but left to himself he would spend hours screwing up nuts and bolts and unscrewing them again. This, then, was used as a reinforcer. When he had done a colour-matching task he was allowed a couple of nuts and bolts to screw and unscrew. Then they were taken away and he was asked to do another task. He was willing to do the tasks because they meant he could manipulate the nuts and bolts, and his colour-matching improved.

Reinforcers for the individual

You will remember that reinforcement is defined as *anything* which has the effect of increasing the behaviour it follows. This says nothing about exactly what is a reinforcer. It does not say that reinforcers are sweets, or nice things, or even that they are things the person likes. Reinforcers may be any of these things, and often are: but these things are not necessarily reinforcers. A reinforcer is recognised by its effect on behaviour: only if the behaviour which is followed by the 'reinforcer' increases can we be sure that it is a reinforcer. When Tom was being taught to dress himself, because he was very fond of his teacher she decided to use praise as the reinforcer. After a week or two, however, Tom was no further forward with his dressing. His teacher realised that, although he liked the praise, he did not like it enough to make the effort to dress himself. She looked for and found a more powerful reinforcer, and Tom's dressing skills steadily increased.

So we make no assumptions about what reinforcer we will use with any particular person. We will not invariably use sweets, and we will not invariably use praise. We have to find out what is likely to be reinforcing to this individual. To do this we often begin, as a first step, by finding out what the person very much likes. We can, if he can talk, ask the person himself; or we can ask someone who knows him very well; or we may offer him a range of things and see which he selects, and whether he selects it consistently. Then, when we have an idea of what interests him most, we can use it and see whether it truly reinforces his behaviour. If possible, we find several reinforcers and use sometimes one, sometimes another, so that the person does not get tired of any one.

Reinforcing appropriate behaviours

Reinforcement strengthens behaviour. Any behaviour. This means that it can work on bad behaviours as well as good ones. No one sets out deliberately to increase a bad behaviour but, especially where attention is a reinforcer, we may find it happening in spite of ourselves. If a person very much wants attention, even angry attention, and if when he pulls his trousers down we leave the other things we were doing, rush over to him, shout and gesticulate at him, yank his trousers up and tell him what a shameless tiresome creature he is and how fed up we are with him for doing it, we may find that, contrary to what we intended, he drops his trousers on many more occasions. We try to ensure that reinforcement follows desirable, and not undesirable, behaviours (see *Extinction* Chapter 7, p.99).

Giving reinforcement

Reinforcement should be given:

(1) When the desired behaviour takes place. Derek was given his nuts and bolts when he had placed a green brick on a green square, not when he was gazing out of the window.

(2) Immediately the desired behaviour takes place. This is very important. Even quite a short gap – five seconds – between the behaviour and the reinforcement can slow down learning. Not only will it be more difficult for Derek to make the connection between green-brick-on-green-square and receipt of the nuts and bolts but, during the five seconds, he may start doing something else, like rocking or grinding his teeth. By the time he gets the nuts and bolts, they may in effect reinforce the rocking or grinding. So the reinforcer should follow straight on the behaviour. This means that with tangible reinforcers (tokens, nuts and bolts, cups of tea) we need to have them right there, between our fingers or at least close at hand, to give as soon as the behaviour happens.

(3) Every time the behaviour happens. This applies especially at first, when the person needs to find that he really will get the reinforcement. Later on, as he becomes more skilful, we will need to give it less often and less regularly (see *Reinforcement schedules* below).

(4) Clearly. This applies especially to social reinforcers. A murmured 'Well done' might be enough for most people, but for a person with a learning disability it may not convey anything much. So the words, the tone of voice, facial expression, should all express warm unmistakable approval.

Negative reinforcement

So far we have been talking about positive reinforcement, and that is what, in effect, we always set out to use. You may, however, come across the term 'negative reinforcement' and it is as well to be clear about what it means. Often you will hear it used when what is really meant is 'punishment'. Negative reinforcement sounds less nasty, but used like this it is wrong. Reinforcement, as we saw above, means strengthening; in behavioural terms either kind of reinforcement strengthens behaviour. Positive reinforcement strengthens a behaviour by following it by giving something 'good'; negative reinforcement strengthens a behaviour by following it with the removal of something 'bad'.

Supposing it was Don's turn to clear up the kitchen after supper and he was being dilatory about it. We could say to him that when he had done it we would treat him to a pint in the pub (this would be using positive reinforcement); or we could stand over him berating him for not doing it until, just to get away from the nagging, he did the task (negative reinforcement). In the first case Don would clear up the kitchen in order to get something positive – a pint in the pub – in the second to gain relief from something negative – the nagging. The two kinds of reinforcement are similar, since with negative reinforcement the 'good' that follows is the relief, but that does require the unpleasant situation to be there in the first place. You can, however, see that negative reinforcement is quite different from punishment, in which the behaviour is followed by something unpleasant, with the aim of weakening the behaviour (see Chapter 7, p.101).

Reinforcement schedules

We saw above that when a person first starts to learn a skill he should receive the reinforcement consistently, every time the behaviour happens. Later on, when the person is becoming more skilful, we need to fade the reinforcement, going from a *consistent*, every-time, to an *intermittent*, every-now-and-again reinforcement schedule. This can be done in either of two ways, on a *ratio* or on an *interval* schedule. Ratio schedules are those that we have been describing up till now, in which reinforcement depends on the occurrence of each bit of behaviour. This is similar to piece rates in factory work, where how much the workers can earn depends on the number of items they produce. Interval schedules, on the other hand, are like the more usual wages and salaries, which are paid regularly, every week or every month.* Similarly, using an interval schedule, the person is reinforced for every interval – five minutes, ten minutes, an hour, half a day, whatever seems most appropriate – in which the desired behaviour is shown. Interval schedules are perhaps particularly useful for dealing with problem behaviours, where the person can be reinforced for each period in which the problem behaviour did not occur. For example, Janey, who was aggressive and disruptive to her group in the ATC, was reinforced for every half-day in which she showed neither of these behaviours.

Both ratio and interval schedules can be either *fixed* or *variable*. Using fixed schedules the reinforcement is given regularly, after every two, or four, or seven, or whatever, instances of the behaviour, or after every three, ten or 30 minutes; while when we use variable schedules we give the reinforcement as often *on average*, but dodged around, so that the person never quite knows when it is coming. For example, if we were using an FR3 (Fixed Ratio 3) schedule the reinforcement would be given after every third, sixth, ninth, twelfth occurrence, and so on: the person would know exactly when to expect it. Using a VR3 (Variable Ratio 3) schedule we might give the reinforcement after the second, then the fifth, then the ninth, then the thirteenth, then the fifteenth, and so on, so that it comes on average after every third occurrence but not regularly after each third. In the same way on a VI (Variable Interval) 30-minute schedule the reinforcement could be given after 20, 35, 40, 15 and 40 minutes, which, although quite irregular, works out at every 30 minutes on average.

Fading the reinforcer

These variable, or intermittent, schedules are particularly important when we want to fade out the reinforcement. Because the person does not know exactly when to expect the reinforcement, he or she is less put out if the gap is rather longer than usual. So, as the person becomes increasingly skilful, it is possible to 'stretch' the schedule, with progressively longer gaps in it. We look forward eventually to tailing off the reinforcement altogether, and to the person continuing with the behaviour without needing anyone to reinforce it.

How long we need to continue to give reinforcement, and how it can finally be brought to an end, depends very much on the individual. Sometimes it just seems no longer necessary. Peter's programme (see

---

* This is not the strictly orthodox description of interval schedules but it is the way we, and many others, use them in our practice.

Chapter 7), in which he was reinforced for not vomiting on the bus, lasted for two weeks, and after this he never vomited again, despite not receiving any special reinforcer after the first two weeks. More usually other reinforcers, of one sort or another, take over. Often a tangible reinforcer may be faded out and replaced by social reinforcers, the person being praised from time to time for performing the task or using the skill. Again, if we teach a person a skill that is in itself enjoyable, once he or she has learnt it the activity itself is reinforcing. Simon was taught to do simple industrial tasks by giving him sips of orange juice: once he had mastered the tasks he enjoyed doing them so much that the orange juice was no longer necessary. Again, even if the activity is not especially enjoyable the person may get satisfaction from the mastery of a skill. Tom was taught to dress himself, using food reinforcers at first; later, although dressing is not a particularly thrilling occupation, Tom felt so proud of his ability to dress himself that this became sufficient to ensure that he continued to do it.

So reinforcement which at first is so important to the learning of new tasks, in the later stages of learning can be gradually faded. Our aim and hope is that the extrinsic reinforcers will eventually be supplanted by social, or better still the naturally-arising reinforcers that we have described above.

Summary

1. Reinforcement is anything which increases the behaviour it follows.

2. There are four main categories of reinforcer: primary, secondary, social and stimulating.

3. When we use the Premack Principle we make use of something the person prefers doing to reinforce his learning of a new skill.

4. We have to look for a reinforcer that is particularly powerful for each individual.

5. Reinforcement should be given:

   · When the desired behaviour occurs
   · Immediately it has occurred
   · Every time the behaviour occurs at first.
   · Clearly.

6. For building up new behaviours a continuous schedule is best.

7. Once the behaviour is established an intermittent schedule is best for maintaining it.

Exercises

1. What difference do you see between the use of reinforcement, and bribery?

2. Can you think of three things that would be reinforcing for you – that you would put out an effort for?

3. Can you think of something, neither criminal nor endangering to your own life, which no reinforcer would be powerful enough to make you do? What is it you get out of not doing it?

CHAPTER 5

Points, Stars and Tokens

Tokens (or points or stars) are one kind of reinforcer, and function in much the same way as does money. Money is of no use to us in itself, but we value it highly because we can exchange it for the things that we want. Similarly, tokens can be earned and then exchanged for a variety of desirable things (the things that tokens are exchanged for are often known as 'back-up reinforcers').

Tokens have many of the advantages that money has. Each is flexible: if we have £20 we can choose between, say, a meal out, a new shirt, or a day in the country. Similarly, tokens can be made exchangeable for a variety of items so that no one item becomes boring. Tokens, like money, are easy to handle and to give: a pocketful of tokens is much easier to cope with than a pocketful of crisps or chocolate, not to mention ice-cream. Tokens can also be given quite often without interrupting the task very much, whereas giving something to eat or to do inevitably means a break. Perhaps the most important advantage of tokens is that they enable us to use as exchange, or back-up reinforcers, the things that adults are interested in. Generally speaking, pieces of biscuit, sweets, snatches of music, and so on are used only for people with profound disabilities; most adults take a livelier interest in more major things such as outings, extra privileges, shopping trips, objects such as pens, books, records, and a whole range of other items. Obviously, it is not possible to give these larger things after each instance of the behaviour. We cannot take someone on an outing each time he peels a potato, but we can give him a token after each potato, he can save them up, and when he has collected the agreed number they can be exchanged for the outing. Along the way, each token signals that the outing is that little bit nearer.

Learning to use tokens

For most people, it is enough to tell them about the programme, discuss it with them, and then give them practice in getting the tokens and exchanging them for whatever back-up reinforcer they want. Some workers have suggested having an introductory period in which tokens are first given out and exchanged without any strings attached, followed by the programme in which tokens must be earned. By the time the programme starts the point of the tokens, and what the person can get from them, is understood, and the person is more likely to be interested in earning them. People with profound disabilities may need to be taught more deliberately how to use tokens; being given a token, then the token being retrieved immediately, and exchanged for the reinforcer; then, when this has been learnt, being given first one, then another token, and then exchanging the two; then building up to three or four and increasing the interval between the delivery of the tokens and their exchange. It may also be necessary for them to be taught how to store the tokens, in a pocket, or a purse.

However, people with profound disabilities have sometimes been found to catch on to the idea of tokens quite unexpectedly. Giles was one of a number of clients whom it had been decided not to include in a token system set up for a small group, because it was thought that he would not be able to grasp what it was all about. When the system had been running for a week or two Giles, who had watched people exchanging their tokens, found a few stray tokens lying on a windowsill, took them to the token shop and indicated that he wanted to exchange them for the items of his choice. Giles was then brought into the programme and benefited considerably from it.

What to use as tokens

Ticks or stars on a chart are easily managed and quite easy to control, although especially with ticks it is important to make sure that they can't be forged. Peter (see Chapter 7) had a programme to help him get up in the morning. Each day he took to his centre a chart on which his mother put a tick whenever he had got up on time. Each tick was exchanged for 30p that he could spend at the centre. One day Peter arrived at the centre with all the days on the chart filled in with ticks. The programme was then adjusted so that each successful day was recorded, not by a tick but by his mother's signature, which Peter was not able to copy.

If more tangible tokens are wanted, for example, for more severely disabled people, any small objects in good but controllable supply, such as beads, discs or even tiddly winks, can be used. They need to be fairly small so that they can be stored; however in one unit it was decided not to use tiddly winks as they could so easily be swallowed. The tokens must also be distinctive, and not easily substituted; in one unit, used matches were suggested as possible tokens, but were ruled out when it was seen that an entrepreneur could arbitrarily inflate his or her supply, just as Peter was able to hep up the ticks on his chart.

Setting up a token programme

Token programmes need a bit of thought. We need to decide on:

(1) the behaviour that will merit a token;

(2) the back-up reinforcer or reinforcers – what the person can exchange ('buy') for the tokens;

(3) the exchange rate – how many tokens are needed for each back-up reinforcer.

(1) The behaviour

Tokens, like other reinforcers, can be used either to increase desirable behaviours or to decrease undesirable ones. In either case, we need to define carefully what are the behaviours whose occurrence, or non-occurrence, will deserve a token. When an instructor in one day centre was asked how she would use tokens with her client, she said 'He'll get a token if his behaviour is acceptable'. This was too vague to be workable. Eventually it was narrowed down to a decision that this blind man, who used his fingers at mealtimes to locate the food on his plate, would be given a token for every five minutes in which, if necessary, he wiped his hands on a damp cloth and not on the clothes of passers-by. If the tokens are to reinforce a positive behaviour we need to say exactly what behaviours will earn the tokens – 'Reg will get a token every time he arrives at a session no more than three minutes after the starting time'.

Similarly, if tokens are to be used to decrease a behaviour, this too should be carefully defined. Janie (see Chapter 7) received her token if she did not hit or attempt to hit anyone, or shout, or throw anything in the half-day up till lunch time, and again in the time after lunch till the end of the day.

(2) The back-up reinforcer

The big advantage of using tokens is that they give us the chance to use a whole range of reinforcers that certainly could not be used for single instances of desirable behaviour, either because they are too expensive, such as cassette tapes, or because they can't be given at the drop of a hat, such as a trip to the sea, or even just a walk. They also allow us to make use of the person's individual preferences: one person may want to be taken out to a pub, another out to tea. Each person's preference can be accommodated.

When a back-up reinforcer is identified we need to ensure that it will be reliably available. With fairly expensive items such as cassette tapes we need to ensure that they are affordable. This is not usually a problem – either they are affordable or they are not. More tricky, as a rule, are treats and outings: if we have agreed with someone that when she has forty tokens she will be taken to watch stock-car racing, we have to know that not only the money for the trip but also the person to go on the trip with her will, without fail, be on hand. (Of course, barring unpredictable disasters, such as flood, fire or mortal illness.) Problems such as potential staff shortages should be considered when the programme is set up. Many people with learning disabilities can understand that an outing needs time to arrange but, if an outing is the reinforcer, it should not be cancelled because it is inconvenient.

(3) Exchange rates

Two things have to be considered here. First, how often do we want the person to get the back-up reinforcer: second, how many tokens is she going to be given. (There is a subsidiary question of how many tokens the back-up reinforcer is 'worth' – a cassette player should require more tokens than a magazine – but this is taken care of in considering the first two questions.)

How often the person should get the back-up reinforcer depends partly on the person herself – how severely disabled she is, how able she is to wait for things – and partly on the stage she has reached in her programme. Very broadly, the more severe a person's disability, the shorter should be the delay in exchanging tokens for reinforcers. This is particularly true at the start of a programme, when it seems important that the reinforcer should be available early on, so that the person finds she really does get it. It may then be better to begin with a relatively minor reinforcer, such as a magazine or a bar of chocolate, which can be earned in a day or so. Later, when the person has had the experience of exchanging tokens for reinforcers and has found that it really happens, it may be possible to work up to the larger reinforcers which take longer to earn.

We must emphasise that these are general guidelines, and in particular cases might not be appropriate. For example, nothing we have said overrides the importance of using reinforcers that are effective for the individual. There is no point in making the tokens exchangeable for a magazine or a bar of chocolate if the person is not interested in the magazine and does not like chocolate. Indeed, occasionally the idea of starting with small, often-exchanged reinforcers may backfire. In one case a star programme was set up for a young woman, the stars to be exchanged for pennies. It soon became apparent that although she got pennies every day she regarded them as beneath contempt. It was not until the agreement was renegotiated so that 60 stars were exchangeable for a pop record that the programme took off. The young woman was so keen to have the pop record that her behaviour in question (complying with requests) improved dramatically, even though it took her several weeks to amass the 60 stars. So there may always be exceptions and our programmes should be flexible enough to allow for this. Nevertheless, generally speaking, the principle that we should start small, with quickly-available reinforcers, and build up to larger and more delayed ones is a useful one.

Fining

For some people, one of the attractions of using tokens is that they can be taken away as well as given: it is possible to use them in punishment as well as in reinforcement procedures. For example, a person who was earning tokens for washing up could have tokens taken away if he shouted at someone, or swore. Alternatively, if the main concern is a problem behaviour, the person can be given a supply of tokens, perhaps renewed every day or every week, and one or more may be deducted each time the problem behaviour occurs.

With these programmes, as with others we have discussed, we need to remember that if they are to work it will be through the effect of the reinforcer, exchangeable for the tokens. If the programme is so severe that the person regularly loses all her tokens, so that she never gets the reinforcer, the tokens will lose their value for her, she will cease to care whether she has them or not, and they will be of no use in helping with the problem behaviour. It is very important that the person retains a realistic chance of collecting enough tokens for the reinforcer to be within the person's reach.

One of the disadvantages of using fining is that it may be very upsetting to the person. Sometimes a physical struggle to remove tokens can ensue, and the person can become so upset that her behaviour gets worse rather than better. One approach to combat this is immediately to offer the person a chance to earn back some of the lost tokens: 'You swore at Julie, and you have to lose five tokens: but you can have two tokens if you apologise to Julie and wash her coffee cup for her'.

Another approach that was effective in preventing resentment over the loss of tokens was taken in a group programme for mildly disabled adolescents (Salend and Kovalich 1981). The aim was to reduce 'talking out' – talking in class without the teacher's permission. A baseline was taken and it was found that 'talking out' happened on average sixteen times in each half-hour class. As a start it was decided that ten times would be acceptable, so the group was given eleven tokens in the form of strips which were fastened to the blackboard where all the students could see them. Every time 'talking out' occurred the teacher removed one of the strips. If at the end of the session there were any strips left at all, the group was entitled to the reinforcement, 20 minutes free time. In this programme the loss of tokens did not result in loss of reinforcement until all the tokens were gone; because the limits were set fairly generously the students always managed to stay within them and the group always received their reinforcement. This, it was thought, was why the resentment often found with fining programmes did not show up in this one. Later, the permitted amount of 'talking out', and the number of strips available, were gradually reduced, still with no loss of reinforcement.

These, then, are ways in which token fining can be used. We ourselves however have not as a rule found fining useful, and now do not use it. Rather than programmes in which tokens are taken away for negative behaviours, we seem to do better with those in which the tokens are given for positive behaviours, and the negative behaviours, if they occur, result in no token being given. Fining is itself a form of punishment and this is discussed further in Chapter 7.

Changing the number of tokens

When we set up our programme we decide on how many tokens we will give and how many will be exchangeable for the back-up reinforcer. We do this rather arbitrarily, and then have to see how it works. If we find the person is not getting enough tokens, or is getting too many, we may have to adjust the programme, in discussion, where possible, with the person concerned.

If the person is earning tokens too slowly, so that the reinforcer seems out of reach and he becomes discouraged, we need either to increase the number that he is given or to lower the 'price' of the reinforcer. Either makes it more possible for the person to attain the reinforcer, and the tokens once more become of value and hence reinforcing. On the other hand, if the person is getting on well and earning liberal quantities of tokens, it may be useful to set our sights a little higher. In this case we may either reduce the number of tokens given, or raise the price of the back-up reinforcer. In practice, it usually seems easier to do the latter, again, if we can, through discussion. If the same reinforcer is being used the person can be told that, as frequently happens in normal life, the price has gone up, and the magazine which last week was six tokens now requires seven; or, if a new reinforcer is to be used, this can be priced rather higher than was the previous equivalent. So, if 30 tokens were needed for a trip to the pub, 35 may be required for a bus ride.

As always, the important thing is not to raise the price too quickly so as to make the reinforcer seem unattainable.

The agreement

When we set out to use tokens, we draw up an agreement. We say, 'Every time Clare does this, she will be given a token. When she has (so many) tokens she can exchange them for (a bar of peanut crisp, or 20 minutes with a tape recorder, or whatever)'. The agreement may be more complex, and may specify more than one behaviour – 'Every time Clare makes her bed, or puts her clothes away, or vacuums the floor of her room' – while it may also specify more than one available exchange reinforcer. When the agreement is drawn up it is discussed, as far as possible, with the person concerned so that they understand and are happy with it. When Janie's instructor wanted to help her overcome her aggressive, disruptive behaviours he discussed this with her; she agreed that she needed this help and agreed to the suggested token system (see Chapter 7).

This, then, is an agreement arrived at between two people. *It should not be arbitrarily changed by one of those people.* So, for example, in Clare's programme we should not suddenly decide that the token for bed-making would only be given if the bed were made with clean sheets or mitred corners. That was not in the original agreement, and should not be part of it unless it is agreed by, or at least made clear to, both parties.

We find that, usually, these unilateral adjustments are made in programmes which aim to deal with problem behaviours. Steve's parents were very concerned that he told lies. A programme was set up between Steve and his parents whereby he was given a transistor radio, which would be withdrawn for 24 hours if he told a lie. When the psychologist visited to see how things were going, his parents said that he had not told a lie but the radio had been confiscated because Steve had been slow about doing the washing-up. The psychologist pointed out that doing the washing-up was not part of the agreement, to which the parents replied 'No, but we had to take the radio away because it worked so well'. They found it impossible to stick to the agreement, and the programme had to be abandoned. On the other hand, Janie's programme laid it down that she would be given a token for every session in which she had not shown any of a number of specified disruptive behaviours: when she arrived late for her session one day the instructor was scrupulous in not including lateness as a behaviour to be penalised. If Janie had been persistently late he might have considered whether the agreement should be re-negotiated so as to include punctuality as one of the requirements, but he did not drop it unannounced into the programme.

Group programmes

One of the advantages of tokens is that they can be used to reinforce the individual behaviours of several people working alongside each other. We are not talking here about formal token economy systems, where tokens are delivered to different people for the same behaviours. We are talking about groups of people working together, each person possibly engaged on a different task: each person receives tokens for individually-assessed performance criteria: and each person later exchanges the tokens for whatever back-up reinforcer he or she particularly desires. For the instructor, or group leader, tokens provide a simple, manageable way to give reinforcement, while for the students, each is working on a task which is suitable for him or her, with goals that are individually set, and with back-up reinforcers that are individually selected.

It is interesting to see how much appeal such a system has. The programme that Giles became involved in was originally intended for only the five most able attenders at a day centre workshop. As time went on the other attenders, all with profound learning disabilities, noticed these five going up to the 'token shop', where the back-up reinforcers were stored, and saw them coming away with the items of their choice. Because these other, less able, attenders looked so forlorn, they too were given a few tokens and were able to select what they wanted: later it was found that tokens could be used with these others to reinforce their skills and desirable behaviours. You can see that this is a neat example of the free gratis way of introducing token use, described earlier. There were a few in the workshop who never caught on to the tokens, but the vast majority did, even though originally it had been thought too complex for them. So tokens, which are especially valuable for more able people, can also be used with people with a wide range of disabilities.

Ending the tokens

Often tokens are used for one particular problem, and when the problem is solved the tokens may not be needed any longer. Peter's programme (see Chapter 7) lasted for two weeks: his vomiting stopped, the tokens stopped, and he has not vomited on the coach since. This was a happy result but we should not rely on things working out so easily all the time. As a rule it is advisable to expect to have to 'stretch' the schedule of tokens (see *Fading the reinforcement*, Chapter 4), giving the tokens gradually less often while still ensuring the behaviour continues. In other cases we have found that once a skill has been learnt we can go on to teaching another, for which the person enjoys earning and then exchanging the tokens. In many other cases the tokens can be faded out as other reinforcers, usually social ones, take over. In Janie's case the token programme helped her to become a much more pleasant person; the other people in her workshop liked her more and were more friendly to her, with the result that Janie was herself more friendly to them, and the tokens were no longer needed.

Summary

1. Tokens, like money, are items which have no intrinsic reinforcing value but become reinforcing because they represent the possibility of obtaining things which are of value.

2. Tokens may consist of small storable items such as plastic discs or poker chips, or stars, ticks or points on a chart may be used instead.

3. The use of tokens may need to be deliberately taught to people with profound learning disabilities.

4. Tokens may be earned, stored and exchanged for a range of major reinforcers which could not be given for single instances of desired behaviour.

5. We need to decide on:

> (a) the behaviour;
>
> (b) the exchange reinforcer(s);
>
> (c) the exchange rate.

6. A token programme should ensure that the reinforcer is realistically and, especially at first, quickly accessible.

7. Tokens can be removed consequent upon undesirable behaviours: in some cases this has been found to make the behaviour worse.

8. As the person becomes more successful we can adjust the programme by requiring a higher level of performance for the tokens, or by requiring the person to give more tokens for the back-up reinforcer.

9. Once the agreement has been drawn up and agreed upon it should not be altered unilaterally or at random.

10. Tokens can be very useful as reinforcers for individuals working in group situations.

11. Tokens can be faded and discontinued:

> (a) when a new behaviour pattern has been established which is independent of the tokens;
>
> (b) when other reinforcers take over;
>
> (c) by gradually stretching the reinforcement schedule;
>
> (d) by moving on to reinforcing a new skill.

Exercises

1. What back-up reinforcer would be necessary to induce you to:

> (i) Go over Niagara in a barrel;
>
> (ii) Take your worst enemy for a fortnight's holiday;
>
> (iii) Go for a five-mile walk in freezing rain and wind;
>
> (iv) Go without sleep for 36 hours.

2. What sort of secondary reinforcer would you use for:

> (i) A mildly learning disabled, unpredictably violent man;
>
> (ii) A blind, moderately learning disabled woman;
>
> (iii) A young woman who always likes to be the centre of attention;
>
> (iv) A person with pica (tendency to put everything in the mouth).

3. You have set up a token programme for a young woman who, although she is often given tokens, never seems to have any and complains that someone steals them. You suspect she may just lose them. What would you do?

CHAPTER 6

Ways of Teaching

Up until now we have been talking about encouraging people to make more, or better, use of skills that they already possess. But sometimes the problem is that the person has no idea of how to do a task; it is no good our being ready with the reinforcer, we will never have the chance to give it to him because he is unable to produce the behaviour we are looking for. So we need to teach him the skill. This chapter concerns ways of setting about that teaching.

Shaping

When we use shaping we reinforce, not the behaviour we are looking for, but approximations to it that come gradually closer to our target. Previously we have talked about reinforcing the desired behaviour; now, as we have already said, the desired behaviour never occurs, but what does occur is a behaviour (X) that bears some relation to the desired behaviour (A). For example, although the person may never sit still long enough to have a meal, he may sometimes sit down on a chair. So we begin by reinforcing behaviour X whenever it occurs. When it is occurring quite regularly we look out for behaviour Y, which is still nearer to the desired behaviour, A, than X was, so whenever Y occurs we reinforce that and we leave off reinforcing X. Then we look out for behaviour W. And so on.

Let's look at an example. Edward is a young man in the Special Care Unit of an Adult Centre who is severely learning disabled and hyperactive. He was extremely restless, always on the go, always moving from one part of the room to another, never pausing long enough to take part in anything. He also reacted badly to physical contact, and went into a frenzy if anyone tried physically to keep him in one place for any length of time. All sorts of efforts had been made to interest him in various activities but one big problem was that there seemed very few things that could be used as a reinforcer – food, for example, he was quite uninterested in, to the point where it was difficult to get him to eat. The one thing he really loved was music.

The Centre staff decided to try to teach him to sit down on a chair, using shaping, and with music as the reinforcer. They made a cassette tape of his favourite music. They watched him flitting round the room, and saw that, by chance, he would sometimes go near a chair and, very occasionally, would sit on it for a brief moment. They decided that whenever he went within two feet of the chair they would switch on the tape recorder, while whenever he sat on the chair the tape would be left running as long as he was seated. Soon he was spending more time by the chair, and was sitting in it more often. It was decided that the tape would he switched on only if he was within one foot of the chair; later if he were actually touching it; then it was switched on only if he was sitting in it. As the tape stayed on while he sat in the chair he began to sit in it for longer and longer, and it was then possible to introduce pictures, colour matching and other activities to him. Soon he was sitting for as long as half an hour, and now he had the music only when he had done some of the activities, and these in turn began to be interesting to him. So from being someone who was perpetually on the move and could not be engaged in any positive task, within about three months he had become, through the gradual shaping of his behaviour, someone who could enjoy all sorts of interesting occupations.

Prompting

Physical prompting. When we use prompting, we help the person to perform a task, guiding his limbs through the action; then we reinforce him for doing it. So if we want to teach Piers to pick up an apple from a fruit bowl and put it on his plate we put our hand over his, guide his hand to the apple, wrap his fingers round the apple and make them pick it up; then, our fingers holding his round the apple, we move the apple onto the plate and release his fingers from it. Then we reinforce him.

Physical prompting can be used to teach actions involving hands, arms, feet and legs; head movements; and movements of the whole person, as when we teach the person to respond to requests such as 'Sit down' or 'Come here'. To teach the former, we position the person in front of the chair; we say 'Sit down', and gently press on her shoulders until she sits in the chair; then we warmly reinforce her. If we want to teach 'Come here', it may be helpful to have a second teacher to help with the teaching: one teacher says 'Come here' and the second gently pushes the person towards the first teacher, who then gives the reinforcement.

When we use physical prompting, and especially when we are prompting movements of the person's hands and arms, it seems most effective if we position ourselves behind the person. Then when our hand moves the person's hand, to pick up a pencil, or to scoop a spoonful of raspberry fool, the movements we make, and that we are prompting the person to make, are the natural ones for that action. If, when we are teaching him to pick up the apple, we were to stand, or sit, in front of Piers, reach out across the table – with which hand? Our left to his right? Or cross our right hand over to his? – we would put our hand back to front over his and the movements we made would be very strange ones. We want him to feel what it is like to do the action, to feel it in his shoulder and arm and hand and fingers, so that he begins to know what to do. We are not, after all, just doing it for him; our aim is that as he feels how to do the action he will begin to do some of it himself. Some physical prompting can be done quite well with the teacher sitting alongside the person (and of course this is less tiring for the teacher if the session is to be a long one, for example a meal time), but if it can be done standing behind the person this may be better.

Gestural prompting. Unlike physical prompting, gestural prompting does not ensure that the person performs the action: what it does is to indicate that the action should be performed, and, to some extent, what that action is. So when we gesture to someone to sit down we point to the seat of the chair, which gives a suggestion of what it is that we want him to do; we help him to understand what is required of him and make it easier for him to do.

Most gestures are made with the arm, or hand, or even with the head, but a very subtle kind of gesture can be made with the eyes – eye pointing. Because this is one that we may do almost without knowing it, we may need to ensure that it is not this that the person relies on to make the correct response; he may be one hundred percent successful when we, with our eye-pointing, make the request and fall down completely with someone else (who will then say, 'He doesn't understand *anything*').

Verbal prompting. When we use verbal prompts, we indicate in words what we want the person to do. This may be a general guide – 'Time to get up' – or can be much more specific and detailed, to guide the person right through an action – 'Hold onto the reins and pommel with your left hand', 'Put your left foot into the stirrup', 'Hold the back of the saddle with your right hand', 'Spring off your right foot', 'Rest your weight on your left foot in the stirrup and swing your right leg over the saddle and sit down'.

Verbal prompting is a useful way of helping people to carry out actions, *if* they understand the words. If in the example above we had been talking to someone with good verbal understanding he would by now be safely in the saddle: if not, he would probably still be on the ground. Our own feeling is that verbal prompts are greatly over-used with people with learning disabilities. We talk on and on, giving a non-stop flow of verbal instruction without pausing to see whether it has any meaning for the person we are trying to help. In many cases physical prompting, if necessary accompanied by some verbal instruction, gets the message over more effectively.

Fading the prompts. When we use prompts, our aim is to help the person to do the task so that he will begin to learn how to do it for himself. As he gets more able to do the task, and is contributing more towards it, so we fade the prompts we give: we do a little less as he does a little more, then a little less still, and so on. Fading prompts is quite a delicate operation, as we try to let the person do as much as he is able to while still ensuring that the task is completed. If we fade prompts too quickly the person may fail.

When we first use physical prompts, for example, to teach somebody to feed himself with a fork, if he does not hold the fork we begin by putting his hand round the handle of the fork and we hold it there, our hand firmly round his. Then, as we feel him holding the fork a little, we use less pressure, then a little less, then still less until it may be enough just to guide the person's hand with a light touch. Then when he is able to do almost all of the movement for himself we may not need to touch his hand at all, but we would at this point follow his hand with ours, so that if he should get into difficulty we are there at once to help. This is known as shadowing, and is a good intermediate stage between giving the lightest of help and not helping at all.

We usually think of fading in relation to physical prompts but gestural and verbal prompts can also be faded. A rigid finger pointed at a chair seat becomes more casual until it is just a flick of the finger, then less even than that; eye pointing becomes less direct, then just a glance until eventually we make sure our eyes do not waver at all in the direction of the object concerned.

It seems important to pay particular attention to the fading of gestural prompts. Often we use gestures or tiny movements without being really aware that we are doing so. We have often encountered the human equivalent of 'Clever Hans', a horse who appeared to have prodigious mathematical ability. When he was given a mathematical problem to solve Clever Hans would paw the ground, stopping when he reached the number which gave the correct answer, and everybody fell about in amazement. Later someone tried asking him questions to which the interrogator did not know the answer, or had the questions asked by somebody hidden from his view, and Clever Hans went on pawing the ground until someone felt sorry for him and stopped him. Hans was not really an equine mathematician; what he was responding to was some tiny involuntary movement made by the interrogator when the correct number was reached. In the same way someone we are teaching may be able to pick up a message, not from what we say, but from some small gesture we make. So if we want to be sure the person understands what we are teaching him we must be careful to fade out the gestures we have used in teaching, especially eye-pointing which we may do almost without knowing it.

Verbal prompts too can be faded: 'Give the conductor the money' becomes 'Give the conductor the m......', 'Give the conductor the......', 'Give......' and then even the 'G......' is faded to a whisper and then fades out altogether.

The point of fading prompts, like the point of teaching the person in the first place, is that he shall be able to do the task or action on his own. So we have to sense just how much the person is able to do, and to let him do all of that and only give as much help as he needs. This is actually very difficult, and requires a great deal of sensitivity on our part, to do enough but not too much. The most important thing seems to be to move slowly, to fade the prompts gradually. Most mistakes seem to involve trying to fade prompts too quickly, with the result that the person fails and may become discouraged. However, if we find that we have gone too fast and the person cannot complete the task, we then go back to an earlier level of prompting and try to fade the prompts more gradually.

Delayed prompting

People with learning disabilities learn best if they are not allowed to make mistakes – trial-and-error methods are not helpful for them. Prompting enables them to carry out a task, even for the first time, without making mistakes and in this way they learn more quickly. We do not however want to *over*prompt, pre-empting what they can do for themselves. So we do not jump in too quickly, but delay the prompt until we see that it is needed to ensure that the task is carried out correctly. Both delayed prompting and fading the prompt can help the person to learn more quickly and surely.

In either case reinforcement is given for the action, even if the person has needed prompting to carry it out. The reinforcement will make it more likely that the person will want to do that action again, and so make it more likely that he will need less prompting next time. As the person becomes more skilful we may move on to giving reinforcement only when less prompting is needed, and withholding the reinforcement if the person makes little effort.

Stimulus shaping

This is another useful learning aid, especially where what is being learned is the difference in the appearance of things, for example different letters or numbers. Using stimulus shaping we begin by emphasising or exaggerating the important areas which need to be attended to: so, for example, if we want to teach the difference between the letters V and U we exaggerate the pointed angle of the V and the flat-bottomed curve of the U.

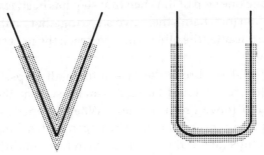

We ask the person to point to, say, V, reinforce him if he is right or tell him if he is wrong, guiding his hand to the correct letter. We do the same for U. When he gets it right, say, eight out of ten times, we reduce the exaggeration:

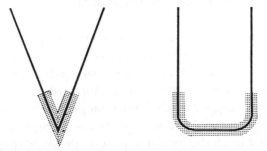

Later we reduce it still further until he is able to pick out ordinary letters as anyone else would.

In this kind of task, which could also include such things as recognising names of things in the kitchen, (flour, sugar), correct TV knobs, the right peg to hang a coat on, and so on, this stimulus shaping method helps people to learn more quickly and permanently than does teaching them by only using and fading gestural prompts. It is worth bearing in mind.

Breaking the task into small steps (or Task Analysis)

Many of the tasks a learning disabled person needs to learn are quite long and complex. Even something as simple as putting on a sock involves getting hold of the sock, getting it the right way round, rolling down the top, positioning it over the toes, pulling it up over the instep, easing it on over the heel. and pulling it up over ankle and calf. If we try to teach all this at once it may be too much. So we break down the task – rather as we have done above with the sock – into small steps; then we teach one step at a time. Although the whole task is daunting, even very disabled people can usually manage one step of it. When that step has been learnt, we teach the next. We then join (or 'chain') these two steps together, so that the person can do both steps, one after the other. Then we teach the next step and chain that to the first two.

We have said that we break the task into small steps, and it seems important that the steps should be really small, so that the person can master it easily and move on to the next. When Kenneth's mother was teaching him to pull up his own pants she began by teaching him to pull them up from his hips (about three inches), then from mid-thigh (another three inches); then, because he was doing so well, she wanted him to pull them up from his knees, which was a distance of about 18 inches; Kenneth floundered, and his mother was disappointed.

We have often seen people make steps too big: we have never seen a programme fail because the steps were too small.

Chaining. We saw above that when two or more steps have been learnt they are chained into a single smoothly-flowing sequence of performance by delivering the reinforcement after the last step in the learned sequence. This chaining can go in either of two ways, forward or backward. When we use forward chaining we teach the first step in the sequence, then the next, and then chain these first two steps. In the example of putting on a sock we would first teach the person to pick up the sock, then to get it the right way round, and we would chain these two together. If we used backward chaining we would first put the sock on the person and pull it up to the ankle (or perhaps a bit further, to the lower calf). Then we would help the person to hold onto the top of the sock with both hands and teach the very last step in the whole process; pulling up the sock to calf level. When the person had mastered this we would teach the next to last step, which would join on naturally to the last and so on. The advantage of using backward chaining (and the reason that we, on the whole, prefer it) is that the person's own actions complete the task and so lead naturally to the reinforcement. Using forward chaining, the person would be reinforced for picking up the sock, and then we would have to take it from him, get the sock rolled up, over his toes, over his heel and up his calf – which does not, to us, seem to give the same feeling of accomplishment. However there is very little evidence to show that one or the other is superior, so, once you have analysed the task into a series of steps, use whichever you prefer.

Restructuring the environment

If someone has a difficulty in learning a task we can look for ways to help him by shifting about the things in his surroundings that affect his learning. To go back to our example of the sock: if the person normally wears rather close-fitting socks which are a bit stiff to get on, we might get a slightly looser pair which will be easier to manage at first. For people who are learning to feed themselves, a plate with one deep side may make it easier for them to learn to scoop up the food. Someone who is very easily distracted may concentrate better in a quiet corner than in the middle of a busy room. Altering the environment may help the learning to get under way.

As with so many of the ways in which we try to help people to learn, we would expect most of these aids to be temporary, and to fade them out as the person becomes more skilful. Our ultimate aim is for the person to cope as far as possible with ordinary things and situations; the aids are just a step along the way.

Imitation

Many of our skills are learnt by watching other people and then copying what they do, but people with learning disabilities do not always know how to copy. In one study in a unit for people with learning disabilities, the teaching method most commonly used was imitation – 'Watch me; do it like this' – although many of the people could not imitate at all. If we can teach them to imitate, it may make it easier for them to learn other skills.

To teach imitation we model (do) the action; we prompt the person to imitate; then we reinforce him. As the teaching progresses, we fade the prompts until, when the person is told 'Do this', he will imitate the action without any prompting. Since at this stage we are teaching imitativeness we may start with quite trivial actions, like tapping a knee, or lifting and replacing a pencil on the table. If possible it can be helpful to have two teachers, one to model the action and say 'Do this' and the second to prompt the action, after which the reinforcer is given by the first teacher.

Once the person has learned to imitate one action, another can be taught, and then the two can be alternated. At this point true imitation begins, when the person has to watch to see what action he should copy. Later other actions can be introduced. Usually, most time has to be spent over teaching the first few actions, with later ones being achieved more quickly. When the point is reached at which the person imitates an action, without prompting, on its first presentation, the person can be said to be imitative, and it may be possible to go on to use imitation to teach him or her useful skills.

Generalisation

The skills that we teach to learning disabled people are those that we hope will be useful to them. It follows then that they should not only learn the skills, but should be able to use them whenever and wherever necessary. For most people this is not a problem: if we learn to tie one pair of shoelaces we can tie others, once we have learnt to drive a car we (usually) have little difficulty in driving others. The skills we master in one situation we can transfer to another. This is obviously very important in enabling us to use our skills economically; if we had to relearn them in every new situation there would be little time for anything else.

For some people with learning disabilities, this transfer of skills is less easy. They may learn a task, and be able to carry it out very satisfactorily in one place, with one person present, with one particular object. But faced with the same task in a different place, or with a different object, they may seem to have lost all their skills. Kate had been taught to dress herself and was able to do this without any help at all; however, when her teacher was called away for a few minutes Kate just stood there, half-dressed. She resumed dressing herself only when her teacher reappeared, even though the teacher did not prompt her either verbally or gesturally, but was just there. Lewis had cooking lessons in his day centre and became very good at managing the gas cooker. However, when he moved into a hostel he was quite helpless – the knobs on the cooker at the day centre were at waist level, while those on the hostel cooker were at eye level. Most people would have no difficulty in making this, quite minor, shift, but to Lewis it appeared to have altered the task so much that he could not attempt it.

This kind of difficulty is fairly common, so much so that it is often recommended that all teaching of people with learning disabilities should include generalisation as an integral part of every programme. This means that we need to be constantly aware of the problem, to forestall it as far as possible, or at least to tackle it if it arises. Kate's teacher, with hindsight, wished that she had sometimes had a colleague stand in for her while Kate was learning to dress; now, with the existing situation, she began by wandering about the room and not paying much attention while Kate was dressing, then spent some time looking through the doorway, then went out for a few seconds, then went out for increasingly long periods. All this time Kate continued to dress herself, until eventually she could do it without her teacher being there at all.

However carefully we plan our programme, it is always possible that generalisation problems will arise because of a change of circumstances. A person may move from home to hostel, or from hostel to independent flat, or the familiar vacuum cleaner may wear out and be replaced with a different model. The important point is that, if this results in the person being apparently unable to do things he had been able to do before, this should not be seen as failure, but as an indication that some more teaching is needed. It may be cheering to know that when a skill has to be retaught in a new situation it is usually more quickly learnt than it was originally – some at least of the original learning sticks.

Working with groups of people

The teaching methods we have been describing in this chapter have all been based on the assumption that teacher and student work together on a one-to-one basis. Although behavioural approaches are used in the teaching of groups this has usually been with children of normal intelligence, and seldom with adults with severe learning disabilities. People who work with groups in, for example, day centres or hospitals, have complained to us that although our descriptions of the behavioural approach sound lovely, it is out of the question for them: 'I can't sit down with one person, I have to be watching out for the whole twenty of them' (or however many there are). This is a genuine criticism, and deserves to be taken seriously.

The problem is, of course, not new. Other people have already looked for ways to use structured teaching within the context of managing a large group. One well-tried approach is known as Room Management (Porter-field and Blunden 1978), and aims to combine interesting and useful activities for a group of people with structured teaching sessions for individuals amongst them.

A minimum of two staff members is needed. One takes the role of the Room Manager who is the overall supervisor and, especially, is responsible for guiding, and giving reinforcement to, each member of the group. The Room Manager has the task, before the session starts, of setting up the room and of preparing the materials that will be needed: making sure there are adequate supplies of paper, pencils, paints, manipulative and sorting tasks, whatever tasks are chosen as appropriate for the particular clients; and also of preparing instruction sheets, which detail the tasks and expected levels of achievement for each client, and record sheets on which to record what is actually achieved. During the session, once the clients are seated, the Room Manager provides each person with a suitable task, giving her the necessary equipment, briefly prompting her to start working with it and putting other materials within easy reach. She (or he) then spends most of her time moving from person to person, reinforcing and praising those who are working, encouraging those who are not, and giving out new equip-ment as it is needed.

The second staff member takes the role of individual teacher. She selects a learning task which is particularly relevant to the needs of an individual in the group, and spends a short time – about 10 minutes – working with that individual only, using the methods of prompting, reinforcement and so on that we have already described. The task chosen should be one in which useful teaching can be done in this very short time. (Indeed, short periods of teaching are often better than long ones for people with learning disabilities.) We find that allowing ten minutes for each person gives us time to move from one person to another, settle to a task and complete it before moving on again. At the end of this time the teacher moves on, leaving that individual to work on other activities which will be overseen by the Room Manager, and goes to someone else. The aim is that as many people as possible will have individual sessions.

If a third staff member is available, she will deal with any interruptions, visitors, phone calls, any client who needs to leave the room, or any occasion of disruptive behaviour. If, however, there are only two staff members available, in our experience it is the individual helper who should deal with these interruptions; if the Room Manager is called away the whole system falls down, while it is less disruptive for the individual helper to leave and return to a teaching session. In fact, again in our experience, once the room management system had been set up, disruptive incidents became fewer and fewer as time went on and clients became more interested in their work.

Room management was designed especially for working with people with profound disabilities. It is, however, demanding work and has usually been used for no more than one hour at a time. This, and the type of tasks originally used (jigsaws, crayons, building bricks) have been criticised, but this is not necessarily a criticism of the Room Management procedure. It is not meant to take the place of other procedures such as individual programme planning, goal setting, time tabling activities and so forth, but to provide a setting in which these can be effectively used.

Summary

1. In this chapter we discuss ways to help the person to succeed in tasks in order to obtain reinforcement.

2. Shaping involves the reinforcement of behaviours which at first are quite distant from, but which gradually come nearer and nearer to, the behaviour we are looking for.

3. In physical prompting we physically guide the person through the action he needs to learn.

4. Gestural and verbal prompts give the person cues to help him carry out the action.

5. All three kinds of prompts can be faded as the person becomes more skilful.

6. Fading is best done very gradually.

7. Prompts may also be delayed to allow the person to do as much as she is able before being helped to complete the task.

8. Stimulus shaping helps a person to carry out a task needing visual discrimination by emphasising the crucial aspects of the task.

9. Even very disabled people can learn tasks if these are broken down into small steps.

10. The steps can be taught one at a time and then, as each is learned, chained to the next step.

11. Either forward or backward chaining may be used: backward chaining may be preferred as leading more naturally to the completion of the task and to the reinforcer.

12. Restructuring the environment can help a person to learn a skill more easily, especially at first.

13. If a person does not know how to imitate we can teach this using modelling, prompting (and fading the prompts) and reinforcement.

14. People should be able to generalise their skills (use them in whatever situations necessary). Generalisation may need to be taught by varying the teaching situation, or by reteaching the skill in different situations.

15. Room Management methods can help to make it possible to do structured teaching of individuals within a group session.

Exercises

1. Why may reinforcement alone not be enough to ensure that a person will carry out a task?

2. Reinforcement should only be given when the person performs the task perfectly. True or false? (Give your reasons)

3. Physical prompting, to succeed, must be done very firmly. True or false?

4. What gestural prompts do we commonly use? What others can be helpful to people who are learning disabled?

5. List of some of the people for whom verbal prompts would not be helpful.

6. If a person responds to prompting we reduce the amount of prompting very gradually. True or false?

7. How would you decide on the number of steps into which a task should be broken down?

CHAPTER 7

Coping with Unwanted Behaviours

Previous chapters have primarily looked at ways in which we can help people with learning disabilities to learn, or to make better use of skills they already possess. This has taken up a lot of the book already and is going to occupy almost all of it after this chapter; the major difficulty for people with learning disabilities is in learning, and our major concern should be to help them learn as much as they can. Some however also need to learn *not* to show some behaviours: behaviours which are dangerous to themselves, or to others, behaviours which interfere with development of other skills, or which cause an excessive degree of annoyance or discomfort to other people.

These constraints on behaviour are not, of course, peculiar to people with learning disabilities. They apply to all of us. If we break a shop window, or beat up an enemy, there is likely to be the wail of sirens followed by a police cell. If we go without washing and wear the same clothes for weeks on end, people will stop talking to us. If we persistently fail to turn up for work, we shall find ourselves out of a job. We like to think of ourselves as free agents, and to a great extent we *are* free to make choices, but if we want to live in a society we have to take account of the needs of others and to conform to at least some of that society's rules. People with learning disabilities, if they want to be part of the society, also need to observe at least some of the rules.

In the past people with learning disabilities have been, as a group, regarded as incapable of making choices for themselves and have been subject to controls of all sorts – on where they live, how they spend their money, who their friends are, what clothes they wear. More recently, there has been a revulsion against this regimentation and a recognition that they have the same rights as anyone else, to live their lives as they choose. These rights are uppermost in the minds of many people and especially of those working most closely with people with learning disabilities who are often reluctant to do anything that might infringe these rights. Especially, perhaps, because of memories of cruel, coercive techniques that have in the past sometimes been practised, they are wary of methods which aim to stop behaviours, and it is right that they should be so. Nevertheless, there are some behaviours which, as we have already suggested, we need to help the person to control. Principal amongst these are the self- injurious behaviours – head banging, eye gouging, self- biting and scratching, vomiting and regurgitation, etc – which, if allowed to continue, can result in serious and permanent damage to the person; and second, violent and aggressive behaviours towards other people. There is also a range of behaviours which, although not physically harmful, result in real disadvantage for the person: repetitive, meaningless behaviours, such as stereotypies, which interfere with learning; those behaviours which make the person noisy, dirty, or smelly so that other people avoid his company. In one way or another these behaviours make life more unpleasant, less rewarding for the person than it should be. So we look for ways to help the person alter or get rid of the problem behaviours.

In Chapters 2 and 3 we described ways of observing behaviours and of carrying out Applied Behaviour Analysis, and we said that the success of subsequent actions depends on the accuracy of this. This is especially true when we set out to tackle problem behaviours. We need to be particularly careful not to jump to conclusions, and not to embark upon programmes because they have worked with other people. Instead, we should take our observations, paying special attention to what may be the setting conditions and trigger events for the behaviour, and to what may be reinforcing the behaviour and might be used to reinforce more desirable behaviours instead. Then, based on this analysis, we set out to devise a programme for this particular person.

As we said in Chapter 1, we aim to tackle problem behaviours using the Least Restrictive Alternative approach. Positive methods will be explored first; if these are ineffective, methods which involve the manipulation of reinforcement will be considered; only if none of these methods is successful, and only if the behaviour is sufficiently serious to warrant it, will we go on to think about the use of aversive techniques (those in which some unpleasant consequence follows the behaviour, described under 'punishment'). Some American workers (LaVigna and Donnellan 1986), have said that we should 'not even consider a punishment procedure unless (we) have carried out a full functional analysis; have failed with no fewer than three carefully designed non-aversive attempts; and (we) absolutely cannot think of any more non-aversive strategies to try'. Whichever method we choose, we discuss it first with colleagues: dealing with problem behaviours is hard work which we tackle better if we have others supporting and encouraging and, if possible, participating with us in it. Punishment methods, which we will come to only as a last resort, should if possible also be discussed with and approved by an ethical committee (see Chapter 1).

Enriching the person's life

Sometimes our observations suggest that a person's undesirable behaviours are brought about mainly because he is unstimulated, deprived, or just plain miserable. In that case we can set about improving his quality of life generally – giving him more, and more interesting, things to do, more variety of experience, more pleasant surroundings, more social companionship. Obviously, this can be quite difficult, and expensive, to do, but in some cases it has resulted in major changes in behaviour patterns. If it is possible, it is well worth trying.

Changing the surroundings

Sometimes we may help a person to reduce undesirable behaviours, not by tackling the behaviours but by altering the surroundings to make them less likely to occur. So, for example, a person who tends to push her plate violently aside so that it skids off the table can be given a dish with suction feet that will make it more likely to stay put. In a very interesting programme carried out in America (Donnellan et al 1984) a young man called Sam, who got so agitated when he was taken into a noisy, crowded places like shops or supermarkets that he was no longer taken to these places, was given a portable cassette player with headphones to wear. With this playing soothing music which screened out other sounds he was able to tolerate the noisy places.

These methods, of course, contain the behaviour rather than getting rid of it, but by containing it they may allow other approaches to take effect. So the person who would violently push her plate aside could be taught to signal 'I have had enough, please take my plate away', which would be easier to do when the plate was not flying off the table. Sam was gradually taught to spend first a few seconds, then a little longer and then still longer, in the supermarket before he got his headphones, until he was able to spend up to an hour in these situations without them.

Building up other behaviours (Differential Reinforcement of Other Behaviours, or DRO)

One of the most positive ways of dealing with an undesirable behaviour is to side-step it; to do nothing at all about the behaviour itself, but to build up another, desirable behaviour instead. Often this can be the obverse of the problem behaviour: somebody who persistently comes into work late can be rewarded for coming in on time, while the times when he is late can be ignored. Dora, who tended to have a runny nose and would wipe it on anything that came to hand, like a tea-towel, was reinforced every morning if she had a tissue in her pocket and every evening when, during the day, she had not been seen to wipe her nose with something unsuitable.

Peter, a young man of 25, had for some time been vomiting on the coach that took him to his Centre, and when this became a daily occurrence the escorts said that they would not take him any longer. The Centre wondered if there was something physically wrong with him, as he was always abjectly apologetic for his vomiting; however his mother said that she could take him out on all-day coach trips at the weekends, and he never vomited on these. It seemed that nothing much would be lost by trying a psycho-logical approach. Peter was told that any day that he did not vomit on the coach he would be given a star to take home to stick on a chart, and that when he had ten stars he would be given a record. Peter earned his stars on the next consecutive ten days that he went to the Centre, and was given his record. He has never again vomited on the coach. Reinforcing non-vomiting, the opposite of the problem behaviour, was enough to get rid of the problem.

The constructional approach

The constructional approach (Cullen and Partridge 1981) takes the build-ing-up-behaviour tactic a step further. It aims to get away from the 'elimi-native model' – simply trying to get rid of unpleasant behaviours – and seeks instead to look at the whole range of the person's skills and to build up behaviours that do the same things for the person, but in more accept-able ways, as the unpleasant behaviour has done. So besides looking for alternatives to the unpleasant behaviour, we need to look at what that behaviour is doing for the person, and try to find some other, more acceptable way for him or her to attain the same end. One example of this is that given on p.97. Here the young woman's unpleasant behaviour was sending her plate of food flying off the table; this was seen not as simply perverse and disruptive but possibly as her way (the only way she knew) of signalling 'I have had enough'. She was taught to make a sign to that effect, and learnt that when she made the sign the plate was removed; and the plate pushing stopped. The virtue of the constructional approach is that not only may it lead to a satisfactory solution of the problem but also it does so from an essentially positive and humane standpoint.

This approach, in which we build up a behaviour which is incompatible with the problem behaviour, is probably the most positive. Even if this is for some reason impossible we always try, when we set up a programme to reduce a behaviour, to set up another simultaneously which will result in reinforcement, for example for learning a new skill. This may be particularly important when we use methods such as extinction or time out from positive reinforcement which involve depriving the person of reinforcement for problem behaviour. Our aim is not that he should be deprived of reinforcement as such, but rather that it should follow positive and not negative behaviours.

Extinction

In the chapter on reinforcement we saw how positive behaviours may be built up and kept going by the use of reinforcement, and that the same can happen with undesirable behaviours. Although we do not mean to encourage these undesirable behaviours, if we look at them carefully we can sometimes spot something which often follows the behaviour and seems to give the person a kick.

When Vincent was sternly ticked off by his mother for calling the visiting psychologist 'fat lady' the smile on his face and his repetition of 'Fat lady! Fat lady!' made it clear that his mother's reprimands, far from lessening, were in fact reinforcing his comments and giving him a kick. If we can identify it, this event that follows the behaviour and that the person appears to enjoy, we can decide that this event will never be allowed to follow the behaviour again. This method is known as extinction, because, when it is used consistently, the undesirable behaviour will usually die out, or extinguish.

Extinction can be a very good method to use if we can identify the probable reinforcer; if, once we have identified it, we have control over it; and if the behaviour is one which is not dangerous, either to the person or to others.

Sometimes it can be difficult to be sure what is reinforcing a behaviour, and we can get it wrong. Kay used to drop cups and plates and dishes on the kitchen floor, and her mother thought that she was doing it because of the horrified attention she got whenever she smashed the crockery. However, when her mother heroically decided not to take any notice, the crockery continued to crash on the floor. It seemed that what Kay really liked was the crashing, smashing noise. It was only when Kay's mother went over to bakelite crockery, which makes a rather disappointing thin little thud as it hits the floor, and which cracks rather than smashing, that Kay gave up dropping crockery.

In the same way we can only use extinction if we have control of the reinforcer and if we can decide when it shall or shall not follow a behaviour. Sometimes we cannot. For example, if a person likes the taste of dirt we cannot deny him the reinforcement he gets from it. If he eats the dirt, the reinforcement inevitably follows. So we cannot use extinction here (of course we could prevent him from eating the dirt, but in this case we would not be using extinction). Similarly, if the reinforcer for clowning about in the workshop is the laughter and applause of the other clients, it may be very difficult to eliminate this reinforcement (although sometimes it can be done).

Extinction should not be used on dangerous behaviours because of what is called the 'extinction burst'. When we first decide that a reinforcer, which until now has always (or often) followed a behaviour, will no longer do so, what characteristically happens is that the behaviour increases. So if the behaviour is an undesirable one it worsens. It seems as if the person is puzzled by the non-arrival of the reinforcement and tries again; then tries harder, or louder, or longer. Still no reinforcement. The person builds up the behaviour to a hitherto unknown crescendo. If *still* no reinforcement is forthcoming, the person usually abandons the behaviour, although sometimes quite slowly at first. This pattern of events is acceptable so long as the behaviour is one which, tiresome though it may be, we can tolerate if it increases, like screaming or swearing; we can grit our teeth and stick it out. But if the behaviour is a dangerous one, like head-banging or playful running across busy roads, any increase in the behaviour could be damaging or even fatal, and we cannot tolerate it. We would do better not even to attempt to use extinction.

We need to know about the likelihood of an 'extinction burst' or we may feel very dismayed when the behaviour increases, and may give up our efforts, saying 'I tried that and it made him worse'. An ATC instructor decided to try to help Janie get over her antisocial behaviours by ignoring them when they appeared, whilst he also reinforced her for periods in which she had been pleasant and friendly. At first Janie stepped up her rude, noisy behaviours, and it was hard for the instructor to prevent himself from stepping in to calm her down. He held out, however, and the behaviours became less frequent and less severe, and Janie became much more pleasant and better liked by the other people in her workshop.

It was especially important, once he had embarked on the extinction programme, that Janie's instructor should not be driven to give in by the increase in the behaviour. If he had done so it would have shown Janie that if ordinary levels of cheekiness and loudness did not bring her attention, extreme rudeness and resounding noise levels would. She would then have been likely to be more rude and noisy than she had been before the programme started. Again, if we think we may not be able to keep it up we had better not even begin an extinction programme; we had better look for something else.

Punishment, as behaviour modifiers see it

Punishments abound in our society, and few of us will go through life without incurring one or another punishment – a slap from an irate parent, early bed-time or no TV; detention after school for misbehaviour in the classroom; a fine for speeding, or for being drunk and disorderly; six months in prison for leaking a confidential document.

The *Concise Oxford Dictionary* defines punishment as a 'penalty inflicted on an offender'; something unpleasant which we have to suffer if we do wrong. Behaviour modifiers view punishment rather differently; they define it as:

> 'Anything which, when it follows a behaviour, makes that behaviour less likely to occur in the future.'

You will notice that this is the exact opposite of the definition of reinforcement given in Chapter 4, p.62. You will notice, too, that the definition says nothing about the 'anything' being an 'unpleasant thing', only that it shall result in a lessening of the behaviour (we are emphatically NOT talking about punishments that involve physical pain, such as smacking). Indeed, some things that we may think of as unpleasant may actually increase the behaviour. Strong verbal reprimands are usually thought of as unpleasant, but in the example above, Vincent did not seem to find his mother's reprimands unpleasant but seemed to get a kick out of them.

So we make no assumptions as to what is a punishment, just as we do not in the case of reinforcement. In each case we have, of course, to make an intelligent guess as to what is likely to work well, but then we have to try it out. The crucial test, in each case, is the effect that it has on the behaviour.

There are two kinds of punishment we can use: when the undesirable behaviour occurs we can either take away something pleasant, or we can give something unpleasant. Each of these methods may be a punishment, the test being whether or not it brings about a reduction in the undesirable behaviour. We will look at each of these in turn.

(1) Removing something pleasant

(i) Time out from positive reinforcement

Using time out is dependent on the person being in a situation that is continuously reinforcing for him; something that he enjoys a great deal is going on – music, a meal, the company of his friends or family, a TV programme. When he shows the undesirable behaviour the reinforcement is interrupted for a short while; he spends some time out of the reinforcing situation. Then the reinforcement returns, and continues unless he again shows the undesirable behaviour, when once again the reinforcement is temporarily lost to him. And so on. Eventually he finds that he has a more enjoyable time, without all these interruptions, if he does not show the undesirable behaviour and this fades away.

A young woman instructor wanted to help Andrea, one of the trainees, to get over her habit of keeping her fingers in her mouth. Not only did this make Andrea unsightly, with two fingers dragging down the corner of her mouth and saliva dribbling down her hand and arm, but the constant pressure on the bottom teeth had pulled them badly out of shape. Andrea was not in the instructor's workshop, so she decided to visit her every day in the lunch hour. For ten minutes she played a game that Andrea loved, where the instructor chased her around the room and when she caught up with her, tickled and hugged her and rumpled her hair. As long as Andrea's fingers were out of her mouth this game continued; however, as soon as her fingers went to her mouth the instructor abruptly broke off the game and turned away from Andrea, until once more she removed her fingers from her mouth. At the end of three months a new baseline was taken which showed that, over 160 occasions in which Andrea was observed, her fingers were in her mouth on only four, when she was also not very well. Compared with the original baseline in which her fingers had been in her mouth on virtually every occasion this was a great improvement. Andrea had also improved in other ways as well, being more friendly and out-going and more willing to approach people than she had been before; but whether this was anything to do with the programme, or whether it was a spin-off from the extra interest and attention that had been paid to her because of the programme, it was impossible to say.

We can use time out whenever reinforcement is continuously available to the person, and when the reinforcer is one we can control (just as in the case of extinction), and this can be used very effectively when attention is the reinforcer. We should perhaps say here that, although attention can be a powerful reinforcer, it is not invariably so. It is fashionable nowadays to say 'We should ignore all bad behaviours'. Apart from the obstacle that many people find this in practice impossible (if for example the bad behaviour consists of attacks on other clients) this would be effective only when attention was the reinforcer. If some other reinforcer is operating, ignoring the behaviour is useless. If, however, attention does seem to be the reinforcer, we may well be able to use time out. If we are chatting to someone who enjoys having a chat, and who then blows a raspberry, we can stop chatting and look away for ten seconds or so. We can then go back to chatting, and only stop again if another raspberry is blown. And so on. Time out is often thought of as involving a much more drastic deprivation of attention than this, by removing the person from the room altogether and, perhaps, putting him or her in another small room. This is such a common misconception that we would like to spell it out:

> REMOVING THE PERSON FROM THE ROOM WILL ONLY WORK IF BEING IN THE ROOM IS VERY REINFORCING FOR THAT PERSON.

If the person is thoroughly enjoying the social scene and the activities going on, then removing him from the room when he shows some undesirable behaviour *would* be using time out, and might well bring about a decrease in the behaviour. (Whether it is physically possible to remove an unwilling grown person from a room with any dignity is another matter.) If, on the other hand, he doesn't much care about the social scene or the activities he was expected to engage in then his undesirable behaviour might increase; it would be negatively reinforced by his being able to escape from the things he disliked.

So time out does not necessarily involve seclusion, and most definitely seclusion is not always time out. We have to be quite clear that quite often seclusion is just seclusion. That has no place in a behavioural programme.

How long time out should last depends partly on how it is being used. If we are using it in a meal-time programme, for example removing the person's plate when the undesirable behaviour occurs, ten seconds, to start after the person has swallowed the last mouthful, is usually enough. Ten seconds is probably long enough to interrupt other similar enjoyable experiences, such as music, or a TV programme. If the time out involves removal of the person to another room five minutes may be enough. In general it seems important not to make the time out period a long one, or the person may forget why he is there and so fail to build up the connection between his undesirable behaviour and what follows it (which is, after all, the whole point of the programme). It has also been found better to start with quite a short period of time out, and if necessary to lengthen it a little. If we start with a longish period, and then reduce it, the behaviour may worsen.

Another problem can be the person's behaviour during the time out period. If, when we turn away or take the plate away, the person creates a rumpus – screaming, banging, hitting out, etc, – we should not turn or give the plate back until he or she has been quiet for at least a short period. We do not want to convey the idea that it was the screaming and so on that brought the plate back. For someone who can understand we may say, 'You won't get it back until you are quiet', but if the person cannot understand the period of quietness may at first have to be very short. Once he or she realises that the plate *will* be coming back, the period can be extended to the ten seconds or so we had decided on.

(ii) Fining

Fining is a commonly used punishment in ordinary life: if we commit some offence we may be required to give up a sum of money, the size of the sum being related to the seriousness of the offence committed. A similar approach has been taken in some token programmes, so that tokens earned for positive behaviours are removed when undesirable behaviours are shown. A problem with this method is that it is very easily seen, by both those giving and those receiving this kind of punishment, as retributive and punitive, and it can lead to a build-up of tensions and hostility. We ourselves have not used this method, which is discussed more fully in 'Tokens'.

(2) Giving something unpleasant

Although the methods described above, which involve at most a brief deprivation of something positive, are often used to tackle behaviour problems, there are times when they are ineffective or cannot even be attempted (see 'Extinction'). Then we may need to look for something else. The methods we are going on to describe all involve some degree of 'unpleasantness' applied to the person, following each occurrence of the behaviour. Once again, we should stress that this 'unpleasantness' is not intended as retribution, nor to make the person suffer. It is intended only to decrease the frequency, or the strength, of the behaviour it follows. So when, for example, we decide on a programme whereby we hold Mabel's hands down firmly each time she slaps her face, what we look for is that she should slap her face less often and less hard. If this happens, then the programme is doing what we want; if the face-slapping does not diminish then, however much Mabel wriggles and protests and seems to dislike having her hands held down, the programme is not useful and we should look for something else.

There are a number of methods we can look at.

(i) Brief restraint

When the person shows the undesirable behaviour, she is held physically still for a short time. In the example of Mabel, described above, when she slapped her face her arms were held to her side for ten seconds. During this time the person holding her did not talk to her, after the first 'No', nor look at her. At the end of this time she was released, but if she slapped her face again her arms were again held down. This probably has a bit of 'time out' in it, in that while the person is being held still she cannot do other enjoyable things. It seems, though, that the physical restriction, although not painful, is something extra that the person may wish to avoid.

It is important to remember that some people may find this physical restriction not unpleasant at all, but rather enjoyable. This may happen in spite of our efforts to make the restriction a neutral, uncuddly affair. If our observations show us that the behaviour is not diminishing, or is increasing, then restraint is not a suitable method for this person.

(ii) Restitution

When we break, or lose, something belonging to a friend we often try to make up for what we have done by mending the object or buying another one. In the same way it seems quite natural that if someone has messed up or created a disturbance in the environment he or she should be expected to put it right. So if Laura throws all the knives and forks on the floor she can be told to pick them up again. If she refuses, or does not understand the instruction, she can be prompted to pick them up. In this case we use prompts in the same way as we use restraints, calmly and neutrally, with no talking after the first instruction ('Pick them up') and using the least amount of prompting that results in her picking up the cutlery quickly and efficiently. We give Laura no reinforcement for picking up the cutlery, whether or not she needs to be prompted to do so (we do not want to reinforce the throwing that necessitated its picking up).

This method can be used for many different kinds of behaviour. Someone who slams doors may be made to close them quietly. Another who smears faeces may be made to clean it up or, if pants are deliberately wet, made to change them and wash them out. Someone who spits may be made to wipe his mouth carefully and to wipe up the blob of spittle. As with other methods, it is important to keep records, of the behaviour and of what is being done. If the behaviour improves, well and good. If it does not, then, no matter how appropriate the method seems, and especially no matter how much it makes us feel that we are at least doing something, we should look for something else.

Schedules

When we were discussing ways of giving reinforcement we saw that the best way to build up a new behaviour or skill was to give the reinforcement every time the person showed the behaviour; that is, to use a *continuous* schedule of reinforcement. Later on, as the person became more adept at the skill, we could move to a *variable* schedule, giving the reinforcer every now and then. When we are using ways to deal with problem behaviours they too work best if we can use a continuous schedule: so that every time Mabel slaps her face we hold her hands down. The method can still work if we can deal with most, even if not all, the problem behaviours, though it may work more slowly. But if we miss out too many, if, say, more than two or three occurrences of the behaviour regularly go unpunished, we may not manage to get rid of the behaviour.

Variable schedules of reinforcement (not of punishment) may be worth mentioning here. If we want to maintain a behaviour, to keep it going, a variable schedule of reinforcement does this most effectively. Many people believe that one reason for some bad behaviours being so firmly established is that they have in the past been reinforced on a variable schedule: that quite often other people have managed not to reinforce the behaviour, but every now and again they have given in. So the person has learnt that if the behaviour does not bring the reinforcement this time, it may the next...or the next...or the next...until it becomes very strongly fixed indeed.

Summary

1. Our main interest in using behaviour modification methods is to increase the person's skills and opportunities of enjoyment.

2. We may need to tackle bad behaviours because:

    (a) they are dangerous to him or to others;

    (b) they hinder his chances of learning.

    (c) they hinder his chance of living in pleasant environments.

3. Ways which side-step the behaviour:

    (a) As a first step we may try making the person's life generally more pleasant;

    (b) or we may rearrange the surroundings to make it less likely that the behaviour will occur;

    (c) another approach is to build up (reinforce) behaviours which are the opposite to, or incompatible with, the undesirable behaviour.

4. Extinction

    (a) We identify the reinforcer which has followed the behaviour, and we ensure that it does not follow the behaviour again.

    (b) When we first discontinue the reinforcement the behaviour may occur more strongly. It is very important that this should not be reinforced.

    (c) Extinction may not be a good method where the behaviour is a dangerous one, or where we cannot control the reinforcer.

5. Punishment is defined in behaviour modification as anything which, when it follows a behaviour, makes that behaviour less likely to happen again.

6. This may be done in two main ways: removing something pleasant, or giving something unpleasant, when the behaviour occurs.

7. Taking away something pleasant:

    (a) Time out from positive reinforcement

        (i) A person who is in a continuously enjoyable (reinforcing) situation has that enjoyment interrupted for a short time when the undesirable behaviour occurs.

        (ii) Time out and seclusion are not the same thing.

    (iii) It is better to use a short period of time out, and extend it if necessary, rather than the other way round.

  (b) Fining

Tokens, stars, points, etc, may be removed following an undesirable behaviour.

8. Giving something unpleasant.

  (a) Brief restraint

    (i) A person may be held still for a short time when the undesirable behaviour occurs.

  (b) Restitution

    (i) A person may be made to put right any disturbance he has caused.

9. Undesirable behaviours are best dealt with on a continuous schedule.

Exercises

1. Give four examples of types of behaviours which we might want to help a person control.

2. What would be the first area we would look to when considering help for a person's undesirable behaviours.

3. What is the technical definition of punishment which we use in this book? How is it different from the popular or commonly used definition of punishment?

4. Why may it be unwise to use the abbreviated term, 'Time Out'?

CHAPTER 8

Recording and Presenting Data

In Chapter 2 we talked about the importance of observing a person's behaviour and everything that went on around it; of getting clear in our own minds what is going on and what we want to do. We talked about some different ways of organising the observation sessions and about the importance of writing down our observations rather than relying on memory. Record keeping *is* valuable, but it is undoubtedly a chore and not everyone will want to or feel they can do it. To them we would say, don't feel all is lost; if you feel you can do the work but can't cope with the recording then go ahead with the work. However, for those who feel they might like the satisfaction of doing so, we look at ways of recording our observations, and of making the results interesting and informative. Keeping records is an added burden to already busy lives; we want to look at ways of doing so that are as easy and painless as possible. We try to get away from hand-written diaries – 'Today all the residents were out but Jill came in at 4 and was upset about something so we calmed her down and she went off to her room to listen to her radio and Terence had lost his keys so we sent him back up the road to look for them but in the supermarket...'. There are times when you need to have a note about all sorts of odd information like that, but it is time-consuming to write and difficult to condense into useful measures of information. We try to simplify the records to make it easy to jot down what has happened – we may lose a bit on detail but we will gain in reliability and regularity of the recordings.

The record sheets we use will differ according to what we are recording and how we set about doing it. There is a basic difference according to the stages of our observations: first, when we are trying to sort out the situation using applied behavioural analysis (see 'Observation') and second, once that has been done, when we want to record the target behaviours in our baseline and in the treatment programme. We could look at these separately.

A(ntecedents)					B(ehaviours)			C(onsequences)	
Date	Time	Place	Others present	Activity	Provoking incident	Victim	Raymond	Others	Raymond
Tues 3 May	1.45pm	Kn	M, C	U	C asked him to dry a plate	C	K threw plate at window	M grabbed R, pushed him into hall, shouted	Didn't resist
Fri 6 May	8.15am	B	-	Dr	Jumper stuck over head (chair)	O (chair)	Sc, K	F held him, took jumper off	Calmed when jumper off

Key:

Place:
Bed: bedroom
D = dining room
Kn = kitchen
G = garden
Gg = garage
H = hall

Other present:
M = mother
F = father
S = Stanley
C = Christine
O = other

Activity:
TV = television
U = unoccupied
Dr = dressing
Sc = scream

Raymond:
K = kick
B = bite
S = scratch

Figure 1: **Raymond: aggressive incidents**

Keeping records during functional analysis

When we carry out applied behavioural analysis we look at the antecedents, at the behaviour, and at the consequences. This is quite complicated. There are many different things we need to look out for and to record and, because we are at this early stage, some of them are unpredictable. However, we can make things easier for ourselves if we list some of the possible happenings, so that if they do come up the observer simply has to put a tick.

Suppose, then, that we want to do a functional analysis on Raymond's aggression at home. We need a section on the *antecedents* – where and when do the incidents happen? Who else is present? What is he doing at the time? Does anything happen that seems to trigger off the behaviour? In the *behaviour* section we need to know what Raymond does – kick, hit, bite, scratch, throw, scream? Who is the victim? In the *consequences* section, we record what happens next – what does his mother, father, brother do? Raymond himself – does he smile, cry, run away? What does the victim do? We then make up the record sheet with as much as possible of this on it (see Figure 1). A key saves space, and helps to make the filling in quite quick, while having the chart already there, with the areas to be recorded already laid out, makes it easier to fill in and so more likely that people will do it. The major drawback to this chart is that it does not leave much room for extra detail, which may be important, so some people may think it worth having a separate, blank, sheet nearby on which they can spread themselves when they really want to.

Keeping records of defined behaviours

(1) Discrete happenings

What records we keep depends on the kind of behaviour we are recording and the kind of recording method we have chosen. The simplest records are those when the recording method chosen is event recording (see 'Observation'). Here we need a simple chart with dates on it, and then for each day we put a tick each time the behaviour happens. The chart for Joe's door-slamming is shown on page 112.

This record gives us a fair idea of how much door-slamming is going on. It does not tell us *when* it is happening: if we want to know that, we could divide the chart up into different time periods; morning and afternoon, or morning (until lunchtime), afternoon (until suppertime), and

Date	Occurrence					Total
19.3.92	✓	✓				2
20.3.92	✓	✓	✓	✓		4
21.3.92	✓	}				1
22.3.92		}	Away for weekend, 9.00 am-10.00pm			0
23.3.92	✓	✓	✓			3
24.3.92	✓	✓	✓	✓	✓	5
25.3.92	✓	✓	✓			3
	Weekly Total					**18**

Figure 2. **Joe:** Door-slamming

evening (until bedtime), or, if we felt the exact time might be very important, into hourly or even shorter intervals.

If we have decided to use partial interval sampling or time sampling,
the record sheet will need to show the intervals we have decided on.
Supposing we had decided to use one of these to record Joe's door-slamming, and to record this for only one hour in the morning and one in the
evening, using 15-minute intervals. Our record would look like this:

	8.00am–9.00am				6.30pm–7.30pm			
Date	8.00- 8.15	8.15- 8.30	8.30- 8.45	8.45- 9.00	6.30- 6.45	6.45- 7.00	7.00- 7.15	7.15- 7.30
19.3.92	......	......	......	......	......	......	......	......
20.3.92	......	......	......	......	......	......	......	......
21.3.92	......	......	......	......	......	......	......	......
22.3.92	......	......	......	......	......	......	......	......
23.3.92	......	......	......	......	......	......	......	......
24.3.92	......	......	......	......	......	......	......	......
25.3.92	......	......	......	......	......	......	......	......

Figure 3. **Joe:** Door-slamming

Using partial interval sampling, we would put a tick if Joe slammed a door at any time in any of the intervals: using time sampling we would put a tick if he slammed a door at a particular point in each of the intervals – say, in the last ten seconds.

(2) Increasing skills

Besides recording the frequency of particular behaviours we will want also to record levels of skills taught, looking for levels to rise and frequencies to increase. There are a number of different ways of recording the results of teaching: by counting achievements; grading prompts; and probes.

Counting achievements (or permanent products – see Chapter 2). This is the simplest. If we are teaching someone a series of tasks, we record when he has mastered each one. So we might record the number of new words a person has learnt to read, or the signs he can make, or the number of garments he can put on or dishes he can cook. If we have broken a task down into a small steps we may record each step as it is mastered, and this provides an encouraging record of progress towards the final achievement, mastery of the whole task.

Achievement often comes rather slowly for people with learning diffi-culties, so this method may be slow to show results, although breaking the task down into (really) small steps helps.

Grading prompts. If the task is one that requires prompting, we can measure progress by recording how much prompting the person needs to complete the task at each stage. For example, if we want to teach Trish to turn on a tap, we may at first have to hold our hand over hers, put her hand over the tap and turn the tap: later we may need to hold her hand less firmly, later still not hold it at all but just point to the tap, while finally she will be able to do the whole task on her own without help. We can then grade the prompts, giving an increasing score as the person herself does more of the task. So the prompts could be graded as follows:

Full physical prompt	= 1
Partial physical prompt	= 2
Gestural prompt	= 3
No prompt	= 4

So if on Wednesday, Thursday and Friday Trish needed full physical prompts to turn the tap, on Saturday only a partial prompt, on Sunday full prompts again, on Monday and Tuesday partial prompts the record would run:

	Wed	Thurs	Fri	Sat	Sun	Mon	Tues	TOTAL
WEEK 1	1	1	1	2	1	2	2	10

The next week's records might be:

	Wed	Thurs	Fri	Sat	Sun	Mon	Tues	TOTAL
WEEK 2	2	2	2	3	3	2	3	17

In this case we have good evidence that Trish is making progress, because the totals are rising. If they were not rising we might have to think about changing the programme.

Probes. When we use probes we monitor progress by, in effect, taking mini-baselines from time to time. So after taking the main baseline we set up our teaching programme, and put it into effect using chaining, prompts, reinforcers and so on as necessary. At regular intervals – say, once a week, or once a fortnight, whatever seems appropriate – we return to baseline conditions: we present the task just as we did originally and see how much the person can now do, compared with what he did in the main baseline.

Supposing we decided to use this method to record Doreen's progress in another programme to teach her to turn on a tap. In our main baseline we take Doreen to the washbasin: we say, 'Doreen, turn on the tap'. Then we record what she does – whether she moves closer to the washbasin, whether she looks at the tap, moves her hand towards it, puts it on the tap; or whether she does none of these things. Then we start our teaching programme, complete with the task broken down into small steps, physical and/or gestural prompts, and of course reinforcement. During the teaching we do not need to keep any records; on one day a week (we decide on Friday), instead of going through the teaching programme we once again take Doreen to the washbasin and say 'Doreen, turn on the tap' – that is we look at what progress she has made with the task. Then we record what she does, using for the record steps in the chaining scale, graded prompts, and so on. Our scale might consist of six steps (because we are going to use backward chaining the last step in the chain, 6, is the first one we will teach).

(1) looks at tap;

(2) stretches hand towards it;

(3) puts hand on tap;

(4) grips tap;

(5) turns tap partially;

(6) turns tap fully;

while prompts could be graded 1-4. Then our weekly record might be as follows:

Week	Date	Stage	Prompt Level
1	2.3.92	1	1
2	9.3.92	1	2
3	16.3.92	1	4
4	23.3.92	2	1
5	30.3.92	2	1
6	6.4.92	2	2
7	13.4.92	3	1
8	20.4.92	3	3
9	27.4.92	4	3

Figure 4. **Doreen**: Turning on the tap

One of the advantages of using probes is that the burden of record-keeping is lightened, as we do not have to record the results of each teaching session; but, as in the example above, we can see the progress being made through the stages, and, within each stage, progress as the prompts are faded.

(3) Graphs

As records accumulate, the time comes when a string of figures becomes difficult to interpret, and we need a better way to show how progress is going. With data displayed on a graph it is easy to see at a glance what has been happening over a period.

Drawing the graph. A graph can be drawn on any piece of paper, preferably lined, while if the graph is to be a detailed one it may be worth getting hold of special graph paper (obtainable from most stationers).

There are two main aspects of a graph: the things that happen (the records) and when they happen (the timing). The things that happen are usually put vertically, going up the page, while time goes horizontally across the page. So we draw a line down the left hand side of the page – this is the vertical axis; and, starting from the bottom of this, we draw a line across the page – the horizontal axis. We label each of the axes. Then we can put each point of our record on the graph in turn, and we can join up these points. As an example we could graph the data from Trish's pro-gramme.

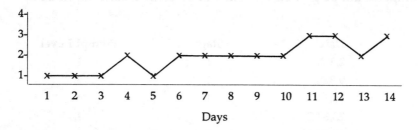

Figure 5. **Trish:** Turning on the tap

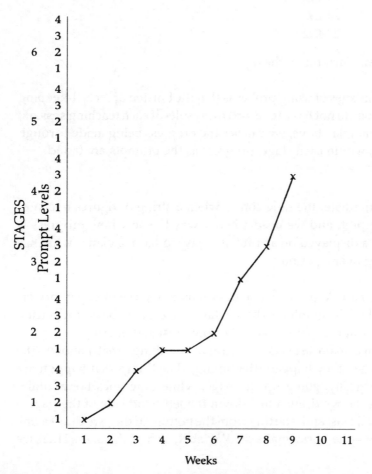

Figure 6. **Doreen**: Turning on the tap (Probes)

We have also made a graph of the probe data from Doreen's programme (Figure 4). Here we have put up the vertical axis not only the stages, but also the four prompt levels for each stage, so that we can see how Doreen is progressing.

It is important to get the scale right, with enough room on the vertical axis for the scores to go up, or down. In Trish's programme there are only four levels of prompts, and in Doreen's six so we know the record cannot be higher than 4 or 6. But supposing we were recording something like the number of words John can say, and supposing we made out a graph like this:

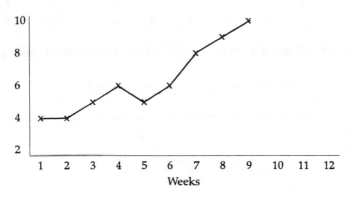

Figure 7. **John**: Number of words said

By Week 9 John is saying ten words, and if in Week Ten he says 12 or 14 there is no room for them. What we must absolutely not do is to try to squeeze them in by, say, halving the scale, saying that we will now put four words where there had been two, and eight where there had been four, and so on. This would give a misleading view of what had happened. If we *do* get the scale wrong, there is nothing for it but to scrap the graph and start again, giving ourselves plenty of room this time.

We must also make sure our graph consists of data which relate to the same topic. So if we begin by counting and graphing the number of words John says, we cannot suddenly decide to graph only the number of verbs he uses, and join that up with the graph of number of words. This would make it look as though John was saying fewer words now than he had done before; again, we need a new graph.

Average scores. You can see that the graph of Trish's scores (Figure 5) goes almost clear across the page, and that was only two weeks' worth. If we expect a programme to last some time it may be better to cut down the number of points on the graph by averaging the scores over time. We can do this for any period we like; often it is convenient to do this for a week. So we add up all the daily scores, and divide them by the number of days – in this case, seven. If we do this for Trish's scores (p114) the total for the first week, ten, is divided by seven which gives us 1.4; the total for the second week is 17, which divided by seven is 2.4. The records for two more weeks might be as follows:

	Wed	Thurs	Fri	Sat	Sun	Mon	Tues	TOTAL	AV
WEEK 3	2	2	3	2	3	2	2	16	2.3
WEEK 4	3	3	4	4	4	4	4	26	3.7

(The average for Week 3 actually came out as 2.2857 so we round that up to 2.3).

We can then put the records for all four weeks onto a graph:

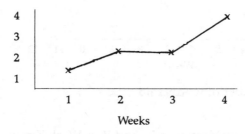

Figure 8

This graph is easier to deal with than one in which each day's individual score is plotted. It also gives us a useful overview of the general progress and irons out day-to-day fluctuations. Another important advantage of using average scores, rather than just weekly totals, is that it does not matter so much whether there are exactly the same number of teaching sessions each week. If, for example, things had gone a bit wrong in Trish's programme (and however hard we try things do go wrong sometimes) and in Week 4 it had not been possible to carry out the teaching on Saturday, Sunday or Monday; if we were using weekly totals, that for Week 4 would have been 14, lower than the 16 she scored in Week 3, and it would have looked as though she had done less well. If we use average scores however her average for the remaining four days works out at 3.5, which gives us a much better idea of how she is getting on.

Percentages. Percentages are another way of managing data. We work out what is the highest possible score the person could make, and we call that 100. Then whatever score the person actually gets is worked out as a proportion of the highest possible score which we then convert into a proportion of 100. This is a percentage.

Let us say that Ralph is being encouraged to improve his appearance and to shave himself properly, to dress in clean shirt and trousers every day, and to have clean fingernails. He presents himself each morning for inspection and gets a token on each of the four counts. In the evening he gets another token if his nails have not been noticeably dirty throughout the day (or, if they became dirty, he went and cleaned them without being told to). So Ralph can earn a maximum of five tokens a day, and 35 in a full week. We can look at the record of the number of tokens he earned in the first four weeks of the program:

	Mon	Tues	Wed	Thurs	Fri	Sat	Sun	TOTAL
WEEK 1	3	2	2	3	4	1	2	17
WEEK 2	3	4	3	3	4	4	Out	21
WEEK 3	4	4	5	2	3	4	3	25
WEEK 4	5	3	5	3	5	Out	Out	21

The highest possible number of tokens Ralph could get is five each day, so for Weeks 1 and 3, when Ralph was at the hostel every day, the maximum for the week is 35. What he actually got in Week 1 was 17. We work out the percentage by dividing his actual total (17) by the maximum possible (35) and multiplying by 100:

$17/35 \times 100 = 48.6$

In the same way his percentage for Week 3 is:

$25/35 \times 100 = 71.4$

These are messy little sums but easy with a calculator. Weeks 2 and 4 are a little different, since Ralph was not at the hostel on all seven days, but on six in Week 2 and five in Week 4. So his maximum possible score in Week 2 is 5 tokens per day on 6 days, = 30, and in Week 4, 5 tokens per day on 5 days = 25. His percentage for those weeks then are, for Week 2:

$21/5x6 \times 100 = 21 \backslash 30 \times 100 = 70$

and for Week 4:

$21/5x5 \times 100 = 21/25 \times 100 = 84$

We can then put these percentages on our graph, and see how Ralph is getting on. We round decimal points to the nearest whole number, so we call the percentage for Week 1, 49, and that for Week 3, 71.

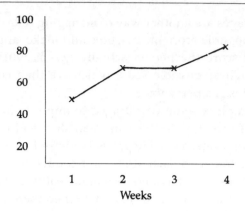

Figure 9.

We can see that Ralph is getting on nicely, and we cross our fingers and hope that this will continue.

Summary

1. Written records which can be put into figures make it easy to see what progress is being achieved.

2. We need a different kind of record for doing a functional analysis on the one hand and recording a target behaviour on the other.

3. Problem behaviours may be recorded as and when they occur.

4. The result of teaching sessions may be recorded from the number of tasks achieved; the level of prompts required; or by the use of probes.

5. Record sheets made out ahead of time make recording easier.

6. Putting figures on a graph makes progress clear.

7. On a graph, time (or number of sessions) usually goes along the horizontal axis and scores on the vertical axis.

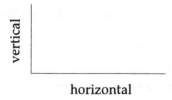

8. Scores may be combined into averages over time in order to get a more compact graph.

9. Percentage scores ensure that we do not run out of space on the graph.

Exercises

1. Where might be the best place to keep the record sheet for programmes designed to:

   (a) teach B to wash a jumper;

   (b) decrease J's screaming/swearing;

   (c) teach F to use the telephone;

   (d) teach M to plant out seedlings;

   (e) reduce K's bedwetting.

2. What recording method would you expect to use for each of these – a, b, c, d, e, above?

Part II

Practice

In Part I we looked at the general principles of behavioural teaching methods, of dealing with problem behaviours, and of ways of recording data and presenting it attractively. In Part II we go on now to look at some of the specific skills that people with learning difficulties often need to learn – self-help, domestic, travel, work and social skills – and to give more detailed accounts of ways that these may be taught.

Part II may be seen as the most immediately useful part of this book, and some people may want to skip Part I and go straight on to whichever section of Part II interests them. While sympathising with this, we feel we should point out that Part I provides the basis for everything in Part II; those who skip may find some of the terms and methods discussed in Part II rather unclear. So if Part II on its own seems difficult, it would be worth going back and having a look through Part I.

CHAPTER 9

Washing and Dressing

Adults take it as a matter of course that they look after their own daily needs: that they wash, dress and feed themselves, that going to the toilet is essentially a private affair that concerns them alone. Indeed, it can be a matter of distress to an adult person if illness or disability forces them to ask for help in these areas. Many people with a learning diability learn these skills as children and are competent in looking after themselves, but for those who are not, special teaching may enable them to achieve this, normal, kind of independence.

As always we start with observing what the person can do already, whether she can do it better in some situations than in others, what reinforcers are likely to work well for her. We then think about how we are going to teach her what she needs to learn and again, the methods we will be describing depend on breaking each skill into small steps, chaining, prompting and fading (see Chapter 6). Let us look at each area separately.

Washing

We need to wash our face and hands and clean our teeth; bath and dry ourselves or maybe use a shower; every so often wash our hair. When we want to teach a person to do these things, in each case we need to break the activity down into small steps which can be taught one at a time.

Washing hands

The steps for hand-washing might be:

   (1) Put in plug.
   (2) Turn on cold tap.
   (3) Turn on hot tap.
   (4) Test water until it is the temperature desired.

(5) Turn off one tap (hot, if water warm).

(6) Turn off cold tap.

(7) Dip hands in water.

(8) Pick up soap.

(9) Rub soap between hands.

(10) Put down soap.

(11) Rub palms together.

(12) Rub right hand over back and down fingers of left hand.

(13) Rub left hand over back and down fingers of right hand.

(14) Rinse hands.

(15) Pull out plug.

If we are using backward chaining we would begin by prompting the person right through the whole process; then, as he or she began to be more skilful, we would aim to fade the prompts, first on step 15, pulling out the plug. Later the prompts could be progressively faded from the other steps. Face-washing is dealt with under 'Bathing'.

Cleaning teeth

Clean teeth not only help the person to look nice but also guard against bad breath. Teeth cleaning is quite a skilful task but can be taught, especially if it is broken down into sufficiently small steps. In this sequence we will include putting the paste on the brush.

(1) Take toothpaste tube.

(2) Unscrew top.

(3) Put top down.

(4) Pick up toothbrush.

(5) Squeeze half-inch of paste onto brush.

(6) Put down toothpaste.

(7) Brush downwards on all outer surfaces of top teeth.

(8) Brush upwards on all outer surfaces of bottom teeth.

(9) Brush downwards on all inner surfaces of top teeth.

(10) Brush upwards on all inner surfaces of bottom teeth.

(11) Brush biting surfaces of top teeth.

(12) Brush biting surfaces of bottom teeth.

(13) Put toothbrush down.

(14) Pick up mug.

(15) Turn on tap.

(16) Fill mug with water.

(17) Turn off tap.

(18) Rinse and spit out three times.

(19) Rinse toothbrush.

(20) Put toothbrush away.

(21) Put mug away.

(22) Wipe mouth on towel.

(23) Pick up toothpaste and top.

(24) Screw on top.

(25) Put toothpaste away.

The main difficulty is to ensure that the person cleans his teeth properly, so the brushing may have to be specified as occurring a certain number of times – say, four times – in any one place. Also it may be necessary to divide up the areas to be brushed, into front, left and right, for top and bottom teeth, inner and outer surfaces, (steps 7, 8, 9 and 10).

Bathing

We could look at the steps we used for teaching 17-year-old Tim to bath himself. His mother had always helped him to bath, and she felt that she ought not now to be doing this and wanted him to be able to bath himself properly and privately. Bathing is a complicated business and perhaps needs to be seen as three separate processes: running the bathwater, washing, and drying.

(a) Running the bathwater

(1) Pick up plug. *

(2) Put plug in plughole. *

(3) Turn on cold tap.

---

* In this case the plug was a round rubbery one on the end of a chain attached to the bath between the taps. If the plug is worked by some other mechanism, such as a lever, these steps would have to be adjusted.

(4) Turn on hot tap.

(5) Keep hand in water, well away from the taps, stirring the water, until the temperature feels right: *or* (if the bath has a mixer tap) keep hand in running water until the temperature feels right.

(6) Watch bath until it has enough water.

(7) Turn off hot tap.

(8) Turn off cold tap.

The trickiest part of this is getting the temperature right, and we supervised Tim very carefully, letting him feel the temperature and tell us when he thought it was right, and then checking it ourselves until we were sure that he was not going to make a mistake and scald himself.

(b) Washing in the bath

Getting into the bath is usually simple, especially if the bath has a handle on each side which the person can hold onto. If a person has difficulty in lifting his legs high enough to get over the side of the bath, a firm stool or steps can help.

When we step into the bath the first thing we do is sit down in it, then lie down or splash ourselves all over to get thoroughly wet. What happens next depends on whether the person is going to wash himself with soapy hands or with a flannel. Tim used a flannel. The steps were as follows:

(b) (i) Face-washing

(1) Dip flannel in water.

(2) Squeeze flannel out.

(3) Rub flannel over front of face (chin, nose, forehead) in a circular movement. This is done without soap to avoid getting soap in the person's eyes though, of course, this could be altered.

(4) Pick up soap.

(5) Rub soap over flannel.

(6) Put down soap.

(7) Rub flannel over right cheek.

(8) Rub flannel round and into right ear.

(9) Rub flannel round right side and back of neck.

(10) Rinse flannel in water.

(11) Squeeze out flannel.

(12) Pick up soap.

(13) Rub soap over flannel.

(14) Put down soap.

(15) Rub flannel over left cheek.

(16) Rub flannel round and into left ear.

(17) Rub flannel round left side and front of neck.

(NB—At this point some people may prefer the person to take a second flannel after he has finished face-washing.)

(b) (ii) *Body-washing*

(1) Rinse out flannel in water.

(2) Squeeze out flannel.

(3) Pick up soap.

(4) Rub soap all over flannel.

(5) Put soap down.

(6) Rub flannel all over left arm and left side.

(7) Rub flannel all over left chest and under left armpit.

(8) Take flannel in left hand.

(9) Rub flannel all over right arm and down right side and under armpit.

(10) Take flannel in right hand.

(11) Rub flannel down left leg, round toes and all round foot.

(12) Rub flannel down right leg, round toes and all round foot.

(13) Rinse flannel.

(14) Squeeze out flannel.

(15) Pick up soap.

(16) Rub soap all over flannel.

(17) Put soap down.

(18) Stand up: *or* lift bottom out of water.

(19) Wash lower part of trunk.

(20) Wash round genitals (for men, easing back the foreskin) and bottom.

(21) Rinse flannel.

(22) Squeeze flannel out and hang it up.

Of course, if the person can't face all this body-washing you could just give him some bubble bath and let him immerse himself in that for ten minutes or so. It works quite well on all but really dirty bits which need rubbing with a flannel. However, you would still have to tackle:

(c) Drying

Tim got out of the bath, and then needed to dry each part thoroughly.

(1) Pick up towel

(2) Rub face and neck.

(3) Rub left foot, including between toes.

(4) Rub left leg from knee down.

(5) Rub right foot, including between toes.

(6) Rub right leg from knee down.

(7) Rub left thigh to knee.

(8) Rub right thigh to knee.

(9) Pat and rub gently around genitals.

(10) Rub around bottom.

(11) Rub front of trunk.

(12) Get towel round back, rub back and shoulders.

(13) Rub left arm and armpit.

(14) Rub right arm and armpit.

The important thing about drying is that it should be done thoroughly, especially between toes and in crevices which may become sore if they are left damp. So, during, the teaching Tim's mother checked each time when Tim indicated that he reckoned he had done enough, and only gave the reinforcer if she was sure that part of him was really dry.

The steps given in each of the three sections are probably appropriate ones, but the order in which they are taken is not on the whole important. For example, although in general we would suggest washing faces first and bottoms last it doesn't matter much whether you wash arms before legs or vice versa. So you can move the order around to suit yourself, though it may be helpful, once you have decided on the order you prefer, to stick to it as it may make it easier for Tim not to miss anything out if he has a regular routine to follow.

Once we have decided on a routine, we then have to decide whether we want to teach it by forward or by backward chaining. For example, if we wanted to use forward chaining we would first concentrate on teaching and reinforcing Tim to pick up the plug, and would then prompt him through the rest of the sequence: if we had decided to use backward chaining we would prompt him through all the steps and concentrate the teaching first on turning off the cold tap.

Using a shower is similar to bathing, with three important differences: first, it is even more important to get the temperature of the running water right and, especially, not too hot; second, Tim (if he were the learner) will have to rinse his flannel in the running water; and third, he will have to balance on one foot to wash the other so a handle on the side of the shower to hold on to is a big help. If he has real difficulty in this, or in standing up, he can sit on a plastic chair or stool under the shower.

Shaving

Unless they decide to go in for a full beard, adult men need to shave every day. Many men with learning disabilities learn to shave themselves, and although in the days of cut-throat razors it may have been rather nerve-racking to allow them to do so, electric razors have changed all that. Usually the only real problem is that he may shave only part of his face, going over the same part repetitively and leaving the other parts out; or that he may do it poorly and patchily, giving him the kind of unkempt appearance that does little for his image. So we need to break down the process, and especially the areas to be shaved, into steps:

(1) Switch on razor.

(2) Rub razor over left cheek.

(3) Rub razor over left jaw.

(4) Rub razor over right cheek.

(5) Rub razor over right jaw.

(6) Rub razor over chin.

(7) Rub razor over upper lip.

(8) Switch off razor.

After Tim has passed the razor over an area he should be prompted to feel the area with his free hand, and if he feels any bristliness, to keep his free hand on the spot and to approach the razor to it and repeat shaving until the area is smooth.

If the razor is mains- rather than battery-powered, Tim will also need to learn to plug it into the socket.

Hygiene

As with many other skills, people who have these skills may not always use them to their own best advantage. So we may have to look for ways to encourage people who can wash, bath, clean their teeth and nails and so on, to do so sufficiently often to keep themselves acceptably clean. Since we are dealing here with skills the person already possesses, we need to look to ways of reinforcing these, and a token programme is often useful. Dawn is a 19-year-old young woman who lives in a hostel. She is a capable young person and is being prepared to move out of the hostel and into a flat with two or three others, and the hostel staff are working with her to increase her skills to the point where she will be able to be confident in her new surroundings.

One of the areas in which Dawn needed to improve was cleanliness. She did not bath often enough, so was smelly, so the other residents did not want to have her around; when she changed her clothes she stuffed the dirty ones back in her wardrobe instead of putting them in the dirty clothes basket; and when she had a period she would not bother to dispose of the pads properly but hid them under the S-bend of the lavatory or in the lavatory brush container. The hostel staff discussed with Dawn the need for her to improve in these ways if she were to be able to move out into a flat, and Dawn agreed that she would like help in this. A programme was set up whereby Dawn would have a bath on Mondays, Wednesdays, Fridays and Sundays; she would report, all glowing and smelling of soap, to a member of staff when she had done so, and would be given a token. Where the dirty clothes and pads were concerned, she was told that the living areas, including her wardrobe, would be checked at random intervals, and that, regardless of whether the checks had been carried out or not, on each day that no dirty articles of Dawn's had been found where dirty articles ought not to be, she would also be given a token.

The tokens were exchangeable for high quality make-up and scent that were normally out of Dawn's price-range. She quite quickly got into the bathing routine and was then given her own bathing chart to keep, staff occasionally making discreet checks on its accuracy. She also soon found it was little more trouble to put dirty articles in the right rather than the wrong places. When Dawn was carrying out the programme easily and almost faultlessly she was told that, for the next six weeks, she would no longer be checked and would receive some elegant bath salts at the end, providing her hygiene continued to be satisfactory – that is, if she had not been noticed as being slovenly. If this had happened the programme would have been reinstated but by this time, helped by the appreciative comments of both staff and peers, these ordinary standards of hygiene had become part of Dawn's normal routine, and the programme has not been needed again.

Using sanitary towels

Michelle refused to wear a sanitary towel when she had a period. She lives in a health service Community Unit and we were asked by some of the nurses who work with her to try and think of some ways to help. What ordinarily happened was that a towel was put in place by a member of staff. Michelle then would sneak off at the earliest opportunity, sometimes as little as two minutes later, and remove it. This resulted in the staff having to give Michelle a bath up to four or five times a day when she was having her period.

Michelle could not speak or otherwise tell anyone why she was removing her sanitary towels. We thought that there were four possible reasons why she might be doing it. Michelle had very little knowledge as to what periods were and may have linked sanitary towels with ideas of handicap and incontinence pads. (Many of the people who lived with Michelle at the Community Unit used incontinence pads although Michelle herself did not.) Second, Michelle may have had an aversion to sanitary towels similar in many respects to a mild phobia. Third, Michelle may have associated sanitary towels exclusively with the bad feelings surrounding a period. Finally, Michelle may have found the bulk of the pad around her crotch uncomfortable.

In the past, the staff had tried many ways of getting Michelle to keep her sanitary towels on. These included using press-on towels, disguised sanitary towels, and buying her frilly knickers, but none of these was very successful. We decided that our goals were as follows: that we wanted to educate Michelle about the basic facts of menstruation, including the fact that all women have periods and use sanitary towels; to desensitise her gradually to having a bulky towel around her crotch; and to get her used to wearing a sanitary towel regularly and for extending periods of time.

The plan we developed to achieve all of these goals involved both Michelle and members of staff in levels of personal intimacy not usually experienced by adults who are not related to each other.

The staff who were involved in teaching Michelle consented and volunteered to take part, and considered it to be part of their job; Michelle herself was not really able since she could not speak to give consent. However, after much discussion we decided that not wearing a sanitary towel set Michelle so much apart from people in the general way that some sort of action on our part was definitely necessary. Since we could not be sure which of our possible reasons for Michelle's behaviour was accurate, we also decided to tackle all of them in the programme we devised.

In the first week of our basic programme we spent a short time each day giving Michelle a sanitary towel to hold and examine briefly. At the same time she was shown pictures (some from advertisements) which associated sanitary towels with normal adult life. Some of these photographs showed adult women putting sanitary towels in their knickers. In the second week, still using the same pictures, Michelle learnt to lay a sanitary towel (a slimline press-on one) in a pair of knickers each day. In the third week Michelle put a sanitary towel in place in her own knickers each day and then removed it. The nurse who was working with Michelle modelled this for her first. In the fourth week Michelle put the sanitary towel in place and wore it for two minutes before removing it. In subsequent weeks the amount of time that Michelle kept the sanitary towel in her knickers was gradually extended. Michelle loved all the time spent with staff while doing all this work, and everyone was full of praise for her for doing so well.

In conjunction with this gradually extending programme, any nurse who felt she could was asked to take Michelle with her when she was changing her own sanitary towel so that Michelle could see that this was something which most women experienced. Everyone who worked with Michelle felt that things had gone very well. However, the success then pinpointed various areas which would need further teaching – particularly the regular changing of sanitary towels when Michelle was actually bleeding – where to throw away soiled towels, and interventions into better and more independent general hygiene such as bathing and hairwashing which Michelle might do for herself.

Using sanitary towels too much

We have, more than once, come across young women who, having learnt to use sanitary towels correctly, began to use them all the time even when they were not menstruating. This can be very expensive and may also be uncomfortable and irritate their skin. One approach may be not to prevent the woman from wearing a sanitary towel between her periods but gradually to decrease the size of the pad used, progressing from normal to small to mini pads and then cutting the size of the pad down, until there is just a piece of gauze left, and finally getting rid of that too. When she is actually menstruating she would of course he provided with normal size sanitary towels to use.

We met someone with an interesting extension of this problem. Jocelyn had developed the habit of putting a piece of toilet paper in her knickers. When she was menstruating she wore sanitary towels and this was no problem, but between times she always insisted on keeping a clean piece of soft tissue in her knickers. Jocelyn had Down Syndrome and her skin was especially dry to start with, while she also had a tendency to thrush and was often very sore. She was not always good at keeping herself clean or putting on clean clothes, and the toilet paper just seemed to make her skin condition worse. Jocelyn agreed that probably it would be better if she stopped putting the toilet tissue in her knickers but she said she just could not get out of the habit. She said that she used the paper 'to keep clean' but saw the sense in stopping using it and wanted to try to. We approached the problem from various angles. Jocelyn's mother agreed to get her appropriate medical treatment for the thrush, to make sure that she bathed regularly and used cream on her dry skin generally and to make sure that she had clean knickers available every day.

At her day centre, her key worker was willing to be part of the scheme. Jocelyn, her mother and her key worker all agreed that during the day she should be able to win points, one for looking clean and tidy, when she came in in the morning, and a further point if she was wearing clean knickers. Then, throughout the day, up to a maximum of four times, her key worker checked whether Jocelyn had toilet paper in her knickers and each time she had not she was given another point. This meant that she could earn up to 6 points a day. In the beginning we set 30 points as a goal; if Jocelyn achieved this she could choose a tape or record as her reward. For the first two months things went very well, Jocelyn blossomed under all the extra attention she was receiving, her thrush cleared up, and she much less often had toilet paper in her knickers. She looked cleaner and tidier and became a more responsible member of the day centre.

Then came Christmas and everyone was busy doing other things and the points were forgotten. In mid January, Jocelyn's key worker checked how things were going and saw that everything had deteriorated. Jocelyn was looking scruffy again, her thrush had come back and she had toilet paper in her knickers again. Everyone felt very disheartened, Jocelyn had shown them how different she could be and now no one was prepared to accept the old standards. Her key worker felt quite angry – if Jocelyn could do it before Christmas why couldn't she do it now? We all sat down and talked about this together. We felt that the deterioration in the situation was not because Jocelyn was difficult or obstinate, but because she needed extra help to achieve even things she wanted to achieve (including avoiding pain). It might be that we would have to go on giving her that extra help for considerable periods of time before we could even begin to think about withdrawing the reward based system again, and that we would have to be very careful when it came to making sure that the new habit had generalised.

The points were reinstated – back to the original six per day, including general tidiness. Again, the difference could be seen immediately. Jocelyn looked cleaner, wore clean clothes daily and dispensed with the toilet paper for much of the time. As time went by we included more items of specific and general personal hygiene and set the total number of points to be earned higher: first 30, then 40 then 50. Once more, everyone agreed that Jocelyn was like a different person and her specific skin problems became much less troublesome. Both her mother and the day centre workers found, however, that considerable time (over a year) passed before they were able to fade the system completely and Jocelyn could maintain a good standard of hygiene for the ordinary reasons of feeling clean and comfortable.

Preparing for menstruation

Mothers sometimes worry about how their daughters who have a learning disability will cope with menstruation, and how they can best prepare them for this. One mother whom we know was faced with this problem and worked out her own solution to it.

Mrs F. had two daughters with Down Syndrome, aged 11 and 12. When she could see they were reaching puberty she went to her doctor and asked, 'How can I prepare them for having their periods?'. The reply she received was, 'That's up to you, Mother'. She went home and thought about it. She bought a book* which had illustrations of children, both boys and girls, adolescents and adults, both clothed and naked. She took the two girls upstairs onto the parents' bed ('That was the best place for a chat') and said, 'We're going to have a chat about young ladies growing up'. She showed them the picture of the naked adolescent girl and said 'You're beginning to look like that', to which the younger daughter replied 'Oh, boobs'. Mrs F said 'Yes, and you're getting a little hair. It means you're becoming young ladies'. She had on the bed sanitary knickers and a packet of pads. She opened the packet and said, 'This is what ladies wear when they're grown

---

* 'Peter and Caroline', by Sten Hegeler, Tavistock Publications, 1957 (translated from Danish)

up'. She showed them how to fit the pads into the knickers. The girls were pleased and excited and the younger one said, 'What do you wear them for?'. Mrs F told them that when girls were grown up they would once a month have a thing called a period, 'a drop of blood coming from where the hair grows between the legs'. She told them the period lasted 3-4 days, 'and I'm going to show you how to put this on so as to stop your clothes getting all messy '. Both girls then put on the knickers, the elder one complaining that it was uncomfortable but Mrs F said firmly 'You have to wear this when you're a young lady – I have to wear it as well'. She told them that from now on they would wear the knickers one weekend each month, starting with that weekend. She explained that they would have to wash between their legs every morning and showed them how to dispose of the pads. Apart from a few complaints of discomfort, all went well, and the family settled into a routine with pads and knickers being worn one weekend each month. About six months later, the family went on holiday, and on their return at midnight the elder girl went up to the toilet, and when she came down again went to her mother and said 'Mum, I've started my period' ('just like a grown-up'), got out all the things she needed and put them on. A year later the younger girl also started her periods, and the only problem with her was that she would go around patting her stomach and saying 'I'm a young lady now'. Again, Mrs F had A Chat with her, and told her 'These are ladies' things, you don't tell everyone'. Both girls had very regular periods, so the day before one was due they took to school a little make-up bag containing knickers, pad, and a paper bag for disposal, so that they had no difficulty when the period started. This approach was highly successful in giving these two girls a smooth introduction to what can be a traumatic event in any girl's life, and the principle of introducing the topic and, especially, of rehearsing the practical routines *before* menstruation starts, seems a valuable one.

Dressing

For most of us, dressing and undressing are tedious routines that we go through almost without noticing. They are essential skills and it is unthinkable that an adult person should be helped to get dressed or undressed unless he or she is quite ill. But for many people who are learning disabled this is a daily occurrence. Some, of course, may have problems that make it impossible for them to manoeuvre clothes sufficiently to get them on, but most can learn to put on garments and to dress themselves completely.

Most of us tend to dress with much of our mind on other things – 'What shall we have for breakfast?', 'Have we got enough milk if they all want cereal?', 'I'll have to catch the 8.12 today, the 8.07 is cancelled' and before we know it we are fully dressed and downstairs. But dressing is a remarkably complicated business. Watching a small child struggling to put on a cardigan shows us how complicated it is and how many separate steps are involved in that process. Again, we need to break each task down into small steps, teach one step at a time by prompting, reinforcement and fading, and then teach the following step and chain this to the previous one.

Assessing the situation

An adult person who is not able to dress independently is likely to have learnt how to do at least some of it, so before we embark on teaching her it may be useful to look at what she can do already. (Here we are, back at observation and analysis again.) So supposing we want to see how much Lucinda can do in dressing herself, we lay out her clothes on the bed – bra, knickers, tights, blouse and skirt: we hand each one to her in turn, and note which she can and which she cannot put on; if there are any she cannot put on entirely, whether she can do any part of the process. We set a time limit of about one minute during which she will be allowed to try to put each garment on; then we put it on partly for her – say, knickers on up to knees – and see whether she can succeed from that point, and we repeat this with each garment. At the end of this we should have a fairly clear idea of how much Lucinda can do and where we should start the teaching. If she is having difficulty with many of the garments we will probably concentrate the teaching on just one: so that each time Lucinda gets dressed she will participate in putting on that one garment (probably one of the easier ones, like knickers) and the rest will be put on for her. Then when she can manage that garment for herself we will move on to teaching her another.

Supposing, then, we wanted to teach putting on knickers. We would work out a series of steps that might be as follows:

Knickers: pulled up from:

(1) Mid-hips.

(2) Lower hips.

(3) Mid-thigh (between thigh and knee).

(4) Knee level.

(5) Mid-calf.

(6) Ankles.

From this point on the task involves more than just pulling the knickers up; it requires Lucinda to put them on. For this, she would need to sit down, on the edge of the bed, or a chair, or the floor if she preferred it. Then:

(7) One foot already through the leg opening, puts other foot through, stands up, pulls knickers to waist.

(8) Given knickers, puts in first one, then the other foot, stands up, pulls knickers to waist.

(9)* Takes knickers, gets them the right way round, puts each foot in, stands up and pulls knickers to waist.

At first, if Lucinda has no idea how to pull up her knickers, we would have to use full prompts, our hands firmly round hers, to make sure that the knickers were pulled up to the proper place. All the time we would try to keep alert to how much she was doing, and to sense whether she was holding the knickers a little more securely so that we could relax our grip a little. Whenever we felt that she was doing this, we would allow her to do as much as she could, fading our prompts but still ensuring that the task was completed. When she could do this stage entirely by herself, not just once but, say, three or four times in succession, then we would move on to the next stage.

When we teach pulling up knickers what often happens is that, although the two sides of the knickers are pulled to the waist, the back and front are still sagging, so it may then be necessary to prompt Lucinda's hands to run round to the front and to the back, and to adjust these before we give the reinforcement.

Putting on trousers is fairly similar to putting on knickers – easier in one way and more difficult in another. It is easier at around stage 8, in that with trousers it is less likely that we will end up with both legs through the same hole; and it is more difficult because the foot has to go down the whole trouser leg and can get jammed. It may then be helpful to have some extra steps between 7 and 8, as follows:

(7a) One foot put through trouser leg to ankle, second foot put through two-thirds of the way, foot pointing to floor, pushes second foot all the way through, pulls up from ankles to waist.

(7b) As in 7a but second foot put halfway through, pointing to the floor.

---

* This step may require special teaching – see 'Inside-out and back-to-front'

(7c) As in 7a, but second foot put quarter way through, pointing to the floor.

During these three steps it may be necessary for the teacher to prompt the foot to point downwards at first, gradually fading the prompt. If necessary three similar steps can be inserted for the first foot, between 7 and 8.

For an upper-body garment, let us look at the steps involved in putting on a T-shirt, working out how to teach this to a young man called Steve.

(1) Shirt put on over the head, Steve's arms pulled through armholes and shirt pulled down to waist level: Steve pulls it all the way down to hip-level.

(2) As before, pulled down to rib-level.

(3) As before, one arm pulled right through armhole, second arm pulled halfway through armhole: Steve pushes second arm right through armhole, pulls shirt down.

(4) Shirt put on over head, one arm pulled right through armhole: Steve pushes second arm into and right through armhole and pulls shirt down.

(5) Shirt put on over head, first arm pulled through armhole, second arm doubled up under shirt against ribs: Steve holds bottom of shirt with first hand, finds armhole with second hand, pushes arm right through and pulls shirt down.

(6) Shirt put on over head, first arm pulled through: Steve holds bottom of shirt with first hand, finds second armhole and completes.

(7) Shirt put on over head, first arm pushed halfway through armhole: Steve holds bottom of shirt with second hand, pushes first arm right through: complete with second hand.

(8) Shirt put on over head, first arm put to armhole: Steve holds bottom of shirt with second hand, pushing first arm into and through armhole and completes.

(9) Shirt put on over head, first arm doubled up against ribs under shirt: Steve holds bottom of shirt with second hand, finds first armhole and completes.

(10) Shirt put on over head: Steve puts each arm through armhole and completes.

(11) Shirt put over head and pulled halfway down head: Steve pulls shirt down to neck and completes.

(12) Shirt put over head: Steve pulls shirt down over head to neck and completes.

(13) Shirt given to Steve, upside down, lower edge of back of shirt into his hands: Steve pulls shirt over his head and completes.

(14)* Shirt on chair: Steve picks up shirt and puts it on the right way round.

So we have now worked out a scale for putting on a lower and an upper body garment, and in general these can be adapted for, in the first case, trousers and skirts, and in the second, vests, pullovers, petticoats and dresses. Garments such as jumpers with sleeves will need extra steps in the scale given for a T-shirt between 2 and 3, and again between 7 and 8, as follows:

2(7)a: Jumper put on over head, first arm pulled right through sleeve, second arm pulled almost through so that second sleeve covers hand: Steve pulls second sleeve up with first hand, and completes.

2(7)b: Jumper put on over head and first arm pulled through, second arm pulled halfway through sleeve: Steve pulls second sleeve up with first hand, pushes second arm through and completes.

Putting on a cardigan/jacket/coat/shirt

Putting on a garment that has to be passed round the back of the body is quite different from putting on one that goes over the head. Much of it is quite simple, but it contains one fiendish trap. We will again use a backward chaining scale, and assume that the person we are teaching, Norma, is right-handed.

(1) Right arm put in sleeve, cardigan pulled up onto right shoulder, left arm put in sleeve, cardigan pulled up just below left shoulder: Norma pulls cardigan up onto left shoulder.

(2) Right arm put in as before, left arm put in and sleeve pulled up to elbows: Norma completes.

(3) Right arm put in as before, left arm put halfway in sleeve: Norma pushes arm through and completes.

(4) Right arm put in as before. Left arm put to armhole: Norma pushes left arm through and completes.

---

* See 'Inside-out and back-to-front'

(5) Right arm put in as before: left arm put level with left armhole. Norma finds left armhole, pushes arm through and completes.

(6) Right arm put in as before: Norma finds left armhole and completes.

(7) Right arm put partly through sleeve: Norma holds cardigan by neck above right sleeve, pulls up on right shoulder, finds left armhole and completes.

(8) Cardigan handed to Norma in right position: Norma holds by neck, puts right arm in and completes.

(9) Cardigan laid out on bed with right shoulder uppermost: Norma picks up cardigan by neck above right shoulder and completes.

(10) Cardigan out in any position: Norma finds right sleeve and puts on.

The fiendish trap is step 6 when, with the right arm in the right sleeve, Norma has to hunt, behind her back, for the left armhole. This is by far the most difficult part of this process but can be helped by a judicious sliding between steps 4, 5 and 6, gradually fading the amount of prompting given for finding the left armhole.

Putting on tights comes somewhere between putting on socks and putting on trousers. The difference from pants is that with them we can do the whole thing holding onto the waist-band, but with tights we have to stretch them on, frequently releasing the tights and taking hold of them again further up the legs, and it is very difficult to pinpoint exactly how this will be done in each case. The difference from socks is that we have to manage both feet at once, instead of being able to clothe first one and then the other as we can with socks. Here then are the steps that we used to teach June to put on her own tights.

(1) Tights put on and pulled up to mid-hips: June pulls them to waist.

(2) Tights put on and pulled up to lower hips: June pulls them to waist.

(3) Tights put on and pulled up to mid-thigh, one side pulled up to lower hips: June pulls other side to lower hips and completes.

(4) Tights put on and pulled up to mid-thigh: June pulls first one side, then the other, to lower hips and completes.

(5) Tights pulled to knee-level, one side to mid-thigh: June pulls other side to mid-thigh and completes.

(6) Tights pulled on to knee-level, June pulls first one side, then the other, to mid-thigh and completes.

(7) Tights put on to ankle level, one side pulled up to knee: June pulls other to knee-level and completes.

(8) Tights put on to ankle-level, June pulls each side to knee-level and completes.

(9) Tights put on over toes, one pulled up to ankle level: June pulls other side up to ankle-level and completes.

(10) Tights put on over toes: June completes.

(11) One side of tights put on over toes, other side given to June scrunched up: June puts other side over toes and completes.

(12) One side of tights put on over toes, other side of tights handed to June half scrunched up: she scrunches it up all the way, puts over toes and completes.

(13) One side of tights put on over toes, other sided handed to June straight: she scrunches it up, puts it over toes and completes.

(14) Tights given to June with first leg scrunched up: June puts it over toes, scrunches up second leg and completes.

(15) As in 14, but first leg half scrunched up.

(16) Tights handed to June to the right way round (if applicable: some tights have heels but many have no heel and can be put on either way round).

Working out ways of putting on a bra has caused us more headaches than any other garment (apart from tying ties, and as many people don't wear ties nowadays we feel we can with a clear conscience leave that alone). But a bra is an essential garment for many women, and, being one of the most intimate, one that they much prefer to put on independently. The question came up in a group of parents attending a course, when Mrs James said that she had not been able to teach her 15-year-old daughter Cathy to put on a bra, because Cathy could not cope with the back fastening. If she tried to do up the bra in the front, she could not get the fastener straps straight and the bra became hopelessly snarled-up. Someone suggested that front-fastening bras were available, but Mrs James said none of these really fitted Cathy. So the group set about devising a method – since there were fathers in the group we could not actually remove our bras in order to test out our ideas, and some of the ideas were pretty weird and wonderful. The one Mrs James decided to try was to lay the bra, inner surface uppermost and fastenings stretched out on either side, on Cathy's bed: then Cathy could lie down on her back on the bra, pick up the fastenings on either side, hook them up, swivel the bra round and put her arms through the straps. It seemed rather a good idea at the time. Cathy, however, poured scorn on it and said she wasn't going to do *that*, she felt it was silly.

In the meantime, a friend of Mrs James' came up with the solution. (So much for the need for professional help.) Cathy sat down in a chair and held the bra by the straps in front of her with the inner surface furthest from her, then swung the bra behind her: she leaned back against the chair, let go of the straps and picked up the fastenings, which, with the bra held between her back and the back of the chair, hung straight and at a convenient level; she did up the fastenings, twisted the whole bra round so that the fastenings came at her back, picked up the straps and put her arms through them. Cathy did that twice under her mother's eye and now she can put on her bra.

Another way that we might try for someone having difficulty with putting on a bra is to do it up first, and then teach her to put it over her head, putting her arms through the straps and pulling it down round her ribs, rather like putting on a T-shirt. This only works if the bra is quite stretchy and has a secure fastening that will not come undone during the putting-on.

Inside-out and back-to-front

Somewhere along the line we have to decide how much we are going to teach. If a person cannot at the outset dress himself at all, then it would be a big step forward if he learnt to put on, by himself, clothes that have been put out for him in the right order. If, however, we are looking towards a much higher level of independence, in a flat or group home for example, then the person would need to be able to choose clothes from the wardrobe that were appropriate for the weather conditions and for whatever he was going to be doing that day: and to put them on in the right order, and the right way round. The latter is often a stumbling block, even for people who otherwise are quite good at dressing. There seem to be two steps here: knowing which is the back and which the front, and putting the garment on the right way round. Many garments already have a label sewn into the back, and it is a good idea to do this for most that have not – hand-made jumpers, slips, tights. Then the person can be taught always to begin the process of putting on a garment by laying it on the bed, or over a chair, front side down and the label nearest him, so that when he picks it up it is the right way to go on. The exception to this back-labelling is socks; teaching the right way round to put on socks seems easier if the label, or a sewn-in thread of a contrasting colour, is in the front. Later it may be possible to fade this by gradually shortening the thread.

Most garments have seams on the inside, and this shows us which way out the garment should be. If the person has difficulty with this we can show him the seams, perhaps prompting him to feel them, and emphasising that they are 'inside'. If the garment is inside-out we can show him the seams on the outside, indicate, maybe by a sad shake of the head, that this won't do, and when he has turned it the right way out give him his reinforcement.

Getting shoes on the right (appropriate) feet is another problem. Sixteen-year-old Ellen lived in a hostel, and although she could do most of her own dressing she often appeared with her shoes on the wrong feet. She herself did not seem to notice this but it cannot have been good for her feet and certainly looked very odd. The hostel staff had made a brave start with this problem by marking one of her slippers, putting a star on the inner sole of her right slipper and teaching Ellen that the starred slipper must always go on the right foot. This was fine until Ellen's school also had the bright idea of marking her shoes, and put a star on the inner sole of her left shoe. Eventually this confusion was sorted out, and the plan was gradually to fade the stars, either naturally through the wear of the shoes, or by using an ink eradicator, so that Ellen has to pay more attention to other aspects of the shoe shape as the stars get fainter. Another method which has worked well with other people is to use a template, drawing on a piece of cardboard round the shoes. If we did this for Ellen, when she wanted to put on her shoes she could first fit them to the template, heels towards her, and then put her feet into them.

Adapting the clothing

When we begin the teaching we make sure that the clothes are quite loose, without constricting necks or cuffs that make it difficult to get them on. This seems particularly important for socks – some kinds of nylon socks are very rigid and unyielding, while others are elastic and much easier to manage. Later, as the person becomes more skilful, it should be possible to go on to more difficult garments if these are in his wardrobe. This applies, too, to differently structured garments. At first, we may want to use very simple garments – T-shirts or sweat shirts without buttons, slip-on shoes, trousers with elasticated waists – in order to maximise what the person can do independently. We are quite often asked 'Why not leave it at that? If a person with a learning disability can learn easily to cope with this type of garment, why put them through all the stress of learning others?'. Of course, if the teaching is going to be stressful, or is most unlikely to succeed (and we are wary of assuming that too readily), then we don't need to go any further.

But if it seems that the person could learn these extra skills, of coping with buttons and laces and closer-fitting garments, then this will enable him to wear a whole range of garments that most non-disabled people wear, and which he otherwise would not. We want to offer him the chance of learning as many of the normal skills that he can and that he wants to.

Drawing up your own scales

We have given a few scales that we think could be useful in teaching putting on one or two garments (and more can be found in *Carr: Helping Your Handicapped Child*). These are meant only as a guide, and it may be that they are not suitable for one reason or another, or that you want to teach putting on or taking off a garment that we have not covered. In either case, you can make up your own scale, working out the appropriate steps. Perhaps we should warn you that it seems pretty much essential to rehearse the steps for real, putting on or taking off the garment yourself. Without this it is amazingly difficult to know what you actually do. We once wrote down all the steps we thought went into threading a needle, miming it as we went along: it was not until we picked up a real needle and thread that we found out, not only that we did it quite differently, but that we held the needle in the other hand from the one we had indicated in our scale.

Summary

Washing

1. In teaching self-help skills we make use of prompting, fading, breaking the task into small steps and chaining. And, of course, reinforcement.

2. Teaching someone to bath himself includes running the bath, and drying, as well as washing all over.

3. Learning to shave with an electric razor mainly involves ensuring that all the relevant parts of the face are shaved.

4. For people who have the necessary self-care skills but do not use them adequately, teaching hygiene usually requires a reinforcement programme.

Dressing

1. Before we begin teaching dressing we need to find out how much the person can do already.

2. Teaching putting on pants involves teaching pulling up the pants from ankles to waist; and getting the pants over the feet to the ankles.

3. T-shirts (and petticoats, vests, etc) require the person to learn pulling down to hip level, pushing arms through armholes and head through the neck opening.

4. Sleeves require extra steps.

5. Jackets, cardigans and so on are especially difficult at the point where the second hand is put in.

6. Tights are like a cross between socks and trousers (but more difficult than either).

7. The problem with putting on a bra is the back fastening: a number of ways of getting over this are suggested.

8. Getting garments on the right way round, and getting shoes on the correct feet, can be made easier to learn.

9. Big, loose-fitting garments are easier at first, then it may be possible to move gradually to closer-fitting, more normal clothes.

Exercises

1. Make up a scale for hair-washing.

2. Which is (probably) the trickiest step in teaching someone to run a bath? Why?

3. Patrick has good self-care skills, yet often looks slovenly. How might we go about remedying this?

4. Why should we bother to teach people to do up buttons and tie shoe laces?

5. How would you set about constructing a scale for putting on some garment we have not mentioned here (say, dungarees)?

CHAPTER 10

Eating and Toileting

Eating behaviours

Feeding

Feeding oneself is such a basic, essential activity that by the time they are adults only the most severely disabled do not have at least the main skills. Others, however, may lack some skills, or may have acquired some poor eating habits.

To teach people good eating habits, or how to feed themselves, we use prompting, fading, chaining, and reinforcement. The reinforcer is nearly always the food itself, and we are careful when we embark on the teaching to use food that the person is especially fond of. Sometimes we may need to use some extra reinforcer, additional to the food being eaten (see 'Replacing the spoon', p.149).

SPOON FEEDING

Occasionally, we come across a person who, although grown-up, is still being fed, and then we may want to try to teach her to feed herself; usually we will begin by teaching her to feed herself with a spoon.

First, we make sure that she is properly positioned at the table, in a chair that is the right height so that the table is at about waist level. We use a dish with sloping sides so that the food will not easily shoot out of it. If the person has a poor grip we may use a spoon with an especially thick handle, or may slip a length of Rubazote over an ordinary handle to make it easier to hold. We stand behind her so that the natural flow of our hand movements fits in with hers. We try to ensure that the food in the plate is not only something she is very, very fond of, but is also fairly tractable and easy to spoon up, like mashed potato, mince or rice (peas tend to skid about). Then we begin. We scoop a little of the food into the spoon, wrap her hand round the spoon, and, with our hand firmly round hers, guide the spoon to and into her mouth, tip the food into her mouth, and then guide the spoon back to the plate. Then we wait while she chews and swallows the mouthful, and repeat the process with another mouthful. This might be enough at first, especially if she objected to the self-feeding idea.

Marcia was 36 years old when her parents asked for help in teaching her to feed herself as they felt they could not take her to a restaurant – it looked so odd for them to be spoon-feeding a grown-up woman. Marcia disliked being touched, which made people uncertain as to whether they could use physical prompting at all. Her parents were confident that she would come to accept it, so the teaching went ahead, but to begin with Marcia was made to hold the spoon for only the first two mouthfuls, when, because she was hungry, she was more ready to hold it. Later on it was possible to extend this to three, then five, then eight mouthfuls, and so on, until eventually Marcia 'held' the spoon for the whole meal.

As Marcia began to accept the idea of having her hand round the spoon, her father, who fed her at home, began to relax his grip very slightly, to enable her to do a little more of the process. He began this fading of the prompt just as the spoon went into her mouth because, with the food almost there, this was the part that Marcia was most willing to do herself. Later he was able to fade the prompt a little when the spoon was about three-quarters of the way from the plate, then about half-way, later still at the point when the spoon was lifted from the plate. This programme is still under way, but if it goes normally, Marcia's father will relax his grip of Marcia's hand gradually a little more, and a little more, as he feels her able to hold and control the spoon, until she is able to hold it by herself. At that point, he will 'shadow' her hand, his hand moving above hers, not touching it unless necessary but right there to help if help is needed.

When Marcia has learnt to take the spoon to her mouth, she can be taught to scoop the food into the spoon, and to replace the spoon on the plate after each mouthful. Replacing the spoon, coming after one mouthful and a long way from the next, may need separate reinforcement – a caress or a kiss, if the person likes this, or a sip of a favourite drink.

USING A KNIFE AND FORK

Once the person has learnt to use a spoon quite well, she can be taught to hold a fork in the other hand and, again by prompting and fading the prompts, to use it to help push the food into the spoon. Later again, it may be useful to teach her to use a knife, both for cutting and for spreading. Spreading can be taught using soft butter, jam, Marmite or any other spread that she likes. Cutting may be taught at first using soft substances like dough, banana or crustless bread, which, for a right-handed person, can be steadied with the left hand while the right hand is prompted to make the back-and-forwards sawing movements. Later she can move on to firmer substances which need more emphatic sawing, like uncooked carrots, bread crusts and apples. Later still, she can be taught to hold the food steady with a fork, and can move on to foods such as potatoes, green vegetables and, the summit of achievement, meat. If we can teach someone to cut meat, instead of wrenching it apart sideways, we really are entitled to a place among the Great Teachers of All Time like Madame Montessori and Socrates.

DRINKING

We teach drinking using whatever kind of receptacle the person finds easiest – one without handles, like a glass or plastic beaker, or a one-handled or a two-handled cup. Whichever we choose, we fill it about half-full with a drink the person likes. A task analysis of drinking will show us the steps involved, such as holding the cup (with one or two hands – even with a one handled cup the other hand can be used to steady it) raising the cup to the lips, tipping in some of the fluid, taking the cup away from the lips and replacing it on the table.

As with the spoon, replacement is the most difficult part to teach and may need prompting, or at least shadowing, and reinforcement, long after she is successful in getting the drink.

Table manners

People who can feed themselves quite competently may still need help in learning to eat in such a way that other people will be glad to share a table with them. This can, in turn, make it possible for these people to be taken on all sorts of outings or expeditions that include a meal in other people's homes, or in a cafe or restaurant, whereas if they were likely to throw food around or grab it from other people's plates they might be left behind.

GOBBLING

Ethel liked her food, so much so that she barely sat down at table before her plate was cleared, and she stuffed one mouthful in on top of another in a way that was unpleasant to watch and not especially good for her digestion. She went to a centre every day, and the other trainees disliked sitting with her, so she was usually isolated at meal-times. Her instructor decided to help her with this. So she began to sit with Ethel at lunch time, and told her she was to eat more slowly. Ethel put one spoonful of food in her mouth and almost at once tried to shove in another. The instructor moved her spoon back to her plate and said, 'No gobbling, Ethel', and removed her plate until Ethel had finished her mouthful and a further ten seconds had elapsed. Then the instructor returned the plate and said, 'Eat nicely, Ethel'. The same procedure was followed each time Ethel tried to put in another mouthful before she had swallowed the last. During the next few weeks it seemed that Ethel was finding it a bit frustrating to have to eat more slowly, and she would 'hide' in the dining-room, or sit with her back to the instructor, apparently to make it more difficult to find her. Nevertheless, within three or four weeks Ethel was eating at a reasonable speed, so long as the instructor was sitting near her.

Another trainee was then invited to come and sit at Ethel's table for lunch and the instructor moved so that she was no longer sitting right next to Ethel, but was near enough to intervene if necessary. When Ethel continued to eat well and other trainees were occupying the other places at the table, the instructor told Ethel that she would be watching her from further away and that each day that she was seen to be eating nicely she would be given a particular large gooey sweet that she loved. On the second day of this programme the instructor noticed that Ethel was not now attempting to hide – could it really be for the chance to get a sweet? It appeared that it was. At the beginning of the fourth week of this part of the programme, when Ethel was continuing to eat well and was enjoying the company at table of the other trainees (who also got a hand-out of a sweet each from time to time), the instructor moved to observing Ethel less openly from the dining hatch, then less frequently; then, as the good eating behaviour became more a part of Ethel's normal routine she was given the sweets occasionally, just as an encouragement, until eventually they were no longer necessary.

EATING TOO SLOWLY

Sometimes a person, although liking her food, takes a very long time over it, so that it is difficult to get on with other activities. Here we may set up a programme in which we work out a generous time allowance for the meal, dividing this up into separate times for the separate courses: let's say; soup – 10 minutes, main course – 20 minutes, sweet – 15 minutes. These time allowances can be explained to the person, and as she is given each course a timer, such as a kitchen pinger, can be set to go off at the appropriate time. If by that time she has finished the course, she can be praised, the plate removed, the next course brought and the pinger re-set; if she has not finished the plate and whatever remains on it are removed without comment and the next course brought in and the pinger re-set. No nagging, no arguments, and no response to pleas for 'just a few minutes more'. Later, as she becomes able to eat at a more normal speed, the pinger can be put further away until it is out of sight, and the programme discontinued.

Where the slowness is caused by the person not liking food – any food – much, this kind of approach is unlikely to work. Bernard ate extremely slowly, sometimes taking over two hours to eat his meat and vegetables. He was underweight and those looking after him were worried about him. A programme like that described above was set up, with the extra proviso that if he finished the food within one hour he would be given a bottle of his favorite sweet fizzy drink. At first his eating times improved, but then, although he still seemed to enjoy the drink when he had it, the time he took to finish got longer and longer. We are still struggling to find the answer to this one.

EATING WITH FINGERS

We eat some foods, like toast or pieces of fresh fruit, quite appropriately in our fingers, while other foods, like stew and mashed potatoes, we do not. Sometimes a person uses his fingers to eat these latter kinds of food because it is quicker and easier than using a knife and fork, but he will be better liked by his fellow diners if he uses cutlery properly. So when he uses his fingers we say 'No', and take his plate away for ten seconds. Or we may just hold his hand still for the same time. Either way, he finds that the food comes more slowly if he uses his fingers, and the meal is more enjoyable if he uses the knife and fork.

EATING WITH MOUTH OPEN

This is another unlovely mealtime behaviour which may make the person an unwelcome table companion and which he may not realise he is doing. It may be enough to remind him persistently to close his mouth, touching him on the cheek as we do so: or imitation might help – sitting opposite him and chewing open-mouthed whenever he does; or a mirror, or some video of his eating, to let him see what he looks like.

STEALING FOOD

Nobody should have to put up with having food taken from their plate. If a person steals food from other people's plates, we try to get the stolen food away from him, and his plate is taken away for ten seconds. If he has already cleared his plate we give a little extra food, or something extra as a treat, to everyone else at the table, ostentatiously leaving him out.

EATING OUT

As well as having meals at home we often want to eat out, in cafes and restaurants. This involves a number of quite advanced skills, and these are discussed in Chapter 14.

Toilet training

Of all the everyday living skills that we try to help people with learning disabilities to acquire, perhaps the most crucial is that of self-toileting. In no other area is a person's dignity and privacy so much involved; in no other area is it so important that he or she should have control and command of him or herself. A few people with profound or multiple disabilities may never learn to cope with their own toileting, but many can. In one American study, people who were profoundly learning disabled, some able to move around only in wheelchairs, learned to keep their beds dry at night. It is always worth trying.

As with so many of the things that we do, we may first want to find out what is happening right now. We need a baseline. This is what the instructors in one Special Care Unit did, when they wanted to try to help Helena, a 25-year-old woman, to learn independent toileting. For two weeks they took Helena to the toilet every half-hour and kept her there for five minutes; each time they noted whether her pants were wet or dry, and whether she used the toilet. They hoped to find some pattern, and to find whether there were particular times when Helena was more likely to want to use the toilet. In fact they could not find any pattern, but they found that, on average, Helena had wet pants three times a day, and she used the toilet on average once a day. So that gave them a good baseline against which to measure the effect of anything they tried to do. They then set up a programme whereby Helena was still taken to the toilet every half-hour, and the same records were kept; but now, whenever her pants were dry she was praised, and whenever she used the toilet she was praised and given one of the chocolate buttons she loved. Soon her wet pants were down to once a day, and she was using the toilet three times a day.

We have said nothing about what happened when Helena's pants were wet. This is because, in this case, nothing special happened except that a clean pair of pants was put on. In some other programmes when the person has wet pants she is made to change them and then to wash out the wet ones. This can be seen as a mild punishment, but it can also be seen as a natural consequence – after all, any of us who has an accident will wash out the pants afterwards. If it is used, however, it is probably better that the pants-washing should be done in a rather distant, cool sort of a way, rather than becoming a jolly occasion for splashing about in the water.

When Helena becomes able to stay dry throughout the day her instructors plan to stretch the intervals between her toileting to, say, every three-quarters of an hour, then every hour, and so on until she is being taken at the same regular times as the other people in her workshop. The instructors plan to continue with the reinforcement of the chocolate button until they feel Helena is really confident and secure in her toileting; then they will occasionally miss it out and just give praise instead; later they will give it more infrequently until it fades out altogether.

Asking for the toilet

We said that, ultimately, Helena would be taken to the toilet at regular times (before and after lunch, at tea-break, etc.). It would be even better if she would take herself to the toilet whenever she wanted to go, as some others in her workshop already do (the toilet is quite near the workshop). If she has problems with this it would be one further step if, instead of having to be taken at set times, she could ask or indicate when she wanted to be taken. For that reason, since Helena does not have speech, she is always prompted to make the Makaton sign for 'toilet' (two little scratches with the index and middle fingers of her right hand on her left shoulder) when she is taken to the toilet; the instructor makes the same sign and says 'toilet' at the same time. As soon as possible, the prompts will be faded, and as she will use the sign every time she goes to the toilet, she may learn to use it herself to indicate that she wants to go.

If sign language were too difficult for Helena, she could be given a small picture of a lavatory and taught to point to this or show it each time she went to the toilet, with the aim that eventually she would do this herself when she wanted to go to the toilet.

Standing up to urinate

Most children, boys as well as girls, learn first to sit on a pot. Later on, most boys learn, often by watching and copying fathers and older brothers, to stand up when they urinate, and this is essential if they are to use the urinals found in most public toilets for men. So if this is not learned naturally, it needs to be taught. Paul, 15 years old and living in a children's home, was clean and dry but always sat down on the toilet, even if he only wanted to urinate. The care staff were worried about taking him on outings in case he was faced with a urinal he did not know how to use. Chris, his housefather, decided to begin teaching him to urinate standing up. He began first thing in the morning when Paul got out of bed, when he always wanted to go to the toilet, and was wearing pyjamas which were easy to manage. When they got to the toilet Chris stopped Paul from sitting down, and pushed up the toilet seat. He told him to hold his penis and aim it at the lavatory bowl. Paul tried to do this, and although his aim was not very good and most of the urine ended up on the lavatory floor, Chris gave him a hug and told him how well he had done – which indeed he had. Over the next few days his aim became more reliable and he gave up trying to sit on the seat. Chris, of course, was concerned that he might not realize that he should still sit down to defaecate, but these fears were unfounded; on the sixth morning, after he had urinated, Paul moved in purposefully, lowered the toilet seat, sat on it and defaecated.

So far so good, and Chris was delighted with his progress. (If Paul had not been as successful in his aim at the toilet bowl Chris had planned to drop a ping-pong ball in it: this makes urinating quite a spectacularly interesting affair, and the ball can be left in the toilet as long as is required, as it does not disappear when the toilet is flushed.) Later on, Chris taught Paul to lift the toilet seat himself and, later still, went on to extend the teaching to the afternoons when he came home from school. At this time, he was fully dressed, so had to learn to cope with trouser zips and underpants. This looks like being rather a slow business, but Chris is keen to teach him to manage urination in this normal, adult way, since his current method, in which he pushes trousers and pants to his ankles, at best looks odd in a public toilet and at worst could make him vulnerable to misunderstanding.

Bowel training

Bowel training goes in much the same way, with enthusiastic reinforcement of any toileting success, although it can be slower, as there are fewer occasions to reinforce. The person can also be reinforced for imitating appropriate toileting behaviour – sitting on the toilet, straining, etc – done by someone else while he watches, while on any occasion that he soils his pants he can, if desired, be made to wash them out.

Wiping

Sometimes a person who uses the toilet appropriately still has soiled pants because he does not know how to wipe himself properly. Again, we have to know how much of this process the person knows – does he know how to hold the paper? How to do the wiping? When to stop wiping? Richard's father found that Richard fell at the first hurdle – he would take several pieces of toilet paper and crunch them up into a ball, after which they were not much use for wiping. So first he had to be taught to take two pieces of toilet paper, and hold them between thumb and fingers: then his father prompted him to move his arm round behind him until his hand was centred over his buttocks; then to apply the paper to his anus, releasing his thumb, in a wiping movement; then to drop the paper behind him in the toilet. Later, Richard was taught to look at the paper after he had wiped and, if it was soiled, to take two more pieces and to wipe again, and to continue doing this until, after wiping, the paper was clean, or very nearly so.

Richard's father could carry out this programme, and Richard could accept it, because they were father and son and had known each other all of Richard's life. The position is rather different for an adult person living away from home with people who are comparative strangers. Alicia is a very capable 19-year-old living in a hostel and working towards going into a flat. She is a very clean, meticulous person but, in spite of her mother having tried very hard to teach her, could not wipe herself clean after the toilet and so often had soiled knickers. Alicia was very self-conscious about this and used to hide the knickers. Her care-worker wanted to help her with this problem, but wanted to do it in such a way as not to infringe on Alicia's rights as an adult to dignity and privacy. She discussed the matter with Alicia, saying to her that she was such a capable person and so good at looking after herself that she would certainly be able to get over this problem; that many people who are quite skilful still occasionally get soiled knickers, so it was not surprising that Alicia had some difficulty: and she suggested that they practice the movements and actions necessary, not in the toilet but in the bedroom, with Alicia dressed in trousers. In this way, the care-worker was able to guide Alicia to make the right movements without intruding on her in the toilet, and Alicia then began to be more competent in the real situation.

Using too much toilet paper

When Richard was being taught to wipe his bottom he got into the way of pulling six or seven sheets of toilet paper off the roll and screwing them up into a ball to use; his father countered this by giving him the boxed tissues that come out folded in pairs, and encouraged him to use one pair at a time. Other people may unroll endless streamers of toilet paper, and these people too may be helped by the boxed tissues, or by being given only the necessary number of pieces of paper (about eight) at a time, these being replenished as necessary.

Night-time training

Learning to stay dry at night is usually more difficult than learning to stay dry during the day, because at night, when we are asleep, we are less likely to notice the signals telling us that we need to go to the toilet.

Parents often lift and pot a toddler who is just beginning on night toilet training, with the aim of cutting down the amount of urine to be contained overnight and so of giving him the experience of dryness that later will extend to the whole night. If this approach is not successful, then there are several other ways in which we can help a person to stay dry at night.

Tokens – reinforcement for dry beds

If the person is capable of controlling his bladder overnight, he may need only some extra motivation to do so. So it may be worthwhile, as a first approach, to offer him some form of incentive scheme, something which he wants very much and which he can get when he has a dry bed in the morning. With adult people this will often be in the form of tokens which can be exchanged either immediately or, by accumulating them, for something he is very keen to get (see Chapter 5).

Bell and pad and pants alarm

The bell and pad apparatus – a pad put on the bed, covered by a drawsheet and connected to a bell which rings as soon as the pad is wetted – is used to help older children who are still bed-wetting, and has been useful, too, for adults with the same problem. However, there were anxieties about the safety of this apparatus, and nowadays pants alarms are more often used. These consist of a pad which goes inside pants or pyjamas and is connected in the same way with a bell which rings when the pad is wetted.

Dry bed procedure

Another method, which has been successfully used in America (Azrin et al 1973) to teach night dryness to people who are very disabled indeed, involves, besides the bell and pad or pants alarm, extra fluids, frequent toileting and practice in correct toileting. After being given extra fluids, the person went to bed and was then woken up every hour and taken (or sent) to the toilet. If he used it within five minutes, he was rewarded, praised for having a dry bed, and allowed to go back to sleep for the rest of the hour. If he did not use the toilet there was no reward, but the rest of the routine was followed. If the bell rang, signalling that the person had wet the bed, he was woken and scolded, taken to the toilet, prompted to change the sheets and was then made to practice using the toilet: he went to bed for three minutes, was got up and taken to the toilet, back to bed for another three minutes, and so on, for 45 minutes. Later, when accidents were down to one a night or less, the hourly wakening and extra fluids were dropped, although any accident was followed by the toileting practice. Later still, when the person had managed seven nights without an accident, the treatment was stopped, although if his bed was wet in the morning he had to remake it. Only if more than one accident a week occurred was training reinstated.

Obviously, this method needs someone to be up and active all through the night in order to carry out the teaching, but it could be that such an intensive effort would be worthwhile: in the original study all 12 adults with profound learning (and in some cases also severe physical) disabilities needed no more than three nights' training, and there were no relapses in a three-month follow-up period. So those were 12 people, at least six of whom had been wet every night before training, who five weeks after the training were almost invariably dry. We must point out, however, that others who have tried to reproduce these results have had much slower and less dramatic success. In one study (Smith, 1981) five young adults with severe to profound learning disabilities, trained by methods similar to those described above, took between 18 and 92 weeks to become reliably dry. Furthermore, they frequently had 'relapses' – several, up to four, dry weeks being followed by several wet ones. So we should not be too discouraged if our efforts are not as immediately successful as those originally described.

If this intensive approach is not possible another, known as progressive lifting, may be worth considering. After the person has gone to bed and to sleep, she is lifted and toileted at a time which, if the bed is already wet, is made earlier and earlier each night until a time is reached at which the bed is always dry. She is lifted and toileted at this time for several nights, then the time is set back a little, say 15 to 30 minutes. If the bed continues to be dry the time can be set back a little more, and so on. The idea behind this is that if she is lifted only just before the time she usually wets the bed, this will be when her bladder is quite full, and she may then begin to associate the feeling of a full bladder with waking. If the waking time is gradually delayed she should be able to hold increasing amounts of urine, while increasingly strong sensations from her bladder will be more effective in waking her.

In the case we have referred to, (Robson 1988) this process was successful, but it took an extremely long time; from the start of the programme when James was lifted at 1.30 am, to the end, when he was lifted at 7.00 am, took just over two years. Nevertheless, after sixteen years of wet beds he became dry and has continued to be dry ever since. In the case of 9-year-old Peter (Carr, 1987) progress was more erratic, with Peter beginning to be dry occasionally all through the night after four months, and becoming reliably dry ten months later. This, then, is by no means a rapid method, but may be worth trying if other methods are unsuccessful.

Leaving off the pads

Whether the person needs training in the day or at night, one of the first things we may need to do is to take him out of incontinence pads. This takes a good deal of nerve, especially if he has never been toilet trained, and we can envisage a terrible lot of wetness around the place without the pads. But it is very difficult to teach good toileting to someone in pads – it takes so long to get them off – while it is not at all unusual to find that simply wearing the pads has prevented the person becoming toilet trained. Dave, who lived in a hostel, had worn pads and wetted them all his life, until one day his careworker decided it was time to teach him to use the toilet properly, took a deep breath and removed the pads. Dave used the toilet from that time onwards and never wetted his pants. That is a real good luck story, but not by any means the only one of its kind.

Summary

1. We can teach a person to feed himself by prompting the correct movements, and very gradually fading the prompts.

2. Putting the spoon, or fork, down on the plate or the cup down on the table may need separate teaching and reinforcement.

3. Better table manners can be taught by taking the person's plate away for a short time whenever she shows the bad-mannered behaviour.

4. Once the bad manners have improved, the teacher has to supervise less closely, moving gradually further and further away, while still ensuring that the good manners continue.

5. In beginning a toilet training programme, we may need to take the person to the toilet very often, perhaps as often as every half-hour.

6. Our aim is for the person to take himself to the toilet but, if that seems likely to be difficult, we try to teach him how to let us know that he wants to go.

7. Men should, if possible, be taught to urinate standing up, so that they are able to use urinals.

8. Bottom wiping can be taught by prompting and reinforcing the correct movements, and by teaching that wiping should be continued until the paper is hardly marked.

9. Night-time training may come about through reinforcing dry beds.

10. If this is not enough, it may be worth using repeated waking, toileting, reinforcement and practice.

11. Progressive lifting involves waking and toileting the person at a time at which he has been found to be regularly dry: then gradually making the lifting time progressively later.

12. Toilet training always involves leaving off incontinence pads or nappies.

Exercises

1. When we teach a person to feed himself, what kind of food do we use?

2. Where do we position ourselves as teacher?

3. Once the prompts have been faded the teacher takes her hands away completely. Right or wrong?

4. How do we teach replacing the spoon on the plate or the cup on the table?

5. Supposing we had removed the plate from a person who had been gobbling or using fingers, and the person tried to snatch the plate back: what would we do?

6. What two methods aimed at decreasing undesirable behaviours were used in the programme to teach Ethel not to gobble her food?

7. How can we encourage a man who is urinating standing up to aim into the toilet bowl

8. How many pieces of paper are needed for bottom wiping?

CHAPTER 11

Home Management

By the time we are adults, most of us expect to have a home of our own. Our homes are places where we can relax, feel secure, and be with our family or friends. For many of us, our homes are the focal point of our existence, while homes must also be looked after if they are to remain hygienic and comfortable. A home must, therefore, be managed.

Most of us learn the skills involved in home management as we grow up in our family home. We see our parents cooking, cleaning, paying bills, discussing whether or not a holiday can be afforded and where to look for a new three piece suite, and we absorb this knowledge as we go along. Many of us then leave our family home, either to share a flat with other young people, or perhaps to start our own families. We may still be inexperienced in many areas of home management and we may make mistakes but, as a rule, enough has sunk in for us to be able to make a good stab at coping on our own.

Some people with learning disabilities have not, for many of their developing years, lived in an ordinary home, but have had to share their homes with many others, in a hospital or hostel. Even if they have been living with their families they may have been protected from the responsibilities which normally come with increasing years. Their families may not have anticipated that they would ever be able to have homes of their own. So when people with learning disabilities do have the chance to move into their own homes there are often many things they need to learn if they are to cope. The main areas we will look at are:

(1) Household chores

(2) Shopping and budgeting

(3) Kitchen skills

(4) Safety in the home.

There are a great many skills to be learnt in all these areas. We will look at just a selection of them.

Household chores

Part of home life involves doing the chores that are associated with it – tidying, cleaning, dusting, polishing and sweeping. People with learning disabilities may have to learn not only how to do the tasks but also how frequently they need to be done.

There is, of course, a good deal of variation about how clean and tidy houses are kept. Some people like to live in impeccable homes while others can tolerate more clutter and even mess. Tidiness can also vary at different times in our lives; for example, when our children were small our houses were more untidy than they were when we lived alone or with just one other adult. Although we all have to find the level of tidiness or untidiness with which we are comfortable, people sharing a house or living together will have to work out between them the standards which will suit them all.

Jonathan and Mary had been friends for a long time when they lived in a hospital. Eventually, they were able to move into a home of their own and Kathy, a community support worker, agreed to work with them, to help them develop a routine to enable them to run their own home.

Jonathan, Mary and Kathy wrote out on a large sheet of card a checklist of all the things that needed to be done each day. Although Jonathan could read, Mary couldn't, so she and Kathy cut out pictures from magazines or catalogues so that she could recognise each task. The charts looked something like this:

MONDAY
Kitchen
> Sweep floor.
> Wash floor.
> Wipe cooker top.

TUESDAY
Sitting Room
> Dust and polish wood surfaces,ornaments and pictures.
> Brush or vacuum chairs.
> Vacuum carpet.

WEDNESDAY
Stairs, landing and hall
>Sweep down stairs and vacuum carpet.
>Dust banisters.

THURSDAY
Bedrooms
>Change sheets on bed, dust surfaces.
>Vacuum carpet.

FRIDAY
Bathroom & Toilet
>Clean toilet.
>Clean bath and basin.
>Change towels.

WEEKEND
Laundry
>Hand wash or use machine at home.
>Do ironing, leave to air, then put clothes away.

Other tasks, such as cleaning windows and the cooker, need to be done less often and routines for these can also be worked out.

This was the checklist Kathy worked out with Jonathan and Mary. Other people may prefer a different regime; nothing is sacrosanct. A balance must be kept between setting goals 'on the clean side' in order to achieve at least a reasonable level of cleanliness and setting standards which are unrealistically high.

Before starting work on items on the checklist, Kathy worked with Jonathan and Mary on the difference between 'clean' and 'dirty'. This applied in almost every situation, whether it was washing the floor, hoovering or dusting. Kathy started with dusting. She physically prompted Jonathan to dust half a table and then asked Mary to say which was the dusted half. She praised her correct answers and corrected wrong responses, explaining why they were wrong, and then Jonathan dusted the second half. They then moved on to the sideboard and reversed roles, Mary dusting one half and Jonathan saying which was clean and which dirty. The same method was used for polishing the furniture, cleaning the bath and so on, with Jonathan and Mary taking turns to be the one who cleaned and the one who made the judgement.

Then Kathy took each one of the items on the checklist and, over a period of time, taught them individually to Jonathan and Mary.

Sweeping and washing the floor

Kathy used the ideas outlined above when she was teaching Mary how to sweep and wash the floor. She showed her how to hold the brush and how to use a dust pan and brush, initially using physical prompts, holding her hands over Mary's and then gradually fading the prompts; and how to use the mop, ensuring she squeezed sufficient water out of it. She encouraged Mary to approach the cleaning systematically, working around the room, under all the surfaces and moving chairs and tables. In particular, when she washed the floor, she taught Mary to work backwards towards the door. She also showed Mary which detergent to use and, just as important, how much – Mary tended to find bubbles more appealing than the task in hand. Kathy found it helpful to keep a small container, which held just the right amount, with the detergent so that Mary could use this to measure it into the bucket.

Vacuuming

Jonathan and Mary had never used an ordinary vacuum cleaner before, as on the ward where they had lived there were only large industrial cleaners. In the flat they had an upright model, and Kathy worked out a task analysis for them, using their own equipment (as below). This would require modification if a different machine were used in differently arranged rooms.

(1) Take cleaner from cupboard.

(2) Unwind the flex.

(3) Plug in at wall socket.

(4) Switch on at wall socket.

(5) Press down lever to release handle.

(6) Switch on machine.

(7) Push cleaner along far side and into centre of room.

(8) Push cleaner along left hand side of room.

(9) Work over to right hand side of room.

(10) Push cleaner around near side of room and door area.

(11) Switch off machine.

(12) Switch off at wall socket.

(13) Pull out plug.

(14) Re-wind flex.

(15) Put machine away.

At first, Kathy carried out steps 1 to 14, while Jonathan looked on, and she then helped him, using physical prompts, to put the machine away (step 15). He learnt this well and then moved on to taking part in steps 14 and 15. In effect, Kathy was using a backward chaining method; she chose this approach, in this instance, because it gave Jonathan the opportunity to watch Kathy doing the task first (modelling) and enabled him gradually to take over more of it himself.

Kathy continued at every opportunity, when vacuuming needed to be done, to prompt Jonathan to take part in more steps, moving on to 13, then 12, then 11 and so on. At each stage he needed physical prompts initially and these were gradually withdrawn as his competence increased.

Cleaning the toilet, bath and basin

Here Kathy felt it was particularly important to stress the meaning and value of hygiene. This included ensuring that Jonathan and Mary used a toilet brush or cloth only for cleaning the toilet, that they used the appropriate disinfectant or proprietary toilet cleaner, and that they always cleaned under the rim of the toilet bowl along with the visible areas. Jonathan was shown how to clean the bath and basin and which kind of cleaner to use. He had to pay particular attention to cleaning the scum ring around the bath and basin and to rinsing away thoroughly the cleaner residue. All this was done mainly by demonstration, until Jonathan was encouraged to do it himself, with Kathy talking him through the task. Gradually, she withdrew her prompting until he could do it independently.

Bedmaking

Making one's bed is a daily chore that has been made considerably easier and quicker with the introduction of duvets and fitted sheets. Once the changing of sheets and putting on new covers has been mastered, there should be few problems in bed making – except, perhaps, in remembering to do it. Mary had always found bedmaking difficult but, when given a duvet and fitted sheets for Christmas and following the programme outlined below, she learned to complete the whole task herself. She learnt in three stages: sheet, pillow, duvet. At first, Kathy helped her through each task, leaving her to do the last bit; then she gradually did more, until she completed the whole of the task. They worked through in the following order:

Sheet

    (1) Find one short side of the sheet.

    (2) Take this to head of the bed.

    (3) Fit end round top end of mattress.

    (4) Smooth sheet down to foot.

    (5) Fit bottom end round foot of mattress.

    (6) Tuck in one side.

    (7) Tuck in other side.

Pillows

    (1) Open out pillow case.

    (2) Push one corner of pillow into bottom corner of case.

    (3) Push second corner in.

    (4) Shake pillow down into case.

    (5) Tuck pillow under flap of case.

    (6) Smooth over.

    (7) Place on bed.

A duvet is done in a similar way. Some duvets fasten at the side, in which case these instructions may need to be adjusted. Mary also had to learn to take off the dirty sheets and duvet cover but, although it took a little practice to do it quickly, she found it much easier than putting them on.

Laundry

Mary and Jonathan were encouraged to have a routine for coping with their laundry. This included:

    (1) Putting all dirty washing into a laundry bag or basket as soon as it was removed.

    (2) Choosing one day on which the laundry was done. (Saturday)

    (3) Sorting the clothes carefully into those to be hand washed and those to be washed in a machine.

    (4) Using the appropriate technique for washing and drying.

    (5) Doing the ironing.

    (6) Putting the clean clothes away.

Jonathan and Mary needed to learn how to use a washing machine. Each working part of their machine had a different coloured piece of adhesive strip attached to it so the routine worked out was as follows:

(1) Put clothes into machine.

(2) Switch on at the wall plug.

(3) Open up the blue container to put in the powder. (How much to put in may have to be taught separately)

(4) Close the blue container.

(5) Press the red knob to switch on.

(6) Turn the yellow dial until it reaches the yellow spot and pull out.

This sequence may vary with different machines, while a twin tub will again required different teaching.

Ironing

After the washing has been done, some of it at least will need ironing. Jonathan first had to learn how to put up the ironing board, which took a long time as the ironing board seemed to have a will of its own.

Jonathan had to understand that (1) the ironing surface needed to be lifted up with his left hand, (2) the leg that it rested on should be pulled sideways until (3) the ironing surface clipped or rested on it at the correct angle. This also involved allowing the leg the board was standing on to move from being upright to leaning.

It was even more complicated to fold the ironing board up again, but Jonathan learnt to turn the ironing board onto its end (where the iron rested). He could then see the lever or clip that was holding the support onto the ironing surface, release it, and allow the ironing board to fold up. Then he put it away in the cupboard again.

Next, Jonathan had to learn about the different kinds of material that needed ironing and at what temperature each should be ironed. Kathy collected a pile of his clothes and together they looked at the labels on them. Kathy had written out some big cards with all the different symbols on them and Jonathan had to match the label in his clothes to the label on the card. Kathy kept telling him to feel the clothes and the textures and to refer to the cards, so that he got the idea that heavy, tough materials needed a hotter iron than flimsy materials.

The iron they used had been chosen partly because the settings were marked with the same symbols as those which are used on the labels attached to clothes. Jonathan, Mary and Kathy had several sessions looking at the iron, and Kathy's drawing, and the labels in their clothes, and Jonathan and Mary learnt to match the iron settings to the labels on their clothes, and to turn the indicator on the iron to the setting needed for any particular garment. Jonathan already knew how to plug electrical equipment in, so he had to learn how to fill up the iron with water and to keep it safely on the heat proof pad of the ironing board. Kathy showed him how the light came on when the temperature was too cool and how it went out when the correct heat was reached.

Finally, Jonathan had to learn the actual ironing of the clothes. Kathy showed him how to do each garment, starting with easy things like handkerchiefs, and then T-shirts, trousers and lastly shirts. Each time he did the ironing he ironed the garments he had mastered and the one new one he was learning to do. This meant that at first he ironed handkerchiefs only. Then he ironed handkerchiefs and T-shirts, and so on until finally he could iron all his clothes.

These are, of course, only a few of the household chores on the original check list, but we hope they give some idea of the methods we have adopted when teaching these tasks, and others can be tackled in similar ways.

Shopping and budgeting

Some people with learning disabilities may never be able to manage all their shopping and budgeting completely alone, but each person can be taught strategies suited to their own level of ability which will enable them to make steps towards independence in this area.

Shopping involves a number of skills, some of which, for example travelling about the streets, and social skills, are dealt with in other parts of this book.

Using local shops

For those of us living in towns, individual shops such as the baker, greengrocer, or off licence are often conveniently situated close to our homes. We develop relationships with the shopkeepers who begin to know us and the sorts of commodities we usually buy. This pattern of shopping has obvious advantages for people who are learning disabled. If they know the shopkeeper, they will feel more able to ask about things they are unsure of and it is less likely that they will be the victims of practical jokes or short changing. A group home close to a parade of local shops could, if the tenants did all their shopping locally, have a large impact on these shopkeepers' takings and this could help to give the tenants some status in their neighbourhood.

Diane lived with two friends in a staffed house. They took turns to do their shopping and usually bought just the things they needed to eat each day, and other things as they ran out. Each of them bought their own personal items such as cosmetics and clothes separately, and they had a house kitty into which each person put £20 each week for food. On week days when they had lunch out, they aimed to spend £6 a day for food, leaving them with £20 for Saturday and Sunday when they were at home more, and £10 over to be used for extras.

Diane's mother lived nearby and she helped Diane and her friends work out their menus. It was easiest to have meals worked out every day for a fortnight as their budget was so tight that it was especially important to plan ahead. Mostly, Diane and her friends followed the rotas although, if they felt bored with them, or had some extra money, they would sometimes treat themselves to something different.

Twice a week, when it was Diane's day to shop, her mother came round early. First they checked the day's menu. The menus were stuck inside the larder door, arranged in pictorial form like this:

Tuesday week 2

3 lamb chops

small cauliflower

potatoes

Then they checked the cupboards to see what they needed. There were no potatoes and they needed to buy the cauliflower and chops too. Diane's mother made the shopping list, which was arranged in columns so that things to come from one shop were all in the same column.

e.g. potatoes   3 lamb chops

cauliflower

They then looked to see if there was anything else Diane needed to get. They checked things like cereal and found that it was running low; they also needed bread and butter and fruit. The list then looked like this:

potatoes	39p	3 lamb chops	£2.50	bread	70p	cereal	99p

cauliflower	50p			butter	69p		

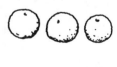

3 apples	30p

3 oranges	60p			milk	36p

£1.79		£2.50	£1.75	£0.99

Total £7.03

Diane took the £6 allocated for the day's budget, plus £1 from the 'extras' money so that she would have enough to cover the things on her list.

Because Diane's mother lived locally, she also knew the shopkeepers. She and Diane had visited the shops before Diane had started doing her own shopping, and her mother had explained to the shopkeepers that, although Diane could understand what they said to her, her own speech was very unclear and that she would always bring a note. She also explained that Diane would be dependent on them to take her money and give her the right change.

The parade of shops where Diane did her shopping consisted of a butcher, a greengrocer and a grocer who also sold bread. There was also a Chinese take-away, a video library, a launderette and a junk shop. From the beginning, Diane's mother headed each column on the shopping list with a picture of the right shop, for example:

greengrocer   butcher   grocer

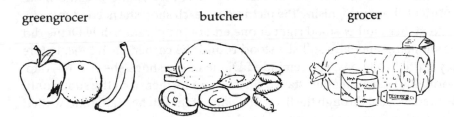

Initially, she accompanied Diane into each shop, prompted her to hand over her list and then prompted her again to hand over her money. At first, when Diane's mother and the house staff had discussed their teaching method, they had hoped to teach Diane to hand over a coin or note with a denomination greater than the value of her purchases and then to wait for change. They had tried various ways of teaching her this, including both table top and real life practice, but it seemed too difficult for Diane to learn the cost of things or the value of money. In the end, it seemed that the only way Diane could pay for her shopping was to hand over her entire purse. This was obviously rather unsatisfactory; however, because the local shopkeepers were willing to co-operate, and because it seemed important for Diane to take her turn with shopping, just like the friends she lived with, her mother went along with it.

Diane and her mother set off for the shops. Diane could tell which shops she needed to go into from the drawings on the top of her shopping list. As they approached each shop, her mother pointed to the relevant picture on the list. Once in the shop, she then prompted Diane to hand over her list and purse to the assistant, put the items into her shopping bag and take back the purse with change in it and the list.

Diane's mother then gradually withdrew the amount of prompting she used. As they approached the parade of shops she prompted Diane to look at the list; 'Do you need to go into the greengrocer's?' Diane looked at the list, found the right picture and looked beneath it to see if anything had been written. If she correctly said that she needed something at the greengrocer's, her mother congratulated her and sent her into the shop; if she got it wrong, her mother explained why it was wrong.

At this stage, Diane's mother was stopping outside each shop on the parade with her and prompting her into the shops where necessary. She then moved back and stood more or less in the middle of the parade but further from the shops, near the kerb. At first, Diane came over to check between each shop; however, before they left home they always spent some time going through the list, and as time went by Diane became more confident about recognising the pictures for each shop she needed to go to.

Next, her mother stood right at one end of the parade while Diane did her shopping and later still she stood round the corner. Each time, before they parted company, she reminded Diane of the shops she had to go to. Gradually, Diane's mother stayed further and further from the shops until she merely went through the list with Diane at the kitchen table and waited there for her until she returned with the shopping.

Achieving some degree of independence for people who are profoundly disabled may, as in this case, involve the co-operation of many people and, in some cases, the realisation that some support will always be needed. Diane's mother continued to help her with the construction and organisation of her shopping list whenever it was her turn to shop. Nevertheless, Diane was able to do a significant part of the shopping and to contribute to the running of her house.

Shopping in a supermarket

This is a much more complex and impersonal task than shopping locally; it has the attraction of probably being more economical and so is a worthwhile skill to learn for people living on restricted incomes. Some local shops are now laid out in a supermarket style and so it is possible to go from quite simple to increasingly complex supermarket shopping.

Junior lived in a staffed group home with five other people; each week two of them did the entire week's shop at the supermarket. They started by constructing a list – always useful for people with a low budget – based on the menus for the week. Not everyone could read, but the house staff had made a series of small cards, each with a photograph or used label of one item on it, and the shoppers sorted these into piles according to the things they needed.

At first, staff went with Junior and Gudrun to their local small supermarket, which was quiet, where they could get used to wheeling the trolley around, queuing at the cash desk and unloading the trolley. Once they could cope with this, they moved to the large supermarket. They started by going on a weekday morning, when the place was quite empty, and just looking round to see where everything was. Most large chain supermarkets change their layout only occasionally, so the staff wrote down a plan of the layout of the shelves, so that shopping cards could be arranged in the order that Junior and Gudrun would come to things in the supermarket. While they went round, a member of staff prompted Junior and Gudrun to look at the cards and search for the items on the shelves. If they missed any, this was pointed out and they were directed back to the correct shelves. Soon the staff were able to stand at the main entrance and wait for Junior and Gudrun to come out. Gudrun could manage money, although Junior could not – whenever a pair of shoppers went out the staff always made sure that at least one knew how to cope with money. When they reached the checkout, they went through a routine which they had previously practised at home; Gudrun took the things out of the trolley and put them on the counter and, when they had been rung up, Junior packed them into bags; when everything was rung up, Gudrun asked how much it came to and then gave the assistant a sum in notes larger than the total rung up and waited for the change. (Further details on using a supermarket checkout counter can be found in the exercises in Chapter 3, and packing shopping in 'Working in a supermarket' in Chapter 13.)

Budgeting

Although learning to budget is an advanced and difficult skill, it is important that people with learning disabilities are given the opportunity to learn this as soon as they are able to recognise the value of money.

Initially, the budget for the week can be planned on pay day, so that no money is spent until all essential bills are paid.

Deirdre lives in a house with two friends and needed some help with budgeting. Her neighbour, Valerie, agreed to help her with this every Friday evening, when they would work out her expenses for the week. They started by talking about Deirdre's weekly income, which was £110, and about her expenses for each week. She wrote out a list of these.

Rent	£61.90
including gas, electricity and local authority taxes	
Food	£20.00
Savings	£10.00
TV licence stamp	£2.00
Two-zone bus pass	£5.65
Total	£99.55

Deirdre was left with only £10.45 to play with each week, although, as the house that Deidre lived in was owned by a housing association, at least all her main fuel bills were included in the rent. Most people with learning disabilities live on very tight budgets like this.

After this, when Deirdre cashed her giro cheque on Fridays she put £10 straight into a savings account, which she had at the same post office, and bought her television stamps at the same time. Later in the evening, Valerie came round and together they sorted out the rest of her money. Deirdre put her food money into a tin in her dressing table drawer, so that she could take money from there as she needed it in the week. She put her bus pass money into one compartment of her purse, so that she could go and buy it on Saturday morning. Finally, she put the rest of her money (£10.45) into another compartment of her purse as spending money for the week.

On the first Saturday morning Deirdre went out to buy her bus pass and while she was out she bought a few extras that she needed, such as deodorant and soap. She could not resist also buying a music tape, and then found to her horror that she did not have much money to see her through the week. So the next Friday evening, Valerie suggested to Deirdre that she put £6 away with her food money, so that she only had £4.45 on her when she went out on Saturday. This way, they made sure that there was some money left for the week. Valerie continued to help Deirdre sort her money out on Friday nights, until the routine was so well-established that Deirdre felt that she could manage alone.

Kitchen skills

Doing things in the kitchen is usually popular – most people enjoy making things they will later be able to eat – while simple cookery is an essential skill for anyone who wants to live independently. Kitchens are, however, quite hazardous places from the point of view of both fire dangers and hygiene, and people with learning disabilities who want to cook must learn to do so safely. We also aim to develop kitchen routines so that, whatever we are doing, basic standards of safety and hygiene are maintained. For example, we would always try to start by washing our hands and wiping work surfaces and to finish by clearing away all rubbish, washing up and wiping worktops down.

Choice of cooker

Most people will cook on either a gas or an electric stove, and each has advantages and disadvantages. A gas cooker provides instant heat which can also be adjusted or turned off instantly, and it is easy to see which burner is on. The disadvantages of gas are that the open flames make it possible for clothing, tea towels, oven gloves and so on to catch fire, while older cookers may have a pilot light which, if it goes out, can cause a dangerous build-up of gas. Electric cookers are safer in that they do not have naked flames or pilot lights but, on the other hand, it is not always easy to see which plate is on, especially when it is turned low, temperature adjustment is more difficult and the plates remain hot for some time after they are turned off. There are some electric cookers with halogen lamps on the plates which light up when they are on and in many cases these are a good choice. However, when it comes down to it, the cooker chosen has to be the one which suits the individual who is going to be using it. If someone is being taught to cook in a different place from where they live, it is also important for the cookers to be the same or compatible. Whichever kind of cooker is chosen, people should be taught never to lean against it. This should apply even when the cooker is not in use, so that it will be less likely to happen when it is being used.

Some ideas on other kinds of equipment – pans, knives, peelers and and so on are available from the Disabled Living Foundation (see Appendix 3).

Some pre-requisite skills

There are some skills which come into so many activities in the kitchen that we would like to deal with these before going on to basic cookery. They are: using oven gloves; using a timer; finding things in the kitchen; and making judgements about cooking.

OVEN-GLOVES

The danger of scalds or burns is one of the major reasons that people with learning disabilities are kept out of kitchens. So, if they are to tackle cooking, they should learn to protect themselves by using oven gloves. At first, they can practise putting the gloves on: then, wearing them, to pick up light easy objects such as empty plastic bowls; then going on to handle heavier pans and casseroles and those with cold water in them, and practising removing lids from these. Later, they can graduate to handling things which are hot, and later still to handling these on top of the stove and getting them out of ovens.

TIMERS

Many cooking operations have to be timed fairly accurately, and probably the easiest way to do this is to use a timer, either one built into the cooker or a free-standing one. If the person does not know how to tell the time, we can follow the same kind of course as that described for Sharon (Chapter 13). So a card could be made up for, for example, boiling rice, with a picture of rice (or of its packet) and with a picture of the timer, showing where it needed to be turned to, once the rice was in and the water had returned to boiling:

When the timer rings, the person can be prompted to test the food, with a fork or skewer, to see whether it is properly cooked. This is quite a delicate operation, and, as in so many cooking processes, can only be learnt by repeated practice and feedback to the person as to whether she has judged rightly (see below), but the timer at least allows her to do other jobs round the kitchen without constantly checking her cooking or forgetting it.

FINDING THINGS

As in other areas, the person may have difficulty in finding the things she wants to use which are put away out of sight. If this is the case, pictures of the most-needed items – sugar, tea, bread, spoons – may be cut out, or labels removed and stuck onto the relevant drawers or cupboards. Then, when the person has thoroughly learnt where these items are kept, the pictures may be removed and, if necessary, new ones put up.

MAKING JUDGEMENTS

Many operations in cookery are impossible to define exactly, but depend on our judgement. We cannot say for exactly how long we should fry sausages or boil potatoes, it depends in the one case on how brown they look and on the other on how soft they are. Because the judgements are difficult to define, they are not easy to teach, but in many cases can be taught, using demonstration, prompting, getting the person to rehearse the skill and make the judgement, and giving feedback.

So, if we are teaching Mandy to boil potatoes, we test them with a fork when they are undercooked, exclaim 'Not done yet!' and prompt Mandy to test them as well. We ask her whether the potatoes feel hard or soft, prompting the right answer if necessary and praising her for getting it right. Then we repeat the process when the potatoes are cooked, changing the wording appropriately. We carry out this process on several occasions, fading our prompts as Mandy becomes able to manage the fork on her own. We also move on to omitting our demonstration and ask Mandy to tell us whether or not the potatoes are cooked. If she is right, we praise her: if (in our judgement) she is wrong, we try to help her to see why this is so. When Mandy judges the potatoes correctly five times out of six, we can probably feel confident in her ability to make this judgement on her own.

Similarly, we can teach people how to judge when meat, toast or sausages are brown enough, and the same kind of approach can be used for many other household skills.

Using a kettle

One of the first kitchen tasks people often want to master is to make themselves a cup of tea or coffee. This also introduces them to the crucial cookery skill of dealing with boiling water.

Sophie and Thomas had lived in a hospital for twenty years where tea was always brought to them in a large urn. They wanted to learn how to make it for themselves and Franco, one of the staff on the ward, undertook to teach them. They bought an electric kettle with a filler indicator on the side and a teapot for two people. They decided to leave the kettle plugged in both at the wall and in the kettle itself, and to fill it with water from a jug.

Franco then wrote down the steps involved.

(1) Take jug to sink.

(2) Open cold tap, let it run for five seconds.

(3) Fill jug.

(4) Turn off tap.

(5) Take jug to kettle.

(6) Take off lid of kettle.

(7) Fill kettle to required level.

(8) Put lid on kettle.

(9) Press switch on kettle.

(10) Put out teapot by kettle, remove lid.

(11) Put two teabags in teapot.

(12) Put two cups and saucers, jug with milk, sugar bowl and tea-spoons on table.

(13) When kettle boils and switches off at once fill teapot.

(14) Put lid on teapot (and cosy if required).

(15) Take pot to table.

(16) Leave for 5 minutes.

(17) Pour milk into cups.

(18) Pour in tea.

(19) Add sugar and stir.

Some steps were more tricky than others. These were 7, 13, 17 and 18 – all to do with pouring in liquid. Sophie and Thomas were able to hold the vessels and pour, but the difficulty lay in pouring in the right amount. With the kettle, Franco marked on the side the level suitable for a pot of tea for two. For the teapot and the cups, it was a matter of filling but not overfilling them, while the amount of milk to go in had to be quite nicely judged, as the level could not be marked on the inside of the teacups. Franco practised these parts of the task several times with Sophie and Thomas, at first prompting them when to stop pouring in the liquid and then gradually fading the prompts.

Thomas had an added difficulty in that he was nervous of handling the hot kettle. Franco overcame this by holding the kettle with him at first, and then gradually withdrawing until Thomas was able to manage on his own.

PLUGGING IN THE KETTLE

At first Sophie and Thomas poured the cold water into the kettle which was already plugged in. Many electrical things, however, need to be plugged in and then unplugged, and Franco decided to start teaching this to Sophie and Thomas, using the kettle. He began with unplugging, with a cold and empty kettle, so that they could tilt it by the handle to see the plug clearly. Sophie and Thomas tended to yank out the plug by the flex, so Franco prompted them to hold the plug itself before pulling it out. When they were able to do this without any prompting, Franco put cold water into the kettle, so that they had to unplug it while keeping it upright. Later, he ensured that they could still unplug the kettle, holding it by the handle, when it was full of hot water.

After this, Franco taught them to put the plug in the kettle. This was more difficult, because they had to make sure the plug was the right way up and that it was inserted at the correct angle. To help them remember which was the right way up, they put a small piece of coloured tape on the top of the plug, which they knew had to face upwards. Franco showed them the holes in the plug and the pins in the kettle that the plug had to fit into, and he tilted the empty kettle, so that the plug and the kettle were at the correct angle in order to be able to see how the two fitted together. Franco had to help Sophie and Thomas by holding his hand over theirs which was holding the plug, and guiding them to put the plug in the kettle. As they improved, Franco withdrew his prompts and, once they had mastered the whole process with the empty kettle, they went on to practise the same procedure with the kettle full of cold water.

Cooking

Cooking needs practise and, for people with learning disabilities, it is important that experience of the different ways of cooking – boiling, grilling and so on – is repeated many times. It can be helpful to teach only one process, for example boiling, at a time, until the person can carry out that one independently before going on to the next.

BOILING

If we want to teach Max to select the right sized saucepan for the food he wants to boil, we may first heap the food together on a chopping board and put an appropriate sized saucepan alongside, and then put the food in the saucepan to show how well it fits; we could also get out saucepans which are too small and too large and show how these were less appropriate. Then we put the saucepans back and ask Max to select the right one. We repeat this with different foods and on different occasions until Max can choose the right one each time.

How much water to use in the saucepan is a tricky question. Most vegetables are cooked in just enough water to cover them, so Max can be taught to put the vegetables in the pan, cover them with water, then remove the vegetables and put the pan of water on to boil. Some things however, like rice, need a lot of water and some like cabbage need very little, and it may be helpful, once again, to have cards made out with pictures of those items that Max often cooks so that he can refer to them when he needs to.

When the pan of water is put on the cooker to boil, the ring or hotplate needs to be turned up full, and this is quite straight forward to teach. Once the food is in, the heat needs to be adjusted to simmer and we teach Max how to judge this from the bubbles or the steam (see 'Making judgements')

Finally, Max needs to learn how to put the food into the boiling water and how to get it out when it is done. These are delicate operations, as there is the chance of splashing with the boiling water. A wire basket or a slotted spoon can get over the problem at both ends but, if these are not used, Max will have to be taught very carefully, again by demonstration, prompting and supervised practice, how to slip the food gently into the water and to pour it out into a colander at the end.

USING THE OVEN

Max will need to learn how to set the correct temperature of the oven for the food he wants to cook and, depending on the kind he is using (an electric oven marked in degrees or a gas oven with numbers), he may be helped by cards showing the type of food and where to turn the dial for that food. If the dial is not easy for him to read, it may be useful to mark it with different colours, so that for example 200° is blue, 250° green, 300° white and so on, the corresponding colours being used on the card as well.

Meat cooked in the oven will, when the timer rings, need to be checked as to its state of readiness by pushing in a skewer, and seeing that the juices that run out are brown, or at least brownish red. If the juices are bright red, we encourage Max to shut the oven door and to restart the timer. We will stress that this is especially important, for health reasons, with pork and chicken.

Dealing with the oven is where Max is going to have the greatest need of oven gloves. We will not allow him to approach the oven unless he is wearing the gloves, and he will find them easier to use if he has had plenty of practice with them beforehand.

GRILLING

Grilling is a relatively simple skill because the food is always visible (at least with an eye level grill) and it is easy enough to test. The main areas that may need to be taught are how to adjust the temperature and, with an adjustable grill level, how high to set the grill pan. Again, these may be taught by demonstration and supervised practice. After that, it is a question of not forgetting either to turn the food or to remove it, and here the timer may help.

FRYING

Frying is a popular cooking method but also rather alarming, because some foods, such as sausages or bacon, can splutter and spit out hot fat. Oven gloves will help, and we teach Max to turn down the temperature, or remove the frying pan from the cooker for a few minutes, if there is too much spluttering. We teach him to put oil or fat into the pan before it goes on the cooker; just as with boiling he will have to learn how to slip the food gently into the pan; and how to adjust the temperature – but without bubbles and steam as a guide this may be more difficult and take longer to learn. Usually, Max will need to turn the food at least once and then to take it out of the frying pan; for some people this may be easier with cooking tongs, while others may prefer two forks or spoons.

When Max is frying, the cooking timer is probably best forgotten; he should never go off to do something else, leaving a frying pan unattended.

Safety in the home

Many people with learning disabilities grow up in a world where they are constantly protected from dangers of all sorts. Because they are thought not able to look after themselves, other people take the responsibility for their safety, on the roads, at work, at home. If, however, they wish to live independently, it is essential that they learn how to do so safely. How much they need or can be expected to learn will depend on their own abilities and their living situation – those in a house with 24 hour live-in staff will not not need the comprehensive skills required for those who are entirely on their own. We cannot attempt a complete outline, but describe below how some basic skills may be taught.

General safety

Basic safety rules, such as making sure that hands are dry before touching electrical equipment and switching off and unplugging it after use, not standing too close to cookers and fires, locking up at night, may be taught by the usual methods of demonstration, prompting, and fading prompts, first in special teaching sessions, then as the situations naturally arise. Once the person seems to have learnt each skill this should be repeatedly checked to make sure it continues to be carried out correctly.

First aid

Perhaps the two minor emergencies most likely to arise are small cuts, and burns or scalds. Max will need to learn where the first aid box is kept, and how to use sticking plasters and bandages; how to wash a small cut, apply antiseptics, check the flow of blood by raising the affected part, and finally to cover the cut with plaster. In the case of burns or scalds, the most important thing for him to learn is to go at once to a cold tap and to run cold water on the burn or scald. If any one of the people sharing a house has epileptic fits, the other occupants may need to learn simple procedures, and who to phone if he does have one.

It may be important, though difficult, to teach when they should apply these simple first-aid measures, and when they should call for expert help (see below).

Telephoning emergency services

In Chapter 13 we describe how a person can be taught to use a telephone, and these methods can be used to teach the dialling of 999. However, there is more to it than that. The person needs to be able not only to dial the number, but also to listen to the questions asked by the operator and to give the correct replies: to

> Give his full name
>
> Give his full address
>
> Ask for the appropriate service
>
> Say why that service is needed

We can first practise doing this face to face with the person, then introduce a two way telephone and take it in turns to be caller and operator.

Jason's father felt it was important for him to be able to call the emergency services and, particularly, the fire service. To begin with, he took Jason to the fire station for a visit; this made Jason realise what the fire service was there for and that the firemen were friendly people. Once Jason was interested, it was easier for his father to practise with him what he should do if he found a fire. Jason was already able to give his full name and address and it did not take long to teach him to ask clearly for the fire brigade and to say why it was needed.

Jason's father then introduced a telephone. Still in the same room, and with the phone disconnected, Jason practised dialing 999, speaking into the mouthpiece, giving his name and address, and asking for the fire service.

Jason was soon able to go into another room, pick up the phone there, speak to his father and give all the necessary information and listen to instructions given to him. Jason and his father practised this several times, and then his father went on to teach Jason in the same way to ask for police and ambulance. Because so much of the procedure was the same as for the fire service, Jason learnt these more quickly. Jason's father could not make sure that Jason would be able to use his telephone skills in a real emergency – it hardly seemed a good idea to set fire to the house to see whether Jason made a good job of ringing the fire service. However, he did the best he could by checking every now and again that Jason knew what to do if a fire broke out, if somebody was very ill, or if the house was burgled.

Reacting to a fire

Fire is one of the most serious emergencies we have to deal with, because of the speed with which it can become dangerous; it has been said that the first two minutes are the most critical time for those in the fire area (Lerup et al. 1980).

So a person living independently may need to learn how to cope with small fires – on the cooker or ironing board for example – and to use a fire extinguisher or blanket; and everyone, whatever their living situation, should be taught how to escape from a burning building. It is unwise to rely entirely on the skills of staff, who may have difficulty in coping with unpractised and panicking residents.

In one study (Bertsch et al. 1984), four people with learning disabilities were taught how to react to the sound of the fire alarm, set off when they were in their own bedrooms. They were taught as follows:

1. Go to the door (crawling is recommended).
   (a) If the door was hot, or if hot air was coming under the door,

      A Leave the door closed
      B Go to the window
      C Open the window
      D Wait for help

2. If the door was not hot, open it
  (a) If they were confronted by (a picture of) a fire

      A Go back into the bedroom and close the door
      B, C and D as above

  (b) If there was no fire, go to the front door

3. Open front door, go outside to meeting place away from the house.
  (a) If the front door was locked or blocked, go to an alternative
     exit and go outside to the meeting place.

Each person was taken through all the steps each time, being prompted if they did not know what to do, hugged and praised when they got it right. When they got it wrong the teacher demonstrated the correct procedure, then got the person to practise it. Later still, as we suggested for Jason, it seems particularly important that fire drills should be held, quite often and some at least when they are not expected. Without these drills, real fires occurring (fortunately) so very rarely, the skills are easily lost. Again, the skills should be practised in other rooms in the house, at the person's work place and so on, to ensure that he or she can use these skills wherever they may need them.

Summary

1. People with learning disabilities who wish to live independently will need to acquire the domestic skills that will enable them to do so.

2. Many of the lists of routines, recipes etc that most of us have in written form can be made up as picture cards.

3. Most household tasks can be taught using demonstration, prompting, fading prompts and reinforcement.

4. Many will also require the person to make judgements (cleanliness, cookedness etc) so a further stage in the teaching involves the person making judgements and receiving feedback.

5. A checklist of jobs and when they should be done can be helpful.

6. Ways to teach sweeping and washing a floor, vacuuming, cleaning toilet, bath and basin and doing the laundry are outlined.

7. Shopping may be made easier with picture lists, both of shops to be visited and of items to be bought.

8. Although kitchens are potentially dangerous places, many people with learning disabilities can learn to use them safely.

9. Before embarking on cooking, people should be taught how to use oven gloves and a kitchen timer.

10. Making a pot of tea involves coping with boiling water, holding heavy kettles or teapots, and making judgements about quantities.

11. Most cooking processes may be taught by demonstration, prompting, fading prompts, and supervised practise.

12. Safety skills should be taught taking into account the person's ability to learn them and his or her living situation.

Exercises

1. How would you set about teaching someone to clean windows?

2. Ashok is a large, friendly young man. How would you set about teaching him to buy stamps at the post office?

3. What safety skills teaching would you give priority to for people living independently?

CHAPTER 12

Travel Skills

Being able to travel independently and to use public transport are important skills for adult people, giving them the chance to take part in all sorts
of activities; going to work, shopping, visiting friends, social clubs, the
cinema. Our roads and transport systems, however, are full of complications and hazards. Parents often suffer intense anxieties when their children first begin to go out on their own, but they recognise that this is an
essential part of growing up. Both normal children and adults with learning disabilities may need some special help to learn to cope safely and
happily with roads, buses and railways, but many adults with a learning
disability have little opportunity to travel on their own, even though they
may be capable of it, because they have always been taken to school and
then to their day centres in special transport. So we may need to offer them
the opportunity to develop more independent travelling skills.

Road sense

There are many ready-to-hand formulae – 'look and listen', 'don't walk out
from behind parked cars', 'the Green Cross Code', 'use zebra and pelican
crossings' – which are just as applicable to adults as they are to children.
Our teaching may need to be particularly detailed and careful, and the
methods we use are prompting, modelling and graded practice. In addition, because road crossing is potentially very dangerous, before we allow
a person to go out entirely alone, we fade the prompts very gradually,
putting a little distance between ourselves and the person, so that he feels
that he is more and more responsible for himself; then, when he sets out
on his own, we 'shadow' him, in the detective story sense of the word, or,
perhaps, get someone whom he will not recognise easily to follow him on
his journey. Then, if he has any difficulty, this person is there to help him
over it, while if all goes well we are reassured that he really can cope safely

and confidently with the journey. (This process is described more fully in the section on 'Going to the local shops'.)

We will start with:

Using a zebra crossing

John has always travelled to his day centre on the hospital coach. His sister, with whom he lives, felt that he could be taught to use an ordinary bus quite easily, especially as one which went all the way to the day centre stopped almost outside his house. The main obstacle to independent travelling for John was an extremely busy road with a complicated road junction, which he had to cross after he got off the bus. The junction had traffic lights, but they did not allow much time to get across. However, about 100 yards along the road there was a zebra crossing, and it was decided to teach John to use this.

The stages involved in using a zebra crossing include:

(1) Stop at the edge of the pavement.

(2) Look left.

(3) Look right

(4) Listen for the sound of approaching traffic.

(5) Look again.

(6) If all is clear, cross.

If the crossing is one of those with an island in the middle, we need to look only in one direction for the traffic and the process is repeated, looking in the other direction, when the island is reached.

When John approached the zebra crossing he would stop (step 1), but only for a moment, and would then step right out into the road without looking or listening at all. This, then, was where the teaching began. John very much wanted to travel on his own and was very fond of the person teaching him, so he started with two advantages. At the beginning of the teaching the instructor physically prompted John to stand on the edge of the pavement while he and his instructor went through the following routine.

Instructor		John
1.	'Now stop here, John' 'Good'	John stops
2.	'Are there any cars coming this way?' Points left	John looks Replies 'No'

3. 'Are there any cars coming this way?' Points right	John looks Replies 'Yes'

THEY WAIT
CAR STOPS

4. 'Can you hear any other cars coming?' 'Good'	John replies 'No' Stages 2 and 3 repeated until all is clear

'Let's cross then'

PHYSICALLY PROMPTS JOHN TO WALK ACROSS ROAD

'Well done, John'

When John crossed the road correctly he was praised by the instructor, but he was also able to buy a newspaper in the newsagent's on the other side of the road, which otherwise he would have to wait for until lunch-time. It is especially important, when we are teaching new skills in public, to try to find reinforcers which can be given immediately but which do not mark the person out as strange or odd (it would certainly look rather odd for one adult to be feeding Smarties to another adult in the street). This can present quite a challenge to the person doing the teaching. In this case, the buying of a newspaper was a normal thing to do, but was also reinforcing for John.

Gradually the instructor was able to fade the physical, gestural and verbal prompts until John could go through the whole process without any help.

Using a pelican crossing

Pelican crossings are light-controlled, and many have the added auditory clue, so that when the green man shows and the bleep sounds we know that we can cross in safety. When we are teaching somebody to use a pelican crossing we always include a 'look and listen' routine, and use prompting, and gradual fading of the amount of supervision required. Using a pelican crossing begins by the person pressing the button to alert the machinery to the fact that someone wants to cross. The person has to learn to wait and look for the green man and listen for the bleep before he moves, but once this is learned a pelican is probably the safest kind of crossing to use. The routine to be learned is similar to that for using a zebra crossing, but includes learning to wait when the red man is showing and to cross only when the green man is showing and the bleep sounds.

In theory, the flashing amber traffic light gives priority to the pedestrian, but not all motorists observe this. It may be safer to teach the person to cross only when the green man is showing continuously and the bleep sounding, and the person herself has checked that it is safe.

Crossing a small road

Most residential areas have a number of small roads without much traffic, and may safely be crossed if the rules are observed.*

(1) Move to a place where there is clear visibility in both directions.

(2) Look to the left.

(3) Look to the right.

(4) Listen.

(5) Ask yourself: is it safe to cross?

(6) If clear, cross, (walking not running).

To teach these rules we would use a routine similar to those described on pages 187–188. It seems best to teach these skills at times when the person would be out walking and crossing roads anyway, and to integrate frequent teaching with jobs and errands which have to be done in the course of everyday life so that crossing the road makes sense as an activity.

Going to the local shops

People with learning disabilities, whether living at home or in a hostel or group home, benefit from being able to pop out to the local shop to get items as and when they want them, so that once they can cross a road safely this is another important skill to teach.

Alice lives in a small group home in a quiet residential area. There are some local shops about half a mile away, and Alice wanted to be able to walk to them, especially at the weekends, in order to buy things she wanted. To get to the shops, she has to turn both left and right, and this she found very confusing; on the one occasion on which she attempted it on her own, she got lost. Alice's goal was therefore to walk to and from her local shops without getting lost. The steps on the journey were as follows (see diagram).

---

*   Although general advice often includes 'don't cross from behind parked cars', in many urban areas this may be impractical and most adults will walk to the edge of the parked car, and then carry out their usual crossing procedure.

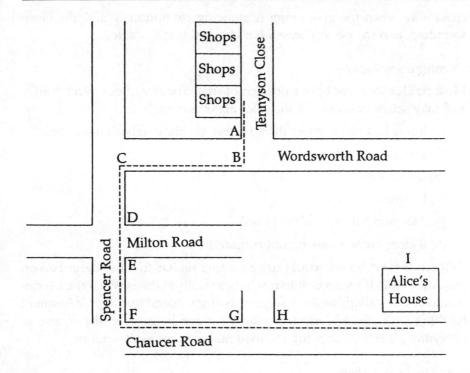

(1) Leave home.

(2) Turn right.

(3) Walk along pavement.

(4) Cross small road.

(5) Continue along pavement.

(6) Turn right at next road.

(7) Walk along pavement.

(8) Cross small road.

(9) Continue along pavement.

(10) Turn right at next road.

(11) Walk along the pavement.

(12) Come to small road on the left. From her side of the road she can see the shops quite clearly.

(13) Cross the road.

(14) Walk up to the shops.

Alice was taught this journey using graded practise with decreasing levels of supervision.

Since she very much wanted to make this journey on her own, actually achieving it was very reinforcing for her. In addition however, when she got to the shops, as well as buying the other things she had gone for she was encouraged to buy a Twix. She ate one half of it, which she very much enjoyed, and saved the other half until she had completed her homeward journey, when she ate that as a reward for accomplishing that too.

At the beginning, Alice and her instructor walked side-by-side all the way to the shops and back again. This was easy, especially as Alice had been given a small map rather like the one above. She had difficulty in following the map by herself, but kept it in her pocket, and found having it reassuring, while it also meant that, if she ever got lost again, she would be able to ask for help and show exactly where she had come from and was going to. Once Alice was quite confident and happy with the journey when the instructor was alongside her, they moved on to the next stage, the instructor walking about ten yards behind Alice all the way. At first, Alice constantly looked round to make sure that she was not alone, but she soon got used to the arrangement. She said that it was rather like being shadowed by a gangster, and it made even buying a pound of apples quite exciting.

At the next stage the instructor walked ten yards behind Alice, until they reached point A. Alice did the last part of the journey by herself, did her shopping, and walked back to the instructor waiting at point A. This was practised again the next day with the instructor standing at point A, but after that they went ahead by leaps and bounds. Each day the instructor waited at a point further back, first at B, then C, then D, and so on, each time greeting Alice's reappearance with a paeon of praise. Eventually, Alice was going all the way on her own with the instructor sitting in her front room waiting for her to get back. Teaching Alice to go to her local shops was quite a lengthy process – it took over 50 journeys – but at the end of it she was able to go out to do her shopping happily and confidently on her own.

The Post Office is an important landmark for those who need to cash benefit cheques and so on regularly, and getting to the Post Office or day centre or other places sufficiently nearby can be taught in a similar way, making sure that the distance between points A, B, C and so on are not too large, and that the person has adequate supervision in the early stages. Our objectives are – as ever – to increase the person's independence, not to get them run over.

Travelling on buses

Many people with learning disabilities are only too familiar with travelling with an escort on Local Authority buses, coaches and ambulances. Travelling on a public transport bus, however, is complicated. The stages involved include:

(1) Walk to the bus stop.

(2) Stand at the stop or at the end of the queue if there is one.

(3) Recognise the number of the bus required (this could involve some table-top teaching before we actually get out on the streets).

At this point, what happens depends on whether it is a one-man bus or whether it has a conductor. We will assume for the moment that it is a one-man bus.

(4) Wait for automatic doors to open.

(5) Get on bus at the front.

(6) State destination or fare to driver.

(7) Give money.

(8) Wait for change.

(9) Go to a seat and sit down.

(10) Know when to get off, looking for a landmark such as a particular shop, house or church at some point before the getting-off point.

(11) Go to door.

(12) Ring bell (if stop is a request).

(13) When bus stops, alight.

If the bus has a conductor, then step 4 is cancelled and steps 5–9 are slightly different, as follows:

(5) Get on bus at the back.

(6) Go to a seat and sit down.

(7) When the conductor comes, state destination or fare.

(8) Give money.

(9) Wait for change.

Probably the most difficult part of this process is step 10, knowing where to get off, and time needs to be spent prompting the person to register that the landmark has been reached.

Standing in a queue

Standing in a queue is an important part of catching the bus, as few things antagonise fellow travellers more than the person who barges to the front. Again, this is a routine which can be learned, involving the person looking to see who is already at the bus stop and going to stand behind the person at the end. We use modelling, physical prompting and fading to teach this, reinforcing the correct behaviour with whatever suits the particular person. In London in the rush-hour many people seem to have more or less given up queueing, and this may also be a problem elsewhere. The skill to be taught here, then, is one of assertiveness, discussed in chapter 14.

Paying the fare

Some people who can travel on buses are not used to handling money, so paying the fare can be a problem. Many people with learning disabilities have bus passes and these, or season tickets, get over much of the difficulty. Other solutions include the person always being given the right money or, especially for a single journey regularly travelled, learning a routine:

(1) State destination or fare.

(2) Hand over money using a coin or note which has been learned to be of greater value than the fare (for example, a 50p piece for a 30p fare).

(3) Wait for change.

The crucial bit in this sequence is knowing to wait for change.

Behaving like everyone else on the bus

Philip lived a good bus ride away from his day centre, and wanted to be able to go there on the bus. However, he would not travel on the bus unless a friend would travel with him and, because his behaviour on buses was so embarrassing, nobody was willing to travel with him, so he usually walked to work. Philip is a friendly, happy person, tall, with a very loud voice. He did not understand money and was not quite sure how to ask for his fare or how to cope with paying, and in order to get over this he spoke very loudly on the bus and waved his arms around a lot, telling jokes to no-one in particular. When he took his seat on the bus, he sprawled across two seats and shouted comments to people he knew over the other side. Philip wanted to be able to travel on the bus like everyone else, and could not really understand where things were going wrong and why nobody would go with him.

First, there were some practical things to sort out. Philip did not have a bus pass, so he was taken to buy one, and this took care of the problem involved in paying his fare. His instructor undertook to travel with him, and found that Philip's behaviour was much better when he was just with one person and deteriorated the bigger the crowd of people with him. He discovered, too, that Philip had never really noticed how other people behaved in public places or thought about what that implied about his own behaviour. So the first sessions took place in the day centre, teaching him to observe other people and to imitate. Teaching him to observe took the form of a game which was carried out walking round the day centre. 'Philip, can you see someone with brown shoes on? With a green jumper? With blond hair? Brown hair? A red dress? Two people talking? Arguing? Smiling? Someone with a sad face?' Philip soon got very good at this, and very much enjoyed these sessions. Next came teaching him to imitate, which started as a game, still in the Centre. The instructor modelled an action and then prompted Philip to carry it out himself, and then reinforced him for this. They began with Philip imitating when the instructor touched his own nose, his hair, then a chair, the floor, a light-switch, then imitating shouting, whispering, smiling, sitting modestly on a chair. Next came a game where Philip and the instructor walked round the day centre and the instructor asked Philip questions: 'Philip, what are people doing in this workshop?', 'How loudly are they talking?', 'Which people are talking to each other?'. Philip had to watch, analyse the situation, and report back to the instructor. Next came applying these skills out in the street and on buses. Philip and the instructor went on a bus and Philip was asked:

Who is sitting on their own?

Who is sitting next to someone?

Who is talking loudly?

Who is talking softly?

After each of these questions Philip had to do the same as he observed the other people doing. Philip managed not to behave embarrassingly when he was just with one person, and he was beginning to observe how other people behaved and what the rules were. Next came the gradual introduction of other friends, first one and gradually working up to four people over a period of about two weeks. Everyone enjoyed these bus trips, partly because they often involved trips to Macdonald's or walks on the common, but also because it was no longer embarrassing to be out on a bus with Philip.

Travelling by train

Being able to use the train has many obvious advantages, especially in large cities; it is quicker and often more direct, and may avoid changes which would need to be made if the bus were used. It is especially convenient for travelling into the centre of a large city in order to go to the cinema, the theatre, other social events or meetings, or to visit family or friends who live at a distance. Using the underground has many aspects in common with using a British Rail train as well as some differences which we can look at later.

Janice was used to travelling by bus from her home to her day centre, but when she got the chance to attend an adult education class in central London one morning a week, it was obvious that it would be very much easier for her to travel by train, and it was decided to try to help her learn to do so. The journey into London involved travelling to the end of the line, so there were no problems over changing trains or platforms. Janice cannot read, but she had learned to recognise certain familiar words like 'TRAINS' and 'EXIT', so the procedure started with an instructor at her day centre teaching her to recognise the name of her destination, 'Holborn'. Janice was already used to travelling by bus, so buying a ticket, stating her destination and being alone on public transport were not totally new to her.

Her journey from home to central London was divided into the following steps:

(1) Walk to British Rail station.

(2) Go to ticket kiosk.

(3) Buy return ticket.

(4) Walk to platform.

(5) Wait for the right train.

(6) When the train comes in, open the door and get into carriage.

(7) Find a seat.

(8) Travel all the way to Holborn.

(9) When the train stops at Holborn, get out.

Janice had to be taught how to recognise which was the right train by learning its head code, and to recognise the name 'Holborn' on a destination board. The journey was taught in the following stages, gradually withdrawing the amount of supervision.

(1) Janice was accompanied all the way from home to Holborn.

(2) Janice was accompanied all the way from home to Holborn, but she asked for her own ticket and opened and closed the carriage doors herself.

(3) As in 1 and 2, but Janice also looked out for her particular land-mark just before Holborn.

(4) Janice was met at her home station, but then went on ahead and went through steps 2-10 with the instructor standing and sitting about one yard away from her.

(5) As in 4, except that the instructor stood or sat about two to three yards away from her.

(6) As in 4, except that the instructor sat on the train in an adjacent carriage.

(7) Janice went through the whole process on her own, except that she was followed through the journey by a person she did not know, just to make sure that things went well.

Janice had also to be taught how to find the ticket kiosk, and how to find her way home again – see *Finding the ticket kiosk* and *The return journey*.

Some people learning to travel may not need all the stages outlined here before they can travel independently, others may need even smaller stages to enable them to learn. The essence of the method is that each step is small enough to ensure success for the person concerned. The stages we have suggested are only a guide.

Buying a train ticket

Some people who are used to travelling independently, like Janice, may make the transition from asking for a bus ticket to buying a train ticket quite easily, but for others this may have to be taught as a special skill. Jack had for some years travelled by train from home to his day centre with his mother, also on her way to work. He knew the journey, which platform to use, and the times of the trains. His mother was planning to change her job and the new job was within walking distance for her, which meant that she would not have to use the train. Neither she nor Jack wanted him to go back to travelling on the Centre transport, but although he was well used to the journey he had never had to buy his own ticket, as his mother had always done this for him, and this seemed to be the major obstacle to his travelling on his own. Jack is a rather shy, retiring person, and was very apprehensive about buying a ticket on his own.

The steps involved were worked out as follows:

(1) Walk to train station.

(2) Go up to the ticket office.

(3) Stand in a queue if necessary.

(4) Approach the window.

(5) State destination.

(6) Offer money.

(7) Take ticket and change.

Jack's greatest difficulty was in asking for the ticket, so this was practised in role-play before he was ever taken to the station. First, the instructor played Jack's role and he played the ticket clerk. The instructor demonstrated to him how to ask for the ticket, to speak clearly and loudly enough, and to get close enough to the mouthpiece in the ticket office window; how to look at the ticket clerk and to pick up the ticket and change. Then the roles were reversed and the routine was gone through again with Jack playing himself. This was done over and over again, pointing out the good things each actor was doing, until the whole process became quite routine. (This approach is dealt with in more detail in Chapter 14.) When Jack felt more confident, he and the instructor went to the railway station and did it for real, with the instructor gradually withdrawing the amount of supervision Jack was given. They had decided in advance that Jack would buy a return ticket, so that he could make the return journey on his own without having to buy another ticket, but this posed the problem of where to keep the return half all day long. Jack decided upon the breast pocket of his jacket as being a good place, and tore the ticket in half as soon as he got it, placing the return half in his breast pocket and keeping the half that he needed for the outward journey in the right hand pocket of the same jacket.

This was Jack's preferred way to look after his ticket, but not, of course the only one. Janice's way was to keep the whole of her return ticket in her purse and not to tear it in two until she got to the barrier at the far end. Sometimes, the person may need to buy a single ticket, and to learn to ask for this, and to give the whole ticket up at the barrier. Many people with learning disabilities have free travel passes (but there are restrictions about when these can be used), while season tickets, which give a great deal of freedom also have to be bought, and both passes and season tickets need to be even more carefully looked after.

Finding the ticket kiosk

It is not always easy to know where to go to buy a ticket. Jack needed to make only one main journey from his home, so he soon learned where the ticket office in his station was. However, if someone is hoping to travel to a variety of places they need to be able to recognise ticket offices in different places. There are two main kinds – a kiosk in the centre of the ticket hall, as in tube stations, or a window or row of windows set in a wall. Usually, although not invariably, both kinds have a sign over them saying 'Tickets', and most ticket offices have a similar look about them, so we need not be entirely dependent on the written word. Learning to recognise the word 'ticket' may be done as a table-top exercise, at least at first. We begin by writing the word 'ticket' in bold, clear letters, on a card, and pairing it with other words which are very dissimilar, such as 'and', 'but', 'come'. Each pair of words presented includes the word 'ticket', and the person is prompted, if necessary, to choose the right one and then reinforced for the correct choice. The range of words to choose from is gradually extended to include both words which are increasingly similar to 'ticket', such as 'blanket', 'sticky', 'cricket', and other words which might well be seen hanging up in stations, such as 'underground', 'exit', 'British Rail', 'ladies', 'gentlemen'. It is possible to buy packs of cards and signs commonly seen in public places which are photographs of the real signs – this obviously makes recognition of the words in the real situation easier (see Appendix 2).

Once the person can recognise the word 'tickets', the next step is to make sure that he can pick out a variety of different types of ticket kiosks in different stations. We do this by taking her to strange stations and asking her to show us where the ticket office is. We prompt, if prompts are needed, and the prompts are gradually faded until the person can, wherever necessary, reliably locate ticket offices.

Train door handles

We avoided these earlier as, luckily, they are not a problem for Janice. However, many of us can have difficulties with some train door handles. There seem to be three common ways of opening a carriage door (apologies to British Rail if we have missed any out). Some suburban services and some trains on the London Underground have a button which, when pushed when the train is actually in the station, open the doors, and this is very straightforward. More common are the type where we have to slide an often very stiff lever on the inside of the door, sometimes needing two hands to do this. Another type requires us to open the window, lean out and open the door using the outside handle. Both these last two types may need more intensive training including, possibly, hand-strengthening exercises, mock-ups of the doors in a place away from the railway station, and physical prompting. This sort of attention to detail is really worthwhile when we want to make sure that a person succeeds in achieving her goal. Chloë knew all the steps involved in travelling from the hostel where she lived to her day centre, but she missed her stop, because she simply could not open the carriage door. She was finally found some way away from her home after the police had been alerted. After we had helped her to learn how to open the doors, she felt happier about travelling by train on her own.

The return journey

Catching a train at a local station is more straightforward than finding the right platform at a central London terminus, but if the person is to make the return, as well as the outward journey independently, we may also need to teach this. Even if a train does not always leave from the same platform, in most busy stations there is a limited number of platforms which are used. Janice, when she was returning home from central London, had to learn to check up to three platforms to ascertain which her train was leaving from. She learned a routine which involved her going first to the most usual platform, and, if the train was not indicated here, there were two other platforms that she could try. Routes change from time to time, and it is important to be able to cope on the day that the points have failed or a flock of sheep has wandered onto the track, resulting in the train not appearing at its usual platform. Janice's teachers made sure that she knew how and where and who to ask for help if she had trouble finding the platform (the methods used are described in the Chapter 14).

Escalators

Escalators are part of the system at many mainline and underground stations, and the ability to use them may be a crucial point in a travel training programme, while they may be encountered also in department stores and shopping centres. Escalators can be rather frightening, especially when they are very deep and the person is not used to them.

Bena attended a social club one evening a week. A group of her friends travelled there by underground, and the only thing stopping Bena travelling with them was her difficulty with escalators. Despite the fact that her friends stepped confidently onto the escalators, Bena was very frightened and refused to set foot on them. The journey was only a couple of stops on the tube, and there were escalators at both ends. Bena could have made the journey by bus and avoided the problem, but all her friends preferred the train and she did not want to travel on her own.

The first step was to discover what Bena's problem actually was. Getting on and off an escalator is often a difficulty but also, particularly with the London Underground, some of them are steep and long, and people may suffer from vertigo. In fact, with Bena, all these things seemed important – every part of using escalators frightened her – and so it was necessary to desensitise her to using them.

The first step was to help her to cope with the depth of escalators on the underground. She was taken to the stairs which run between the 'up' and 'down' escalators. She was encouraged to hold firmly onto the hand-rail of the steps with her right hand; the teacher held onto the elbow and lower arm of her left arm, and together they walked firmly down the stairs. Since Bena was very keen to travel by train, she practised using the underground stairs several times a week, the physical prompt to her left arm being very gradually withdrawn, until she was much more confident about their height and could walk up and down the stairs without being prompted.

Next, Bena had to learn to get on and off escalators. This was practised first using a small escalator in a local branch of Marks and Spencer's. The programme went as follows:

(1) Bena reached for the handrail and the teacher held Bena's left lower arm and elbow.

(2) The teacher said 'Let's get on to the escalator now'.

(3) Bena and the instructor stepped forward together onto the middle of the top step. (The escalators in Marks and Spencer's are good for this, as they have plainly painted yellow lines on either edge, showing where it is safest to stand.)

(4) Bena held the hand-rail firmly with her right hand while the escalator travelled downwards. The teacher kept hold of Bena's left arm all the way down.

(5) Three steps away from the bottom the teacher said 'Let's get off...'

(6) 'Now'. As the last step was reached, the teacher physically prompted Bena to step off the escalator.

Just as in the programme to teach walking up and down the stairs, the physical prompts were gradually faded until only a gesture was required to encourage Bena to step on and off the escalator, and later even this too was faded. When Bena was quite confident about travelling on the Marks and Spencer's escalator, the same process was repeated in an underground station, although by now Bena was so much more confident that the programme proceeded quite quickly. The reinforcement in this programme was two-fold; first, Bena wanted very much to travel with her friends and knew that she needed to overcome her fear of the escalators if she was to do so, but second, when she got to the bottom of the first escalator in the tube she was given her ticket, which she looked after and was able to give in at the other end, and she was very proud of being able to do this.

Summary

1. Travel skills are an important part of independent adult life.

2. The main methods used in teaching these skills are prompting, fading, modelling, and graded practise.

3. If the person is already attempting to travel, we begin by looking at what he can do already.

4. Reinforcement for success needs to be immediate, but in this case it is important to find reinforcers which do not mark out the learner as being rather peculiarly treated.

5. We begin teaching road-crossing in the simplest, safest place we can find, often a pelican crossing.

6. Road-crossing involves physical prompting and close supervision at first, both then systematically faded.

7. Fading the supervision may be a very slow process, involving increasing the distances between the person and the teacher, and at the end supervision by someone the person does not know.

8. Going out to local shops may be taught after road crossing.

9. Travelling on public transport involves some social skills as well as the practical ability to handle money, recognise numbers and signs, etc.

10. An important skill is knowing where to get off public transport.

Exercises

1. What can you remember being the most worrying thing about learning to cross the road when you were a child?. How would you go about teaching someone to cope with this?

2. Do you feel there are ethical concerns about having somebody, who is being taught to go to the shops independently, shadowed by a stranger?

3. What, for you, are the most tricky parts of a train journey you often make?

CHAPTER 13

Going to Work

Until the late 1970s, people attending day centres (Adult Training Centres) tended to be occupied with routine repetitive industrial work and not much else. There was little further education, or training in daily living skills. Pamphlet No.5 (1977) from the National Development Group suggested that Adult Training Centres should change the emphasis of their work; many adopted this idea and in doing so changed their name to Social Education Centre. Industrial contract work was largely abandoned, and much time was spent in teaching social, domestic and independence skills (rather like those described in the bulk of this book).

The pendulum has now swung back some way. People with learning disabilities, like other people, want to work. They see that having a job, besides bringing in far more money than is offered by the SECs, confers status in the normal world. Despite the many problems (the poor kinds of work available to them, the difficulty of finding jobs, the complications to be sorted out between wages and benefits) many people with learning disabilities are eager to find and to keep jobs. One of our tasks is to help them to do this as well as they can. Much of the published work in this area* focusses on people already employed in sheltered workshops, and looks at ways to develop their skills, especially the skills needed for the particular job in hand, and how to keep production flowing. We have ourselves done little of this, but have usually been concerned with people embarking on work experience or a new job with the Pathways or other similar schemes, who want help with the practical aspects of their new lives. What follows is a description of some of the ways in which we have tried to do this.

---

* An excellent introduction to the whole area of work for people with learning disabilities is given by Whelan and Speake (1981).

Time-keeping

Good time-keeping – arriving punctually and keeping good time when going to and coming from lunch and tea breaks – is important for any worker. In addition, an average SEC day is much shorter, and has more substantial breaks in it than does the normal working day. So important elements to be learnt on work experience courses are arriving on time, staying all day – a rather longer day than usual – and occupying time and structuring the day when actually at work.

Arriving on time

In order to get to work on time, we need to get up promptly, organise getting dressed and having breakfast, travel to our workplace and check in. People with little to do during the day may find getting out of bed a problem, and they will need to change from, say, staying in bed until 11.00am to getting up at 7.00am. This is not easy, and we have known several people who almost lost the possibility of employment because they did not manage to arrive on time in the first week. One of these was Emerson, (mentioned in Chapter 1) who arrived late for work because he had difficulties in getting up in the morning.

Since returning to live with his parents after leaving boarding school, Emerson had always found it difficult to get up in the mornings. He had the opportunity to go on a work training scheme, the aims of which were to teach basic carpentry skills, and to develop good work habits in people who were not used to being at work all day. In his first week at the workshop, Emerson was late twice and he was told that, unless his punctuality improved, his place would be given to someone else. Emerson was extremely keen to make a go of his opportunity, and his parents decided they would try to help him get up in the mornings.

The usual pattern in the mornings was that Emerson's mother would call him and he got up; but after going to the toilet he would go back to bed again. His mother used to call him several times and each time he would get up and then go back to bed. Finally, he would come downstairs in his pyjamas and eat his breakfast while watching TV. Then he had to be detached from the television, get washed and dressed, and be out of the house by 8.15 in order to get to the workshop by 9.00. His mother felt that she was not very good at getting him up, so his father offered to try to structure the early morning routine for him so as to help him leave the house on time.

Although we had a pretty good idea of what happened in the morning, as outlined above, his father started off by looking carefully at what Emerson did each day. Emerson needed a great deal of help and supervision in his washing and dressing, but his father felt that this could be worked on later. To both of them, the most important thing was to stop Emerson wasting time by going back to bed, and by watching television, and to make sure he left the house by 8.15.

First they decided to change the usual routine. They decided that Emerson should not keep getting up and then going back to bed, and that he should wash and dress before he came downstairs. They worked out a new routine.

6.45   Mr Paterson gets up.

6.50   First call to Emerson.

6.55   Second call to Emerson with a cup of tea.

7.00   Mr Paterson takes Emerson to bathroom for a wash.

7.15   Emerson dresses in the bathroom with Mr Paterson's help.

7.25   Cartoons on TV.

7.35   Television switched off. Emerson goes to kitchen for breakfast.

7.55   Cartoons on TV.

8.05   Emerson organises the bag he takes his packed lunch in and puts on his coat, all with Mr Paterson's help.

This timetable took into account the needs of all the Patersons – Mrs Paterson liked to sleep on in the morning, but Mr Paterson was always up early, often before 6.45, so calling Emerson did not put him out. Emerson could dress quite quickly with his father's supervision and they both agreed that the TV cartoons were a good reinforcer for his dressing. Cartoons were the only bit of TVam which Emerson actually liked, and usually he spent a lot of time watching things he was not interested in, in order to catch the cartoons. With the new timetable and with cartoons as the reinforcer, Emerson had more time to eat his breakfast and pack his bag – both of which he liked doing.

Emerson and his father drew up the timetable as a checklist, so that each morning they ticked off each item as it was completed, and this also gave Mr Paterson the chance to let Emerson know how well he was doing in keeping to the schedule. Although the timetable looks fairly tight, Mr Paterson and Emerson both felt that it meant that they had less of a rush in the mornings. It also enabled Emerson to leave the house and get to work on time, and he succeeded in keeping his workshop place.

Keeping to time at work

Once at work, there are various time schedules which must be met there, including going to and returning from lunch and tea breaks. Sharon had just started work as a chambermaid in a small hotel. She was working shifts and this meant that her breaks occurred at different times on different days. She found this confusing and tended to go off for her tea or lunch break at the wrong times. Her job had been found for her by the Pathways Scheme, which meant that, for the first six weeks, she had a partner, one of the established employees, to work alongside her. Sharon's partner, Asmina, agreed to help Sharon learn the times of her breaks. We drew up two cards* for Sharon, to show her how the clock should look when it was time, first to go to and then to return from her lunch and her break.

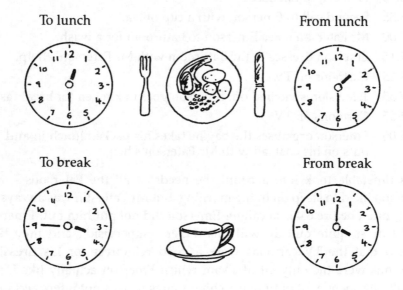

At first, when Sharon arrived at work each day, Asmina sat with her for a few minutes. She showed her the cards and told her that the clocks on the cards showed the times at which Sharon was meant to go to lunch (pointing to the correct one), come back from lunch (pointing), go to break (pointing), and come back from break (pointing again). Asmina then asked Sharon to show her which clock she would look at to tell her when to go to lunch. If

---

*   The cards were adapted from those described by Sowers et al (1980).

she got it right, she was praised. If it was wrong, she was shown the correct one and was asked to show it herself again. Then Asmina asked her about the other clocks on the card. Asmina carried on with this until Sharon had got eight consecutive answers right. Then they went to the real clock in the hotel's staff rest room and Asmina moved the hands of the clock until they matched the going-to-lunch clock on the card. She asked Sharon to point to the clock on her card which matched the real clock face. When she got it right, she was given a great deal of praise. If it was wrong Asmina said 'No' and explained why. Then they went on to the returning-from-lunch clock, and so on, until Sharon could match each clock on the card with the corresponding time on the real clock.

Sharon had two sets of cards, one for an early shift and the other for a late shift, and she had to learn to match the times on the clock for all eight possible times (four on each shift card). This took quite a lot of time. However, as well as working like this with Sharon every day, Asmina also intervened at Sharon's real lunch and break times. For example, if Sharon attempted to go off to lunch before the exact time for lunch, Asmina would tell her it was the wrong time, get out her clock card, make her compare the clock on the card with the real clock and then help her to wait until the two matched up correctly before she went to lunch. Similarly, if Sharon was late in going to her breaks, Asmina would tell her to go, but also go through the card with her before she left.

At the beginning, particularly at the shorter tea break, Asmina and Sharon found that the instruction took up nearly the whole break period, so that although Sharon did have a break from her work, neither she nor Asmina always had enough time for a cup of tea. Luckily this only happened a few times, and Sharon soon became quite reliable about leaving for and returning from her break at the right time.

Interestingly, all this instruction did not teach Sharon to tell the time. She remained totally dependent on matching the clocks on her card with the real clock – and this she could do very accurately. When her shifts changed, new cards were made and she had to be retaught the new times, which she learnt much more quickly than she had the original times. The skill she had been taught was a matching skill and not, at that stage, a time-telling skill, but it helped her to cope with an important part of her working life.

Queuing for lunch

In Chapter 14, we mention that many SECs have now reorganised their canteens so that members have the experience of queuing for and selecting food in a way which is similar to that in which factory canteens are organised. This means, of course, that many people are able to make the transition from getting their lunch in the SEC to getting their lunch in a work setting without much extra teaching. This, however, is not always the case. Albert had been gaining work experience at a gas meter factory and had been doing very well. At first, he had gone each day from 9.00-12.00 and had then gone back to the SEC for lunch. The works manager wanted him to start doing a whole day. This would have meant his staying for lunch, and Albert's lunch time behaviour left much to be desired. In particular, being extremely fond of his lunch, he had always refused to queue for it but would barge straight to the front of the queue, no matter how many people were there before him. If the serving hatch was not yet open, he would rattle the grille until it was opened for him. If any of the instructors tried to get him to take his place at the back of the queue, he made an enormous fuss, so for the sake of peace and quiet they had got into the habit of letting him have his own way. The other members at the SEC were annoyed by all this, as they did not think that it was fair, and staff realised that this behaviour would not be tolerated in an ordinary factory. They pointed this out to Albert, and agreed to help him to learn to queue properly.

We tackled this first at the SEC. We assumed that Albert was extremely hungry and that the meal itself would be a reinforcer. We used a desensitisation approach (see Chapter 15). First, we encouraged Albert have a slightly larger breakfast (he often went out without eating anything), so that he was not so hungry at lunch-time. Then, in week 1, it was arranged that Albert should be first in the queue for lunch, having been organised to arrive at the canteen before anyone else, so that he did not have to jump the queue.

We progressed as follows:

WEEK 1

Monday	Albert alone in queue, grille opens at once
Tuesday	Albert alone in queue, grille opens after 15 sec
Wednesday	Albert alone in queue, grille opens after 30 sec
Thursday	Albert alone in queue, grille opens after 1 min
Friday	Albert alone in queue, grille opens after 2 mins

In effect, we were desensitising Albert to waiting. It went very well, so that, in Week 2, we felt we could extend the times for which Albert waited.

WEEK 2

Monday	Albert alone in queue, grille opens after 2 mins
Tuesday	Albert alone in queue, grille opens after 3 mins
Wednesday	Albert alone in queue, grille opens after 4 mins
Thursday	Albert alone in queue, grille opens after 5 mins
Friday	Albert alone in queue, grille opens after 6 mins

By the end of Week 2 Albert could wait quite happily for six minutes without rattling the grille or making a fuss. In Week 3, we started introducing other people. We arranged for another SEC member, an easy, good-natured man whom Albert liked, to walk into the canteen with Albert, before the proper opening time, and to stand just ahead of him at the grille. Albert was chatting with his friend and did not mind being second in the queue. Later we introduced another person and again gradually extended the waiting time. So this stage went like this:

WEEK 3

Monday	One person in queue in front of Albert, Albert waits 1 min to be served
Tuesday	One person in queue in front of Albert, Albert waits 2 mins to be served
Wednesday	One person in queue in front of Albert, Albert waits 3 mins to be served
Thursday	Two people in queue in front of Albert, Albert waits 2 mins to be served
Friday	Two people in queue in front of Albert, Albert waits 3 mins to be served

As you can see, doing this sort of thing depends on our having control of what goes on. However, the results were so encouraging that everyone was willing to put themselves out to make it work. At the beginning, those who stood in front of Albert were hand-picked and the whole thing was stage-managed to happen in the ten minutes before the canteen really opened. By the end of Week 6, Albert could wait for up to ten minutes with up to ten people in front of him.

It was at this point that it became no longer possible to stage manage what happened. At 12.30pm everyone streamed into the canteen. However, at the beginning of Week 7 the instructors made sure that Albert was in fairly early – he did not go straight to the front of the queue, but took his turn, about tenth. We were worried at this stage, because other factors which we could not control, such as the noise and clatter of 50 people having lunch, came into play. If this had affected Albert, we would have had to go back to square one and devise ways of desensitising him to the noise, or to anything else which seemed important. As it happened, by the time we got to the stage of introducing Albert to the main lunch queue, he was so used to the idea of queuing that, with careful supervision, he was able to fit into normal lunch-times quite easily. Soon after this he went on to staying all day at the factory, having his lunch in the factory canteen like everyone else.

Using the telephone

Using the telephone is an important everyday skill. It is particularly useful when we are working, because it enables us to phone in if we are sick or unable to arrive on time, while some people need to use a telephone as part of their jobs.

Nadia had begun working in a supermarket belonging to a national chain. Although they are very caring employers, the managers are very particular about knowing if their employees are taking the day off for illness. Nadia decided that she would need to be able to use the telephone when she started work; she would also then be able to phone her mother when she wanted to. Nadia lives in a house of bedsits with a public telephone in the ground floor hallway. We decided that there were two aspects of this skill that she needed to learn: first, number recognition, and second, the mechanics involved in using the telephone.

Nadia's friend Mary agreed to help her, and they began with number recognition. Mary laid out some cards, each with a number on it from 0 to 9. She laid these out in random order, and pointed to each in turn asking Nadia what it was, and noted which ones she knew. Next, Mary named each number in turn – 'find me number 7,' 'find me number 3'. From this, it seemed that Nadia had difficulty with '2' and '5' and confused '6' and '9'.

Mary started first with '2' and '5'. Using three-inch printed cards, she put the two cards on the table and asked Nadia to give her one of them. If Nadia was unable to do this, Mary guided her hand to pick up the correct one. She then put that card back on the table and asked Nadia for the other (naming it). From time to time Mary changed the position of the numbers on the table, so that Nadia did not always have to pick up, for example, the one on the right hand side. We thought that we would then move on to making sure that Nadia could recognise numbers on a smaller scale, for example large numbers on a calendar, then in ordinary type-script, and finally in handwriting, but within two sessions of working on '2' and '5' Nadia could distinguish between them reliably in a variety of sizes and scripts, including the numbers on a telephone dial.

The figures '6' and '9' proved to be rather more difficult. After several sessions of being guided to pick up the one asked for, Nadia was still confusing them. So we used stimulus shaping (see Chapter 6). We put two different colours along the tail of each number, as shown.

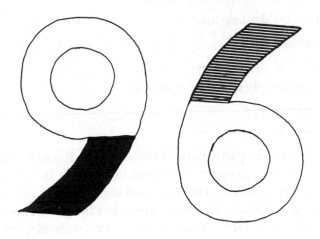

It is the position of the tail which is, after all, how we normally differentiate between the two numbers and it was these positions that we emphasised. The colour was then faded towards the tip of each tail, thus directing Nadia's attention to the position of the tail, and quite quickly she learnt which number was which. Nadia's knowledge of all the numbers was then rechecked, including using different sizes and styles of type.

We then moved on to teaching Nadia how to dial her work number. First, we decided just to practise dialling the number. This was done in the evenings as it was unlikely that anyone would be at Nadia's work place to answer it. Mary used backward chaining and a real telephone. With the telephone number written on a card in front of Nadia, Mary dialled the first six digits of the work 'phone number and directed Nadia's finger to dial the last. This was rewarded by the 'phone starting to ring. Mary and Nadia practised until Nadia had no difficulty with it. Then Mary dialled the first five and Nadia the last two. As Nadia got more skilful, Mary allowed her to dial progressively more of the number, until she was dialling the whole of it.

Having sorted out dialling the number, Nadia and Mary then worked on using the coin-operated box. The stages they worked out were as follows:

(1) Go to the telephone.

(2) Put 10p ready in slot.

(3) Lift receiver in left hand.

(4) Hold receiver the right way round.

(5) Listen for the dialling tone.

(6) Dial correct numbers.

(7) Listen for the ringing tone.

(8) Listen for the 'phone being picked up.

(9) Listen for the pips.

(10) Press in 10p.

Point 4 turned out to be particularly difficult for Nadia, and Mary had to show her how to have the part with small holes, with the wire hanging down, opposite her mouth, and the part with the large hole against her ear. This, and the learning of the numbers were in fact the parts of the teaching which took all the time. With Nadia, the other parts seemed quite straightforward and were learnt quickly. At the final stage, Nadia 'phoned into work one day when she had a day off to check her starting time the next day and was tremendously excited when she got through and was able to talk to her supervisor. Nadia's next goal was to learn her mother's number so that she could 'phone home whenever she liked, and she learnt this quite easily.

The phone in Nadia's house was coin-operated, with the numbers on a dial. If her phone had been a push button one, or if she had needed to use card phones we would have adapted our teaching to these, slightly different, tasks.

Structuring a working day

A 'real' job involves being in the workplace for much longer periods of time and with much shorter breaks than people who have attended SECs are used to. Structuring the time at work can also present problems, especially if the work does not of itself fill the entire day.

Teresa was gaining some work experience at one of the city farms. She worked in the staff snack bar and the job consisted of making an urn of tea three times a day for the morning and afternoon breaks and lunchtimes, and selling drinks, crisps or confectionery at break times. Teresa's initial timetable was as follows:

9.00	Start work
10.30–11.30	Staggered tea breaks for staff
12.00–2.00	Staggered lunch breaks for staff
3.30–4.30	Staggered tea breaks for staff
5.00	Finish work

Although Teresa was given an induction period and shown what to do, after she had been working for a week on her own there were many complaints, as staff were arriving for the first tea break at 10.30am to find that the tea was not yet made. Teresa was finding it difficult to anticipate how long it would take to do everything she needed to do, but she herself was also complaining that she was bored and that there were long periods of time when she had nothing to do. John, Teresa's key worker at the SEC, went along to the farm to see how she spent her day – it went something like this.

9.00	Arrive at work. Teresa made herself a cup of tea and sat on a chair at the door of the hut, watching the rest of the staff getting on with their work.
10.15	Teresa had made no attempt to start getting ready, so John suggested that she begin filling the urn.
10.30	The first group of staff started arriving, although the tea was not quite ready. John helped Teresa out so that they were not kept waiting too long.
10.30-11.30	This was quite a busy time, with a new group of staff arriving every 20 minutes for their tea.
11.30	Teresa was free again, with no washing-up to do, as everyone used plastic cups.
11.50	John again prompted Teresa to fill and boil the urn – this took about 20 minutes.

12.00-2.00	Lunch time was quieter than the tea breaks, as most people brought a packed lunch, so they just bought a drink and some bought sweets or crisps. Both John and Teresa had time to eat their own lunches in this time.
2.00-3.30	Teresa again had very little to do. This was her official lunch break.
3.30-4.30	This was as busy as the morning break, with everyone wanting drinks in quick succession and wanting cake as well as crisps and sweets.
4.30-5.00	Teresa cleared up and put things away.

John and Teresa went for a drink after work and discussed how the day had gone. Teresa had all the skills to do the job but, because she was not planning her day very well, she was becoming flustered and making mistakes such as not giving people their change properly. She also had cut up the cake as she was going along, so some people got bigger pieces than others. John and Teresa decided that they needed to work out ways for Teresa to do her work more efficiently, and to work out what she could do during the time when work was slack.

They started by making a list of the jobs to be done and then turned this into a daily timetable. By the end of their discussions it looked like this.

9.00	Start work.
9.05	Put on small kettle for a drink for Teresa. While the kettle is boiling fill the large urn.
9.15	Make herself some tea.
9.30	Lay out sweets, crisps and so on on the counter.
10.05	Switch on urn.
10.15	Sort out change into piles of pennies, etc. (John later got her a wooden box with separate compartments in it for each kind of coin.)
10.25	Put tea into pots and fill from urn.
10.30	First customers arrive.
10.30-11.30	Serve staff.
11.30	Refill urn, wash out teapots.
11.40	Replenish stock; sort out money; generally clear up, (throw away dirty plastic cups, wipe down counter). Switch on urn.
11.55	Put tea in teapots.

12.00-2.00	Customers came into the hut only sporadically during this time and Teresa was able to keep the tea pots filled and stock laid out quite easily. Teresa said she liked this time best, as she was kept busy enough not to be bored but not so busy as to be frantic, and was able to keep the place tidy as she was going along.
2.00-3.00	Teresa's lunch hour.
3.00	Fill urn, generally tidy up.
3.10	Switch on urn; cut up cake; sort out change.
3.25	Put tea into pots and fill with boiling water.
3.30	Tea breaks begin.
4.30	Wash out urn; wash out teapots; put stock away; generally clear up.
4.55	Return petty cash to site manager; go home.

John made Teresa a timetable chart to remind her of what she had to do and when. It used both words and pictures and looked like this:

Arrive work

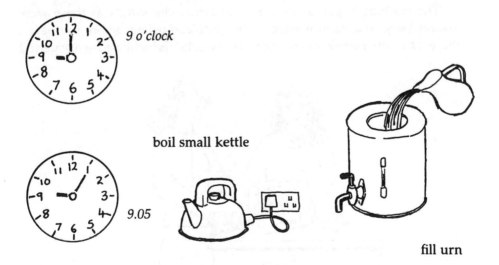

9 o'clock

boil small kettle

9.05

fill urn

etc. etc.

Teresa still found that there were quite a few times during the day when she had very little to do, so she decided to take some knitting in with her to do in her lunch hour, as well as in quiet times. With her working day better organised, Teresa found her work much more satisfying. She also received plenty of compliments from the other staff about how much better she was getting on, and as a result found that she liked them more.

John was able to stay with Teresa for several more days and to prompt her through the stages on her timetable. Teresa was keen to make a success of working and she welcomed the extra help John was able to give her. She very much enjoyed the improved relationships with her workmates, and also her wage packet when she received it at the end of the week.

Working in a supermarket

Supermarket work is quite often available to people with learning disabilities, and there are many different sorts of work they take on, including giving out baskets, packing goods at the check-out, and filling shelves.

Rajni accepted a job in a large supermarket chain which, found for her by the Pathways scheme, meant that she had a work partner for her first six weeks. The Pathways officer and the work partner, Christine, agreed that packing shopping at the check-out was the most problematical task which Rajni would be doing and decided that they would spend some extra time at the beginning teaching her how to do it.

The teaching began away from the actual check-outs as these were always busy, and Rajni needed to be quite competent before she began there. The store manager agreed on a two weeks' induction-to-work period

for her, and offered us the use of the staff rest room so that Rajni could learn her job away from public view. This was a very positive start, as we would not be faced (as we were with Teresa) with people complaining before we really knew that anything was going wrong.

Christine and Rajni first went round the shop collecting a typical, quite large, weekly shop – this helped Rajni to learn her way around the shop, and Christine encouraged Rajni to suggest the sorts of things she thought an ordinary family would buy. They took their 'purchases' up to the staff room and arranged a table and chair to simulate the check-out and put the 'shopping' out on the table.

The art of packing shopping consists in putting heavier, harder things at the bottom, and softer lighter things at the top. Christine and Rajni decided to start with making sure that Rajni could sort out what was heavy and what was light, what was soft and what was hard.

They began by going through the shopping and comparing various items. Christine would present two items to Rajni, saying 'Which is the heavier?'. Rajni found that she could not always tell by looking which was the heavier, but if she held one in each hand it was much easier. Christine corrected her if she made a mistake, explaining why and making her try the comparison again. In fact, the judgements to be made did not need to be very accurate, just so long as Rajni could distinguish between very heavy and very light things (so as not to put the tinned tomatoes on top of the crisps). Next, they went through 'soft' versus 'hard' – much easier to teach, as a gentle prod tells all. Rajni started by giving slightly too vigorous a prod, and in order to preserve the curd cheese Christine showed her a way of giving a soft press with the inside of her thumb which was unlikely to cause any damage.

Christine felt that it was also important for Rajni to be clear about the distinction between foods and cleaning materials. They talked about how it was particularly important to keep fresh foods away from soaps, as food can easily pick up detergent smells. Rajni learnt to tell from the smell of the packets which were those containing soap.

Together, Christine and Rajni developed a way of packing so that Rajni could deal with whatever came along, heavy, soft or soapy. Rajni started by opening three carrier bags, then, as heavy items came along she loaded them into the first bag. When the bottom of the first bag was full with heavy things she started to put them into the bottom of the second. Soft things could then go into the top of the first bag and soapy things into the third. They practised a similar method with cardboard boxes, Christine giving Rajni continuous feedback and praise when she got it right and explaining to her fully where she had gone wrong. They spent the first hour of every day at work practising this for the first two weeks, before Rajni tried it 'for real' in the shop. By then she was really very confident. However, they chose to start her packing in the real shop at a quiet time, so that she did not feel too flustered or under pressure, and they regarded themselves as having been extremely lucky to have had a manager who had been able to allocate specific time for training once Rajni was at work.

Working as a cleaner

We have not been involved with this training ourselves, but mention it here because it is such an heartening example of how, with the right help, people with very severe disabilities can do and keep a real job. Susan, a woman with multiple difficulties including no hearing, no sight in one eye, and a history of problem behaviour, was taught over a period of 6 to 8 months to do a cleaning job in a pub. A great deal of staff input was needed over that time but, eventually, this enabled Susan to hold down a real job, to the satisfaction of her employers, for real pay.*

This work demonstrates that a person's disabilities need not prevent him or her from working in real employment, with all the benefits that result from this, if we are willing to put the time, the energy, the resource-fulness and the resources into the teaching.

Summary

1. Many people with learning disabilities wish to work in real jobs for real wages.

2. Ways of teaching (industrial) production skills are dealt with in other publications.

3. Good time-keeping is important for any employee, and may be taught by analysing the events in the time sequence and teaching these systematically, providing visual prompts where necessary.

4. Work-related skills, such as queuing for lunch appropriately or using a telephone, may need to be taught to enable a person to keep a job.

5. A person with learning disability may need help in organising her working day so that she is both efficient and happy in her work.

---

* Kings Fund 1985

6. If a particular part of a job is likely to be difficult, it is worth spending time practising this before the person begins work in earnest.

7. With careful, systematic teaching, even people with very severe disabilities can hold down a real job in the real world.

Exercises

1. How would you go about teaching someone to select the correct clothing for working as a gardener?

2. Which skills do you consider to be the crucial ones necessary in order to obtain and keep work?

CHAPTER 14

Social Competence

Some people with learning disabilities have problems in social situations. They find it difficult to meet people, to keep up a conversation, to ask the way, or for what they want in shops or restaurants, so training in social skills is often suggested to help them. This training has been developed in the last few years and it is only very recently that it has been offered to people with learning disabilities.

What is social competence?

We think that social competence consists of three main aspects. The first is a person's observed behaviour during a social interaction; how she appears and what she does. The second consists of the person's thoughts and feelings; how competent she feels herself to be. The third is the person's ability to initiate and sustain social roles and relationships; for example, worker, housewife, parent or friend. These aspects of social competence seem to be independent of one another. For example, you can be a good mother while feeling that you are not a good mother, or you can have an intimate and loving relationship with one person, even though you tend to be abrupt and difficult socially. Most of the teaching and training of social skills has, in fact, concentrated on the first aspect – that is, how people behave in interpersonal encounters – and much of this chapter will be about how people can be helped to learn specific social behaviours. It is quite likely that the second and third aspects are just as, if not more, important than observed behaviour and we will talk a little at the end of the chapter about how these other aspects of social competence can be tackled.

People with learning disabilities can often be picked out in a crowd because of their socially naive or gauche behaviour, and helping them to greater social competence may be one way to help them achieve a dignified and normal life in their local community.

How do we go about it?

Teaching social behaviour can be done in groups, or with individuals; either way may be effective, and either must be tailored to each person's needs. There is a format commonly adopted for teaching social behaviour involving role play, modelling, practice and feedback. Many teachers now use video feedback and find this extremely effective, but video is not always available and other ways of giving feedback have to be found. Not all attempts to teach social behaviour have been successful, but here are some hints about what will help it work.

Setting it up. We aim to have between four and eight people attending the course and two group leaders. Normally, the people in the group agree to come to every session and the membership is limited to the original participants. However, circumstances do not always allow for this and we have run a social skills group at a 'drop-in centre' which was for anyone who happened to be on the premises that day; we have also run groups without co-leaders, and with more than ideal numbers. These things are not necessarily to be recommended, but a less than ideal group may be better than nothing so don't be too put off if you find that your group does not meet all the rules.

Role-play and feedback. Role-play is not psychodrama and we don't have to be budding Laurence Oliviers to do it. It is a way of practising something by pretending to do it before we have to do it for real. So, for example, we pretend we are in a restaurant ordering a meal. Other people in the group pretend too – one would be the waiter and another our companion in the restaurant. We can then practise different ways of doing things, looking at the menu, deciding what we would like and can afford, catching the waiter's eye, and so on. We can see what it is like to do these things, and find out what other people's reactions are. We also have the chance to hear from other people watching how they think it has gone, whether we did it right or what we could do better. The joy of role-play is that, having had this feed-back, we can then try again and see if we can make a better job of it the second time around. If we have video, we can film and refilm ourselves, see what we really look like and how we have improved our performance. Even without video, we can still get feedback on how we did from other people in the group. Although it can be quite scaring to face criticism from other people, in this situation this is usually positive and helpful, since they, too, are going to have a turn at role-playing and will have to face criticism from us. The group leader, of course, needs to set a good model for this and to comment positively about each person's performance. In fact, modelling plays a great part in role-play in this setting. Often the group leaders (we usually have two if we can) begin the session by acting out the scene themselves, so that everyone has an idea about how to start, and the courage to do it when someone else has done it already. Most people with learning disabilities that we have worked with soon become very astute at noticing the common mistakes that their friends make and suggesting positive alternatives.

Choice of subject for the role-plays is important. Again, in the past we had a fixed agenda of the sorts of things which we thought it would be a good idea to teach, ranging from things like eye-contact, facial expression and body posture to larger-scale situations like returning faulty articles, going for an interview, or asking someone for a date. We now think that this sort of fixed agenda is not such a good idea, and that, to be effective, role-plays have to be linked to real things that have happened to the person concerned, preferably that week. This sort of approach obviously takes careful management in a group, so that everyone's interest is maintained while something which is not directly relevant to some people is being worked on. It is, however, very difficult to learn much from role-plays unless they are realistically linked to events in the person's own life.

Frequency and numbers of sessions. In the past, groups often ran for 10 to 12 weeks, meeting for 1 to 1½ hours each week. Most people now seem to agree that it is better, if possible, to meet more frequently over longer periods of time – we recently formed a social skills group which ran for 30 weeks. Many social education centres now try to include social skills in their curriculum so that these sessions are part of the daily timetable, but if this is not possible it may be a good idea to have 'booster sessions' some time after initial training has been completed.

Starting off. The best way we have found to start a group is with introductions. Some people may not know the others and even those that do will probably not have had much practice at either introducing other people or at trying to remember what they have said. Introductions are also a good way of breaking the ice in a group, and show from the beginning that the group can be fun. Certain skills which will be emphasised time and time again such as listening, and reporting what others have said, are used right from the first session.

We quite often start a group with a name game, to help people remember each other's names. One of our favourites involves asking each person in turn to give her name and to talk about why she was given it. In another game, everyone gives her name and then talks about any nicknames that she has been given. There are lots of variations on these games, but the emphasis is on introduction, not, at this stage, introspection. The group leaders usually start these games and try to keep it as light as possible.

In a session on introductions, the group leaders often begin by giving a demonstration to set the ball rolling, and to suggest the sort of questions we ask when we meet someone for the first time – 'What is your name? Where do you live? Who do you live with? What school did you go to?' (five or six questions are enough for the first time). We then split the group into pairs and send them off into the corners of the room to introduce themselves to each other, with a time limit of two minutes each way. The introductions can be practised several times with the group dividing into different combinations of partners, although we need to beware of over-repetition and boredom. Bringing the same topics or themes up in different sessions and different contexts will help this. Using the video, if you have it, makes everything more entertaining.

Many people with learning disabilities find these introductory exercises very difficult to do, so we reinforce successive approximations to the skill we are aiming for, not criticising but praising the good things that they do. We have found that people with learning disabilities learn quite quickly how to respond positively to other people, and support each other's attempts to learn new skills. In a small group, individual members soon become less shy about role-playing in front of the others and, even in a large group, we have found that people who are embarrassed at first actually enjoy it in the end. We think that this may be partly because of the lengths to which we go to be positive – we aim never to be critical.

Generalisation and reinforcement. Role-playing may be radically different from performing the behaviour in real life, and the reinforcement involved may be quite different too. A good role-play of, for example, returning faulty goods, may bring a spontaneous round of applause from the rest of the group, or 'Well done' all round, or may be the signal for a break for tea and biscuits. This, however, is not what would happen in real life. Here, the reinforcer for a 'successful performance' would be the exchange of the faulty goods for perfect ones. This is, of course, what we are leading up to.

Practising a skill

Supposing the task is to enquire about a job at the Job Centre, the sequence might be as follows:

(1) discussion of the task;

(2) demonstration by leaders;

(3) several people take turns practising the task.

Once the person has learnt to cope with the role-play, the next step is to try out the new skills *in vivo* – in a real situation, first with back-up support and then alone.

(4) going to the Job Centre and trying it out, with help;

(5) going to the Job Centre and trying it out, alone.

The sequence 1–5, or any part of it, is repeated as often as necessary. The real life practising of skills may need to be repeated very frequently before the person can use them confidently whenever necessary.

Some instructors/teachers have set up situations where they have briefed people in the street, a restaurant, a shop, (more easily in the hospital or training centre), to be especially kind and helpful to the person who is practising the skill she is learning. This is a way of bridging the gap between the arbitrary reinforcer used in the role-play to the natural, but probably more subtle, cues available in day-to-day life. It requires considerable organisation but is a good idea if we can manage it.

Homework. One way in which we increase the number of real life opportunities to practise skills is by setting homework. As an extension of the theme of the social skills session, the group members are asked to carry out some simple tasks before the next session. For example, the theme of a session had been 'talking to people you don't know very well at work' and Peter had practised this in the session. We then set him the task of sitting at lunch with people he did not normally sit with and initiating a conversation with them. Peter kept a record of whether he had done this each lunch-time until the next social skills session, putting a tick on the small card we had given him on each day that he managed to complete the homework.

At the beginning of the next session, the first thing we did was go through the homework, and Peter was able to say which days he had achieved his goals and what had happened on the days that he had not been able to do it. After he had reported back on his homework the four other people in his group did the same. Their tasks were similar but not exactly the same; for one it was to pass the time of day with her neighbours at home, for another to try to speak to people he did not know at a social club he attended, for another to speak to someone at lunch at work. Each task was specially chosen to suit the needs of the person concerned.

Commonly, a session will begin with reports back on homework done and a recapitulation of the previous session. It is clear that most people we have worked with remember the situations acted out elsewhere in the role-plays much better than they do points made in general discussion. Because of this, we try to make sure that all the major points we tackle are not just discussed but also made the subject of homework and acted out in reality.

Finally, where possible, we would try to make sure that the skills we were teaching a person were acknowledged, reported and reinforced through their daily social interactions. We may do this very simplistically, as on p.226, when Hilary's attempts at making eye contact are responded to by instructors at her SEC. Or (and rather more difficult) we might try to make arrangements with a group of people within a whole social network to support and encourage complex social skills which may initially have been learned in a group or individual session.

Some skills training areas

The topics we focus on in a social skills course are those which are the most relevant for the people concerned. Sometimes, this may be a problem of controlling temper, or we may need to look at more general skills of which anger control is only a part. Certain topics come up again and again, and we will describe how we tackle these.

Eye contact

When speaking to other people, we normally make intermittent eye contact, sometimes looking at them quite intently for a few moments, and then glancing away. The amount of eye contact that is thought appropriate varies in different cultures and in different social settings, but both too much and too little can seem odd.

Hilary not only did not look at people when she spoke to them, but actually turned her head away, giving people the impression that she was not interested in them. In the group, we talked about the different effects eye contact can have and everyone practised talking to a partner for two minutes while purposefully looking away. This was videoed and the video therefore included Hilary behaving very much as she did normally. The other people in the group commented on how difficult they found not looking at the person they were talking to and how it interfered with their conversation. We then tried the opposite tactic, and spent two minutes talking to our partners, gazing without pause into their eyes. Almost everyone found this very embarrassing as we normally only stare deeply into someone else's eyes when madly in love. Hilary found this part of the exercise very difficult, but she made an attempt at it, and other members of the group, including the leaders, commented on how hard she had tried.

The group leaders then demonstrated a two-minute conversation with a normal amount of eye contact, and other members of the group tried it out in pairs in front of the group, with the rest commenting on how they had done. (It helps in these circumstances to give people a topic, like 'What I've done in the evenings this week', to talk about, otherwise they don't know where to start.) We videoed them, and Hilary was videoed again. When we played it back the group said how much easier it was to understand what she was saying when she looked at the person she was talking to, and Hilary herself noticed the difference between the first and second videos. We carried on practising eye contact for the rest of that session.

In this particular case Hilary was not singled out for work on eye contact, as other people in the group also needed help, to differing degrees, in this area. However, everyone knew that this was a major difficulty for Hilary and in subsequent sessions people remembered to comment upon Hilary's eye contact in the role-plays, no matter what the general theme was. At the same time, the instructors in the SEC which Hilary attended reinforced appropriate eye contact with warm smiles during their day-to-day contact with her and Hilary liked this very much.

Recognising emotions

Here we are talking about both expressing emotion and the recognition of emotion expressed by other people. Karen was often confused about whether people were happy, sad or angry, and did not really know how you could tell. This was particularly distressing for her as it often made her feel that people might be sad or angry because of something that she had done, whereas often they were not in fact sad or angry at all.

Karen was in a social skills group, and one of the earlier sessions was on the topic of understanding emotional expression. We started by looking at photographs of people and trying to guess what they were feeling by the look on their faces. With some people, it may advisable to start straight off with real people expressing emotions. In Karen's group, however, everyone seemed very shy, so photographs felt like a safer initial exercise.

We have found that photographs are much easier for people with learning disabilities to understand; they often find line drawings difficult to interpret.* We then played a game like charades where each person was given a card with an emotion written on it. Each person in turn, starting with the group leaders, had to act the emotion on his card while everyone else guessed what it was. We each had several turns, and did it in a couple of different ways. First, we had to sit on our hands and try to express the emotion with just our faces. Karen found this almost impossible; all she could produce was a massive grin. We then tried it standing up so we could. use our whole bodies as well as faces. Everyone found this much better, although at first, due to both poor acting and poor guesswork, most people guessed only the more extreme emotions. Boredom, thoughtfulness, anxiety, were much more difficult to portray than anger or sadness. Karen soon became much better at guessing the emotions expressed by other people, although she still found it difficult to show them herself.

Expressing emotion appropriately

All this session concentrated on facial expression, as one component of the expression of emotion. However, to round the afternoon off, we decided to role-play a scene in which the expression of emotion played a central role.

We outlined a scene in a pub where someone, perhaps slightly drunk, knocks into you and spills your drink all over your good clothes. How to react? The group leaders acted out a possible solution first, and then everyone talked about what they might do. Initial solutions included 'punch them in the nose', that the spilled-over person be given £10 to cover the cost of the dress, or bought a fresh drink. Everyone then took turns to re-enact the scene with their own solutions. As groups like this get off the ground, the participants become more confident in putting forward their own variations in the role plays.

A difficulty can be that, with the group leaders always acting out the scenes first, people merely duplicate the models given by the group leaders instead of finding their own solutions. We don't think that there is any easy way of getting over this, apart from promoting the confidence of the group participants and helping them recognise and build on their own initiatives.

---

* It is possible to buy ready-made photographs like this (PTM are one source, see Appendix 2). Alternatively, you can make your own, although it can be difficult to get any emotions other than the most stark extremes. Most magazines are full of people looking happy and occasionally thoughtful, serious, or at least neutral. Pictures of people looking sad or angry are more difficult, but can sometimes be found in newspapers.

This is done, we think, in this context by an overriding atmosphere of positive reinforcement and acceptance.

Other factors in the expression of emotions, such as tone of voice, posture, gestures, etc, can be experimented with in the group by the same approach; first pinpointing and practising the minutiae and then establishing the context with a role-play of situations pertinent to the individuals concerned.

Taking part in conversations

There are many skills involved in talking to other people – taking turns in speaking, asking questions, answering the question which has actually been asked, finding out about the other person and their interests, not being preoccupied with talking about yourself (a common fault), and knowing when, and when not, to interrupt, to name but a few.

We would normally start this topic with a general discussion of what is involved, but move on as quickly as possible to more specific examples which incorporate the details and give an opportunity for practice. One particular example of taking part in conversations arises when we meet new people, when it can be difficult to know what to talk about. Edward had recently started part-time work in a large supermarket. He found the people there very kind, but he did not have occasion to speak to anyone much while working. At tea and lunch breaks he used the company canteen but sat alone, and when other workers sat near him he had only been able to reply to their questions in monosyllables, unable to think of anything to say to them.

We started by Edward directing two members of the group to act out what had actually happened. They did this amid great hilarity as Edward felt that they captured his own inarticulateness extremely well.

We then talked about the various aspects of the difficulty. First, answering just 'yes' or 'no' in reply to questions does not give the other person much to go on and he soon gets discouraged; we need to give him a bit more information so that he can respond to this or find similarities in his own experience. Second, what could Edward find to say? Other people in the group suggested that he ask about the person himself, how long he had worked there, what department he was in, about his family and hobbies. We all decided that what this occasion required was small-talk and it was therefore not right to launch into a detailed history of the whole of our lives, but just to give some information and, particularly, to be interested in what the other person told us. Finally, everyone gave suggestions of other topics which might be discussed, recent television programmes, films, items in the news, etc. The group then split up into twos and went off into separate corners of the room for five minutes to try out the whole approach.

We then came back together again and re-ran our original role-play, with Edward playing himself but trying to respond in different ways to the approaches made by 'workmates' in the canteen. Other people then took turns in playing Edward, while he tried to be the other worker. All this was very difficult for Edward, and his behaviour during this first session only changed a little. However, now that everyone knew exactly what Edward found particularly hard, they were able to give him appropriate roles and work to do in subsequent weeks' sessions, and also homework, as described earlier in this chapter.

As time went by Edward did talk to more people during his breaks at work, and felt that he had more to say to them. He did, however, remain rather passive and tended to wait for people to approach him before he started speaking.

Asking for help and information

People in our groups are often concerned with asking for help or information, and we usually spend some time on these subjects. Some of the topics suggested are real emergencies, such as an accident or a fire, and how to deal with these is often covered in the more general teaching in a school or social education centre. Knowing how to ask for help in the street if we are lost, or in a station if we are unsure about which is the right platform for our train, are also recurring topics.

Katherine lived in a hostel in one part of the borough, and attended a day centre in another. Some people made this journey by train and Katherine wanted to do so too. A complex training programme was initiated which enabled Katherine to do more and more of the journey on her own. There still remained one major difficulty: the journey involved a change of trains at Clapham Junction. Katherine knew which platform was the right one for her second train. However, Clapham Junction being Clapham Junction, there seemed to be many occasions when, for one reason or another, the train came in on a different platform. Katherine could recognise numbers under 20, but not words, and had considerable difficulty understanding the public address system. On the station, the obvious solution was to ask the platform staff, but Katherine found this extremely difficult and asked us for help. She had problems in recognising who were the platform staff and then she felt unsure about how to tell them where she was going and ask them for the information she needed about platform numbers. Katherine was not a member of a group, so we set up two

distinctly different learning situations for her. The first was a discrimination task which itself was on two levels. She had to learn the difference
between, first, ordinary clothes and uniform, and second, between uniforms. We used photographs for both the first and second parts of the task.

We started with pictures of adults in their street clothes compared with
a picture of a man in a British Rail platform staff uniform. We showed the
picture of the uniform first with one other picture which was very dissimilar to it (for example, Picture 9), and then changed the picture with which
the British Rail uniform was paired in a hierarchy of increasing similarity
to a uniform ending with the most similar, a man in a dark suit. We then
went on to the recognition of differences between uniforms. To do this
properly, we needed colour photographs with sufficient detail on them to
be able to see the differences between the clothes. The various photographs
we used were:

Pictures of people in street clothes

(1) man in dark suit
(2) man in light suit
(3) man in overalls
(4) man in jeans and pullover
(5) man in cords and leather jacket
(6) woman in trouser suit
(7) woman in shirt and skirt
(8) woman in jeans
(9) woman in dress
(10) woman in skirt and blouse
(11) woman in top coat.

Pictures of people in uniform

(1) British Rail platform staff
(2) Police
(3) Traffic wardens
(4) Tube ticket collector
(5) Army
(6) Navy
(7) RAF

We then moved out into streets and onto station platforms, and in particular to Clapham Junction to check and reinforce Katherine's discriminations
in real life, as well as to ascertain such things as where the platform staff

usually stood, and what routes she might have to take between platforms if the train were changed from the expected one.

As a further stage, Katherine needed to learn ways of approaching the platform staff once she had identified them and then ways of asking them which platform her train was due to come in on. We decided that, because it was difficult to predict the situation in advance, Katherine would follow the same ritual every day. That is, she would alight from the first train, make her way to the platform that her train was expected in on, and then ask the platform staff if this was the right platform.

To begin with, we practised in role play various ways of doing this. Katherine was very reluctant to do this part of the work as she was shy and hated talking to strangers, but this made it all the more important that she should feel able to do it, so we practised that much harder. This part of the process went on over a period of six months. Meanwhile, Katherine travelled to work every day with Alice, a woman who lived in the same hostel and attended the same SEC. However, Alice preferred to travel alone and was only prepared to continue to accompany Katherine for a short time.

We then moved on to Katherine travelling alone and alighting from trains and asking directions whilst being shadowed. This was practised 15 times before Katherine felt confident enough to try it alone, and even then the 'shadow' was only withdrawn gradually. Eventually, Katherine was able to do the whole journey completely on her own, which made her extremely proud. However, she never really learnt to be flexible about the whole procedure, so that the hostel staff were continually aware that, if something unexpected happened, like Katherine not being able to find any platform staff, or if all the trains were cancelled because of bad weather, she would be left not knowing what to do. The only thing we could do about this was to make sure that, every day, when she had completed the journey, she 'phoned the hostel staff to let them know that she had arrived safely, while she would also 'phone if anything went wrong. Everyone felt that, although there was a slight risk involved (and Katherine bore out our apprehensions on one occasion by getting the wrong train and going all the way to Portsmouth), we had done everything we could to equip her to make the journey independently and that this was sufficiently important to her self-esteem to make the risk worthwhile.

Giving praise and handling criticism

This section could just as easily be called 'handling praise and giving criticism' as both the giving and receiving of praise and criticism can be difficult. We have not found abstract discussion and introspection about why this should be difficult to prove particularly useful, so most of our work has concentrated on handling practical situations.

In one group, an example was brought up, after we had discussed the general area, of something that had happened recently. Dario lived in a local hostel where he shared a room with three other men. All four were quite good friends. However, someone in the room kept borrowing Dario's electric razor and leaving it by the sink in the room, uncleaned. Dario did not know who was doing this, but it was annoying and he wanted it to stop.

Dario had two problems: first, he had to find out who was doing it; and second, he had to ask them to stop it without becoming 'bad friends' and spoiling the nice atmosphere in their shared room.

In our group we discussed how and when Dario might go about finding out who had borrowed his razor. The main alternatives seemed to be either to ask each person individually, or to choose a time when all four were in the room together. Dario and the other members of the group practised both ways of doing it. In the end, Dario said he thought asking everyone at once would be the best way for him to tackle it, so we then practised what he might say, and how the other men might react.

This sort of exercise is good for everyone, as people experience both sides of the situation, and have the chance to try out different solutions.

Because Dario would be speaking to three other people, he had the opportunity to respond to three different reactions within a short time, and to moderate his own reactions accordingly. In the role-plays, many people, when asked if they had used the razor, responded quite aggressively, and our experience of running groups like this in SECs and hostels suggests that this reaction is quite common. We concentrated on finding positive solutions and alternatives to aggression, which included teaching people deep-breathing exercises in order to control themselves and developing moderating strategies such as talking the situation over with a third party before responding. Other situations which might call for similar solutions include dealing with someone you live with who keeps on turning the TV over, moving to allow another person to sit down on the sofa, or getting others to take their turn with the washing up.

When we get on to giving praise, we often find that in our groups, because of the way we organise them, most people have got the idea long before we come to formal teaching about it. As we said previously, the whole ethos of the group is a positive one, looking for the good things which people do and letting them know about them. Receiving praise may also be problematical, and people sometimes have to practise receiving praise without qualifying it. This again can be turned into a general game, so that the whole group is always on the lookout for it and picks anyone up who starts saying 'Yes, but...'

Eating out

Eating out is a topic embraced with much enthusiasm by many of the people we work with. Eating skills in general have already been discussed in Chapter 10, and here we would like to look at the social side of eating and at the skills which go with it.

There has been in recent years an expansion in the variety of restaurants and cafes available locally, from MacDonalds to pizzas to curry houses, each of them requiring slightly different skills which may have to be taught separately.

Many SECs now have cafeteria-style lunches where we have to queue for our lunch and make choices about the food we want. This is, of course, more like (and is meant to be like) a works' canteen, and we talk about using this sort of facility in Chapter 13.

Using a cafe such as MacDonalds is an intermediate step between the canteen and a proper restaurant. For one group we worked with, who were particularly keen on eating out, we constructed a hierarchy of eating places which gradually extended the number of skills necessary. The hierarchy looked something like this:

(1) the canteen at the SEC;

(2) a canteen in BHS;

(3) MacDonalds;

(4) a Wimpy Bar;

(5) a pizza house;

(6) a Berni Inn;

(7) a curry house.

When constructing the hierarchy we felt that the differences between 6 and 7 were rather large, but everyone was very keen to finish with a curry, and so we pushed on. We decided from the beginning that the best way of tackling this project was *in vivo* practice and, accordingly, everyone started saving up. Fortunately, it turned out that we could eat quite cheaply up to 6, and so the course of training was not prohibitively expensive for anyone.

We decided to look in advance at the particular intricacies and new behaviours required in each setting in the protected atmosphere of our group, to practise them and feel competent before we stepped over any thresholds. As with many items in this chapter, we used role-play, feedback and social reinforcement. What follows will give you some idea of the sorts of difficulties which were pinpointed as we went through:

(1) The canteen at the SEC: everybody was used to this and nobody saw any problems with it;

(2) A canteen at British Home Stores: this was very similar to the one in the SEC, except for (a) the amount of choice, and (b) handling money at the end when your tray was full;

(3) MacDonalds: (a) it was a different sort of queue, (b) the food was not displayed, (c) choices had to be made from printed lists, (d) things had to be got out of their paper containers, (e) plates etc had to be disposed of into a dustbin at the end;

(4) A Wimpy Bar: (a) you sit straight down at a table, (b) you are given a menu, (c) you have to tell a waiter what you want, (d) you have to wait for the food, (e) they leave the bill on the table, (f) you have to get up and pay at the cash desk on your way out, (g) you can leave a tip if you want;

(5) A pizza house: (a) the selection of food is different; (b) everything is written down, usually without pictures, (c) the layout of the menu is a whole subject which itself needs to be learnt, (d) several courses may be ordered, (e) there may be a separate drinks menu, (f) you have to catch the waiter's eye to order, to get extra drinks etc, and to pay, (g) payment is made at the table, (h) change and/or tips have to be negotiated;

(6) A Berni Inn: (a) often in a larger building and a much larger room, (b) tables often have to be booked, (c) you have to tell the waiter who you are and be shown to your seat, (d) there are excessively white tablecloths which are a source of embarrassment if you are inclined to spill things, (e) the cutlery used may be complex and involve learning rules, such as work from the outside towards the middle, (f) which side is your bread plate? And which side your wine glass? (g) you may be expected to taste your wine, (h) you may have to choose your sweet from a trolley, (i) coffee may be offered without your ordering it, (j) the waiter may help you on and off with your coat (can prove awkward later if you've left your money in the pocket);

(7) A curry house: (a) strikingly different sort of food and subsequent difficulties in understanding the menu, (b) may be eaten in unusual ways, several people sharing dishes between them, (c) usually you are not given a knife, (d) water may already be on the table, (e) knowing what to order with what, (f) may need to ask for and pass dishes on the table, (g) complexities of dividing up the bill when everyone has had bits of everything.

Each small step in this great long list was practised and re-practised in our group first. When everyone felt competent, we went out to a British Homestores for our first lunch. Not until we had completed this stage successfully did we move on to MacDonalds and go through the same process, and later to each of the restaurants on our list, finishing up with a curry. We have to say that this has been one of the most enjoyable groups that we have run recently.

Making and sustaining relationships

This area, of making and sustaining relationships, could take up a whole book in itself, and the complexities involved are beyond the scope of this one. However, there are a few small things we would like to say in the context of social competence.

Friends and social lives

Most of us agree that having and seeing friends is an important aspect of our lives. Although not everyone supports this, and there are tremendous individual differences, making friends and keeping them is a topic which often comes up in a social skills group, and as a starting point, we can often begin with suggestions about where to meet people and what to say to them. Most people we talk to have some friends, from school, from their place of work or day-time occupation, and from where they live (particularly those who live in hostels). Most people attend a club like a 'Gateway' club and most speak very positively about it. Only very few have friends outside the 'disabled' world and even fewer attend any activities which are integrated with the general population. Some (but very few) have social lives which could be described as a 'mad, gay whirl', but even these seem to be segregated activities.

As things are at the moment the social lives of many adults with disabilities are very different from the social lives of single adults in the general population. The trend in the general population is to meet friends from school or work who introduce you to their friends whom you meet in pubs or at parties and with whom you then go to the pictures, dancing, sporting activities and so on, or whom you invite to your house. Adults with learning disabilities partake in almost none of these activities. They are tremendously limited by their inability to travel alone and by lack of money, and they do not themselves expect to have that sort of social life. The social life they expect is one which is organised for them by other people, and in which they are picked up at home and dropped off again in mini-buses.

Certain steps are now being taken to counter this trend. The Campaign for People with Mental Handicaps, Action Space and Citizen Advocacy Alliance are both promoting support for people with learning disabilities in integrated activities. Nevertheless, these have not yet influenced the style of social life available to most people.

Boyfriends and girlfriends

Many people attending Social Services' day centres do have boyfriends and girlfriends, and many more would like to. The people we see in social skills groups may not be representative in this way, as presumably they have come into the group or been encouraged into the group because of their poor social skills and not having a boyfriend/girlfriend is an obvious area in which they can see that they are failing. In fact we managed to upset considerably an otherwise lively and happy group by spending a session talking about girl and boy friends. None of them had one.

In the context of the group people do from time to time bring out difficulties of a sexual nature, and we have included sessions which could more easily be described as sex education. This in itself is an immense subject which we do not have the space to address in this book. Useful information on this subject is available from the Family Planning Association unit (address in Appendix 3).

Self-image and social roles: people first

As we said at the beginning of this chapter, social competence has three main aspects. We have discussed ways of teaching and modifying behaviours at some length. Interventions on the other two aspects, self-image and social role, have not been developed to any level of sophistication in most areas of psychological intervention and any advances of technique or theory tend to filter through to people with learning disabilities only slowly.

The self-image and social roles of people with learning disabilities are partly historically determined. People with learning disabilities were thought to be like children, innocent and naive, who needed to be protected and kept with their own kind. Since the Government White Paper, 'Better Services for the Mentally Handicapped', (HMSO 1971) when it became government policy to close the large, long-stay hospitals for people with disabilities, attitudes, particularly within the profession, have changed. Many people who previously would not have been thought able are now living in hostels, group homes, and their own flats. These moves have obviously influenced the types of social roles available to people. The institutional role is still commonly available in the surviving long-stay hospitals; however, the roles of worker, housewife, neighbour, etc are now possible.

The other side of this is the ability of people with learning disabilities to take up new social roles. Being treated as incapable inevitably leads to loss of self-esteem, inability to take on responsibilities or make decisions, and low status in relation to people in authority. The major work that has been done to change the self-image, assertiveness and perception of self-status in people who are learning disabled is in the area of self-advocacy. An excellent and informative book on this subject is *Speaking for Ourselves* by Paul Williams and Bonny Shoultz. This book sees quite clearly that the way forward for people who are learning disabled is to change their status in society and that the only way that this can be done effectively is for them to learn to tell other people what they want. The book explains in detail how to set up self-advocacy groups, describes the role of the leader, and gives examples of existing groups both in this country and in America. The outcome of long-term participation in these groups does seem to be to raise the consciousness of the people in them to points where they can re-evaluate their own self-image in much more positive ways, and take a more active hand in determining their own futures.

The people who have taken part in self-advocacy groups do seem to us to be more able than many of the people that we work with. However, we think that if more resources were available, this movement could be extended to less able people, and for the small group of people who really cannot speak for themselves there are also the options of legal and citizen advocacy where another person takes on the obligation of ensuring that the person with learning disabilities has access to all the privileges which go along with their status as a citizen.

Summary

1. Social competence consists of three independent aspects; observed behaviour, self concept, and social role.

2. Most work has been done on the behavioural aspect of social competence.

3. Social behaviour can be taught in groups or individually.

4 It is taught most effectively if the subject of each session reflects the experience of the person concerned.

5. Methods of teaching most often used include role-play, modelling, repeated practice with feedback, and *in vivo* experience .

6. Teaching is more effective if it takes place in frequent sessions which continue over long periods of time.

7. The reinforcement used in role-play and practice sessions may not be those present in real life, so means have to be found to bridge the gap between the two.

8. Homework is sometimes given to aid generalisation of the skills.

9. Teaching may focus on both the minutiae of social interactions, such as eye contact, tone of voice, or on larger scale situations which use these skills, such as returning faulty articles or talking to someone we don't know very well.

10. The development of new social roles, better self-esteem and social assertiveness may most adequately be dealt with by self-advocacy programmes.

Exercises

1. What are the advantages and disadvantages of teaching social behaviours in groups?

2. Give three ways in which we might help a person who has learned a social skill to generalise it.

3. How would you go about teaching a group how to ask the person who lives upstairs to turn down his record-player, which he plays persistently and loudly at 2.00am?

4. In a course on social competence and self-assertiveness, how would you go about running a session on being able to say 'No' to offers of rides in cars from strangers?

CHAPTER 15

Disturbed and Problem Behaviours

In Chapter 7 we looked at ways to help people get over all kinds of difficult behaviours. Some behaviours, however, seem to be special problems because they are so common, or cause so much anxiety, or are so difficult to cope with. We have taken an extra chapter to try to look more closely at these topics.

Because these special problems cause great difficulties, it is particularly important that we take great care in approaching them. We need to be very much aware that each is an individual problem: even if we have met a similar one in another person we will have to approach it anew when we meet it in someone else, and we cannot take it for granted that what we did last time will be the right thing to do now. Always, we need to carry out a functional analysis – look at the behaviour, look at the circumstances surrounding the behaviour, look at the consequences of the behaviour; and then base our intervention on what we learn from this. Because we know that challenging behaviours and lack of skills go hand-in-hand, we need to adopt a constructional approach, aiming, as far as possible, to build up skills that will take the place of the problem behaviour.

As a rule, we would begin by observing the person carefully (see Chapter 2). Alternatively, if the situation is puzzling, if we feel uncertain as to what antecedents and consequences are the most relevant to the behaviour, it could be worthwhile using analogue methods. These involve deliberately setting up some particular conditions, one at a time, which we think may have a bearing on the behaviour, and other conditions we think are of less relevance. So, for example, if Dan slaps his face, and if we are not certain whether he does it because he wants attention or because he doesn't like doing things he is asked to do, we could have one set of conditions, lasting about 15 minutes, in which every time he slapped himself somebody went to him and attended to him; and another in which he was asked to do tasks and every time he slapped himself the asker desisted; and probably a third set of conditions, as a control, in which he was left pretty much alone. It might be necessary to run these three conditions several times but, at the end, we might have a clearer idea of what were the important factors in Dan's face-slapping. Analogue methodology is a hightech approach and probably should be undertaken only with some expert psychological assistance but, in especially difficult cases, it could be worth asking for this (Iwata et al 1990).

Because challenging behaviours may exasperate us, we should determinedly approach them using the Least Restrictive Alternative; we ourselves, using it as a matter of principle even when we felt that it stood little chance of solving the problem, on occasions have been astonished to see it successful, making the more stringent methods we thought of using unnecessary.

Above all, these problems are not for one person to tackle alone. They are difficult and, in some cases, dangerous. To tackle them, we need a team approach, where ideas can be sounded against those of others, where one person's strategy may be supported or modified by those of people with other experiences. And here, above all, the support and advice of professionals should be sought and should be available every step of the way.

Masturbation

Masturbation is not in any way harmful, but is embarrassing for other people if it is done publicly. We do not want to attempt to prevent it altogether – for some people with learning disabilities, masturbation may be the only source of sexual satisfaction available to them – but we may well want to specify where and when it should happen. We need, then, to teach the person that he or she can masturbate in the privacy of the bedroom or in bed at night, but not in the sitting room, garden, street, shopping centre, sportsfield or anywhere else where there are other people. This is taught by preventing or stopping the person from masturbating when he does it in public and, at first, taking him to his bedroom, saying 'You can do it here', and leaving him alone for a while. Later, when he has learnt that masturbation is not forbidden altogether, but is allowed in conditions of privacy, it may become necessary to refuse permission for it to be done at all at times when other tasks need to be tackled. It should not interfere with learning, nor become a way of escaping from daily tasks.

Showing affection

Some people with learning disabilities seek affection and physical contact in ways that would be acceptable in a three-year-old but which are inappropriate in an adult. This is difficult to deal with, because we do not want to refuse either to give or to take affection from someone who needs it, yet, if we are aiming for people with learning disabilities to be accepted in ordinary communities, this kind of over-demonstrative behaviour may be a real barrier.

Elsie is 45 years old and would approach strangers to hug and kiss them. She became particularly attached to Karen, who is the domestic supervisor in the home where Elsie lives. Karen is a warm-hearted person who did not want to brush off Elsie's affectionate approaches and in any case was flattered that Elsie should seek her out. Elsie was one of the residents who, it was hoped, would move into a house in the community, and other workers in the home worried that this kind of behaviour would seem very odd in ordinary surroundings. This was discussed with Karen, and she saw that it might be better for Elsie if she could learn more adult ways of greeting people. She began to fend off Elsie's advances and to say to her 'No, it's not such a good idea to kiss everyone, just grasp my hand'. Gradually Elsie learnt that she should shake hands with most of the people she met, and to reserve hugs and kisses for members of her family and for special friends.

Stereotypies

Stereotypy, as we use it here, means a brief piece of behaviour that is repeated over and over again and which does not have a recognisable end result. Stereotypies include rocking, either in a sitting or a standing position, finger-snapping, head-weaving, hand-flapping, twiddling, spinning and twirling, amongst other things. Harold's kind of stereotypy consisted of endlessly throwing things into the air, preferably balls, but if those were not available, his own shoes.

Although these activities are not dangerous either to the person herself or to others, they can interfere with other, more useful, activities while they also make the person doing them look peculiar.

Why people perform these stereotypies is not fully understood, but there are various possible explanations. Often people seem to do this when they have nothing else to do, so the stereotypies act as a stimulus and as a shield against boredom. In this case, obviously, it is helpful if the person can be given plenty of interesting things to do, and sometimes this may be all that needs to be done to counteract the stereotypies. In one unit, the level of rocking, twirling and so on was markedly reduced in the group as a whole when a structured activity programme was introduced into their day. In other cases, more deliberate teaching efforts may be needed. Dave used to sit in a corner of his workshop twiddling a piece of silver paper all day, and refusing to join in any of the workshop activities. Using an edible reinforcer (orange juice) his workshop instructor, over a period of about three months, taught Dave to do very simple industrial tasks. Once he had learnt these, Dave found them so enjoyable that he would do them voluntarily, and the twiddling disappeared, at least while he was working.

In other, quite opposite, cases the stereotypies may be acting as a shield against a plethora of stimuli coming in from the outside world. Sam, the young man quoted in Chapter 7, when he was in a noisy, crowded environment would repeatedly snap his fingers and make piercing vocal noises. Careful observation suggested that Sam did this in order to screen out the noises coming to him from outside, but the stereotypies were so obtrusive that he was no longer taken on outings. He was given a portable stereo cassette player and headset, and a tape of soothing music, and was reinforced for wearing the headset while he was in shops and other noisy places. Within a few weeks he could be taken out without resorting to his stereotypies, so long as he wore the portable tape system, and later he learnt to do without this for increasingly long periods, before being once again given the headset. In this case, the stereotypies, far from providing stimulation to counter boredom, were aimed at reducing the stimulus level Sam experienced (Donnellan et al 1984). Obviously, we need to try, using the observation and behaviour analysis methods described in Chapters 2 and 3, to ascertain which of these two functions – providing stimulation or protecting against it – a particular person's stereotypies seem to have, as the approach we take will be very different in each case. To explore this, we could put the person, first, in a quiet room by herself with little to occupy her, then add noise from a radio, then take her into a crowded room. In each situation we would observe the level of her stereotypies and, from this, should get a good idea which approach to treatment we should take.

Phobias

A phobia may be defined as an extreme and unreasonable fear of some thing or situation. Many non-disabled people suffer from phobias, and the things or situations they are afraid of are usually potentially dangerous; people develop phobias of, for example, heights, or snakes, or air travel, but not, as someone has said, of onions or socks. However, the fears that phobic people develop are out of proportion to the real dangers involved. One young woman for example had a phobia about spiders. Now some spiders – some South American, Australian and African spiders – are indeed very dangerous, but not the ordinary British spider of which this, highly intelligent, young woman was so afraid that, when she saw one nestling in the corner of a ceiling above a doorway she got down on her hands and knees to go through the door. People with learning disabilities can also develop phobias. These can interfere with the smooth running of their lives, and we may want to help them get over them. The main method we use is desensitisation.

Desensitisation involves drawing up a hierarchy of the person's fears, starting with a situation that is not at all frightening, and going on to one that, although tolerable for most people, is extremely frightening for the phobic person. Let us take spiders as an example. With most non-disabled people, the hierarchy will begin with a real spider, albeit perhaps safely in a jam jar and dead. If this were still too frightening, whether or not the person was disabled, we would work backwards, through photographs, models and drawings, until we reached the point where the person was quite unworried. That then is where we start. If it had been at the simple drawing we might then go on to more realistic drawings, to photographs, to models, to films, and then to real spiders – first securely shut up in jars and placed well away from the person, then brought gradually nearer, then allowed out of the jar far away and later nearer, and finally, perhaps, the spider moving about over the person's shoes and clothing, perhaps even hands.

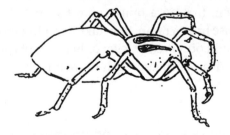

With someone who is not learning disabled, or is only mildly so, we can draw up the hierarchy with her help, finding out from her which is the next step on the scale; whether, for example, a model spider or photographs of a real one would come after realistic drawings. With a person who is more severely disabled, we may have to use our own judgement and draw up the hierarchy as best we can, knowing that if we find we have got it wrong we will have to change it. We make the steps in the hierarchy as small as we can but, again, we may find we have to make them smaller still. If, when we first showed a photograph of a spider, that was found to be too frightening we might have to start with a photograph of a smaller, or more distant, spider.

When we have drawn up the hierarchy we can begin the treatment. We present the person with the lowest level of the hierarchy – the simple drawing. We make sure the person is quite calm and unworried about it. With a non-disabled person we may ask him to rate his own anxiety level, from 0 to 10. With a disabled person we may have to judge from her demeanour – expression, restlessness, tension – whether she is anxious or relaxed. If she seems quite relaxed we move on to the next level, the more realistic drawing, which gives her a small twinge of anxiety. We make the situation she is in, complete with the minimally-anxiety-provoking thing, very comfortable, pleasant and enjoyable. We talk calmly with her, and if it seems appropriate we do relaxation training with her, mainly through teaching her to do slow, deep breathing exercises (see p.256–7). She remains in the situation, not leaving or avoiding it, until even the trace of anxiety disappears, and we can present the drawing to her without her feeling any distress. Then we move on to the next level in the hierarchy and repeat the process. In this way we gradually work up the hierarchy until she is able to encounter spiders with no more distress than most people show, and certainly does not crawl through a doorway to avoid one on the ceiling.

How phobias are established is not always clear and may differ from one person to another. In some cases at least, it seems that the person may have had some genuinely frightening or unpleasant experience, and was then so nervous of any recurrence of this experience that he (or she) avoids all possible chance of it, to the point where even things remotely connected with the experience are avoided. Since the experience is avoided, the person never learns that it is harmless, and so his fear of it continues, or even increases.

Using desensitisation, then, we expose the person to a very low level of the feared experience; the person is not allowed to escape it and, indeed, we make the whole situation so pleasant and enjoyable that he feels very little urge to escape it. By staying with the experience, he eventually loses what little urge to escape he had. The person has then experienced this low level of the frightening experience, and has been able to recognise it as harmless. We may then go on to the next stage in the hierarchy and go through the same process until that, too, is perceived as non-frightening; and so on, through all stages of the hierarchy.

Let's look at the hierarchy we developed to deal with a real phobia. Rose is a middle-aged lady who was phobic about having her hair washed. When this had to be done, she would scream and struggle, and it took two people to hold her down over the basin while another did the washing. The sequence of events began with Rose being sent upstairs to collect her towel from her room at the hostel where she lived, and then going along to the bathroom. The first part could be accomplished with encouragement and coaxing and 'the scene really starts' when she got inside the bathroom door. So we drew up the hierarchy as follows.

(1) goes upstairs

(2) goes to bedroom

(3) collects towel

(4) goes to bathroom door

(5) goes inside the bathroom door

(6) goes to the stool

(7) sits on the stool

(8) leans forward

(9) leans forward with head over basin

(10) leans forward with head over basin and spray is run into the basin (not over her hair)

(11) Rose passes a dry sponge over her hair, her hand being prompted if necessary

(12) Rose passes a slightly damp sponge over her hair, prompted as above

(13) Rose passes a damper sponge over her hair

(14) Rose's hair is made noticeably wet

(15) after her hair is made wet, a tiny drop of shampoo is put on Rose's finger and she is asked to rub it on her hair, after which it is sponged off

(16) Rose is given more shampoo to rub on her hair

(17) Rose is prompted to hold the spray and let a little of it run over her hair

(18) onwards. Rose gradually holds the spray over progressively more of her hair until she is rinsing her hair

This hierarchy includes some items that had not been in the hairwashing sequence before, but which were inserted in order to make the steps in the sequence smaller and more tolerable for Rose – for example the use of the sponge.

The programme for Rose specified that she would be taken towards the bathroom and the point at which she showed the first signs of anxiety – hesitating, trembling or sweating, looking nervous, hanging back – would be noted. After that, she would be taken each day to the place *just before* this point, and she and her hostel worker would stay at that place for about five minutes. When Rose had stayed at the just-before place for about five minutes without showing any anxiety, she would be given a sweet (her reinforcement) and praised for her sensible behaviour; the trial would be over and Rose would return to her usual occupation. When Rose had been able to carry out this step on two consecutive occasions, the hostel worker would, on the next occasion, move her along to the next step in the hierarchy. If Rose showed no anxiety at this point, the procedure would be repeated: if, on the other hand, she showed any of the symptoms, she would be made to wait quietly at this point, the hostel worker would talk sooth-ingly to her, until the signs of anxiety disappeared. She would then remain there, calm and relaxed, for about five minutes, would be given the sweet and the praise, and then go back to whatever she had been doing before. This step would then be repeated until, again, on two consecutive occasions Rose showed no anxiety at all. Then the next step in the hierarchy would be tackled. In this way the whole hierarchy could be worked through gradually.

One thing that might have made Rose more anxious about hair-washing was the possibility of getting water and soap in her eyes, so it was planned to buy her a pair of goggles to put on, probably between steps (7) and (8), and let her practise wearing these, first separately, then in the hair-washing sequence.

Sometimes it is not possible to work out a hierarchy and carry out a desensitisation programme; there may be practical difficulties, or there may simply not be time, for some reason, to go through all the steps in the hierarchy. We may think of using one of the methods which come under the overall title of 'flooding'. Flooding has been described as 'jumping in at the deep end', in contrast with desensitisation, described as 'wading in at the shallow end'. So with desensitisation, as we have seen, the person starts with a minimally-feared situation and is gradually brought to face up to the situation in its more and more realistic state; with the flooding technique we are describing here, known as exposure, the person has to face the realistic level of the situation straight away *and is not allowed to avoid or escape from it*. In this way, the person is forced to undergo something which, because he has always hitherto avoided it, he has never had the chance to experience as harmless. Once he does this and finds that it is harmless his fears may diminish and the phobia disappear.

Henry lived at home with his mother, and had numerous phobias; one of these was with the switching on of the central heating, and another was concerned with wearing crumpled pyjamas in bed at night. Henry was not disturbed by the central heating as such but, if the day turned chilly and his mother decided half-way through the day to switch on the heating, Henry would become very upset, throw himself about in his wheelchair and lash out at his mother until the heating was turned off. At night, he always went to bed in a pair of clean pyjamas, but if he woke up in the night and found them rumpled (as indeed they were bound to be) he would call out to his mother to change them, and this would happen sometimes four or five times a night. Henry had no language, so he could not tell us what frightened him about being in rumpled pyjamas or how fearful he was, but his behaviour indicated that he was always extremely anxious at these times. Henry had suffered from a serious lung condition in the past, and his mother was afraid that it might be dangerous for him to become distressed, so when he demanded to have the central heating turned off, or to have a clean pair of pyjamas, she always acceded to his demands.

At length, however, she felt the situation was getting out of hand and she asked for help. In each case the treatment approach was similar. Henry's medical state was checked out and he was found to be in no more danger from becoming upset than would be anyone else. His mother was reassured on that point, and then told that, if she turned on the central heating, it was to remain on as long as it was needed, no matter how much fuss Henry made; if he tried to hit her, she should leave the room. To deal with the pyjama problem, the psychologist took all but one pair of Henry's pyjamas away with her, so that his mother could tell him quite truthfully that there were no spare pyjamas in the house and he would simply have to sleep in the ones he wore when he went to bed. Henry did make a fuss over the central heating issue, but not nearly as much of a fuss as his mother had feared, and soon accepted that it was turned on and off when required. Where the pyjamas were concerned, the first night that he was told there were no spare ones available, he slept right through and never again needed to have his pyjamas changed during the night.

Rituals

What we are discussing here are states which are often described as obsessions. 'Obsession', however, refers more properly to compulsive thoughts, while 'ritual' refers to compulsive actions. Often it is hard to know what are the thoughts that a person with a learning disability is having, but we can see compulsions and rituals taking place. Compulsions are closely related to phobias but, instead of trying to avoid a situation, the person seems to feel he must carry out some action, sometimes over and over again. In non-disabled people, the purpose seems to be to reduce anxiety, and it seems reasonable to assume that the same applies to people with learning disabilities. Again, the treatment consists of not allowing the person to carry out his rituals, and letting him see that disaster does not follow. However, because we cannot always discuss this with the person, and because preventing the ritual altogether may result in extreme distress and agitation, often we approach this, like so many other things, gradually, and reduce the ritual by degrees.

Jed is 25 years old and lives in a hostel, spending holidays and weekends with his family. Jed has many compulsive behaviours. As one of these he would, as soon as he arrived home for the weekend, remove all the cups and glasses from the kitchen cupboard and hide them around the house. This was very inconvenient for the family, but attempts to stop him from removing the cups and glasses made him very upset and difficult. So a gradual approach was adopted. His parents marked with adhesive tape all but two of the cups and glasses. They told Jed he could take all the marked items, but the unmarked ones had to stay in the cupboard. Jed accepted this with equanimity, and would even point out to his mother the ones he could and could not have. Later, the adhesive tape was removed from two more cups, then from two more cups and one glass, then from three more glasses, and it is planned to continue this programme until all the cups and glasses are clear of adhesive tape and remain ready for use in the cupboard.

Jack's ritual was very similar to those seen in non-disabled people. Jack attended a Day Centre, and at morning coffee, lunch and tea-times he would check that his coat was in its locker. To do this, he would wait until he was the only person left on his landing, for example when everyone else had gone down to lunch. He would then go to a cupboard and, from the inside door take down a key: go to another cupboard where spare blankets were kept, unlock it, and take from under the blankets the key to his locker: unlock that, check his coat, and then go through all the previous ritual in reverse. If, at any point, he was interrupted, he would go back to the beginning and start again. Sometimes the rituals would occupy hours of his day. If he was asked why he did these things he said simply, 'I must'. Jack could become violent when his ritual was interrupted, so in this case gradual changes were made in the environment in which they occurred. First, the row of keys in the first cupboard was removed, and the blanket cupboard was left unlocked. Jack now went straight to the blanket cupboard and got out the key to his locker from under the blanket. Then the blankets were removed, and the key to Jack's locker lay in a corner of the cupboard. Then the cupboard was moved out and Jack was given the key to carry in his pocket. At this point, the programme stopped. Jack still went through the ritual of checking his coat, but it was much shorter now, and he was no longer missing his lunch, as had often happened. The ritual was not eliminated, but it was much diminished. Sometimes, this may be the best we can manage: it is still better than nothing.

Self-injurious behaviour

One of the most distressing problem behaviours we meet in people with learning disabilities is that of self-injury – for example, head or body banging, eye-poking, self-biting, scratching and pinching. Self-injury is more common in children and in those who are more severely disabled, but is also found in adults and in those who are relatively mildly disabled. Attacks of this kind, by people on themselves, may be so severe as to produce dangerous, even at times life-threatening, injury to them.

Why people should set out to harm themselves has been much discussed, and many theories have been put forward, from those based on psychoanalytical ideas to those based on biochemistry or developmental theories. Two of the most useful, from the point of view of arriving at ways of dealing with it, are, first, that self-injury has been learned as a way of providing the person with stimulation, perhaps in an otherwise rather boring life; and second, that it has been learned as a way in which the person can get what he wants.

The idea that self-injury may act as stimulation arose partly from the observation that people living in understimulating environments – for example those in hospitals where there are few staff compared with the

patients – are likely to show these behaviours; and partly from the observation that these behaviours declined if the people were given other things
to do. The idea that people may learn that self-injurious behaviours are a
way to get what they want harks back to what we know about reinforcement (Chapter 4). The behaviours may first take place by accident, such as
an accidental bang on the head, or perhaps as a result of some illness –
sometimes children with earache will rock or bump their heads to counteract the ache. This fortuitous event may then produce a response from the
outside world – parents or teachers may show concern or sympathy, or at
least focus attention on the person who has suffered the hurt. Often, too,
they search for the reason for the behaviour – 'What is the matter? What
does he want? What can we do to stop him doing this?' If this sequence is
repeated often enough, the person learns that, when he self-injures, things
go his way, and he injures more often. Once the behaviour brings about
serious injury, or at least the possibility of this, the person has the world
more or less at his feet; for fear of the injury he may be given anything he
wants, allowed to avoid anything he does not want. These are very powerful reinforcers. Perhaps this makes it more understandable why a person
should be willing to hurt himself, sometimes quite badly [*] – he is willing to
do so because he gets so much out of it.

Our approach to the treatment of self-injury begins, as does all other
work in this field, with careful observation of the person's behaviour,
paying particular attention to antecedents and consequences – what goes
on before the behaviour occurs, and what happens after it. From these
observations we may be able to see whether the behaviour seems to
function more as a stimulus – if the person does it more when he is on his
own, or has nothing to do – or whether he seems to be doing it in order to
get what he wants. If it is the first, then we need to give the person plenty
to do and occupy him as much as we can. If possible, it may also be useful
to occupy him in a way that relates to his self-stimulation. For example, a
girl who poked her eyes a great deal was thought to do this partly to get
the effect of flashing lights which this action produces, so she was given a
piece of apparatus which, when she pressed the switches, produced a series
of bright flashing lights. She very much enjoyed this and would spend a
considerable amount of time with the apparatus instead of poking her eyes.

If the observation and analysis suggest that the person is being reinforced for his self-injury, then it seems self-evident that we should try to

---

[*]   There is also some evidence that people who constantly injure themselves may release
     substances into their blood stream that make the injury less painful (Richardson &
     Zaleski 1983).

make sure the reinforcer will not follow the behaviour. If we saw that, whenever Clark bit his wrist he was taken for a walk ('we find that always calms him down') and if we knew he very much liked going for walks, surely we would then decide that he would never be taken for a walk when he injured himself?

We should think very very carefully about this. If we did this, we would be using an extinction programme (see Chapter 7). You will remember that when we use extinction, we have to allow for the possibility of an extinction burst – that is, for the behaviour to get worse at first. Where self-injury is concerned, this implies serious risks. We feel that this kind of approach should not be undertaken without professional help and support and so we will not discuss it further here. Similarly, we will not discuss the use of aversive treatments – following the behaviour with something unpleasant; for example, a taste of lemon juice or the smell of ammonia. These kinds of treatments have been used but, again, we feel that they should only be undertaken with professional guidance and help.

If we can identify the reinforcer for the behaviour, there are two strategies we may think of using. First, we can ensure that the person gets much more of the reinforcer at times when he is not self-injuring. So if Clark is fond of walks, we could make a special effort to get extra help so that he would be taken out for walks a great deal of the time, even if this meant he did not participate much in other activities. Later, we might ask him to do one tiny part of a task – if it was table laying, put one spoon on the table, if it was dressing, put one arm into his coat before he was taken out. Later still, the tasks could be gradually extended.

The other strategy would be to teach Clark a better way to show us that he wanted to go for a walk. If he had some words, we could teach him to say 'walk'. If he could not, we could teach him to sign or to point to a picture to let us know what he wanted. At first, we would have to take him for a walk very often when he let us know that this was what he wanted, but later this too could be modified as discussed above.

Protective clothing, restraints and drugs

Often, our first reaction on seeing a person injure himself is to try to protect the part that suffers the injury, or to construct some kind of restraining device that will prevent the injury being carried out. So for a person who bites his arms, we might bandage or cover his arms in some sturdy material, or look for some kind of face mask which would make it impossible to bite, or for arm splints that would prevent his arm from going to his mouth.

Most people who work with a person who self-injures will make use of some kind of restraint at some time. Such restraints have their value, especially in allowing some relative safety in which other programmes can be carried out, and especially if, despite the restraints, the person can still carry out ordinary tasks, such as eating, or using his hands to handle tools and materials. Restraints do have some disadvantages, however. They may cause skin irritation where they are worn. The person wearing a restraint may show astonishing ingenuity in by-passing the restraint in order to carry out the self-injury: one boy who was fitted with a helmet to prevent his banging his forehead went on to bang his cheeks, nose, chin and finally the back of his head, moving on to injuring a new area as each was protected. Most serious of all, perhaps, is the tendency for restraints themselves to become reinforcing. Why this should be we don't really know. It may be that the restraint is a signal that, while it is in place, the person will be safe from pain (although paradoxically, it is he who inflicts this pain on himself.) This leads to the situation where, when a person self-injures, he is put into some protective clothing: this then becomes reinforcing, and the person finds that he has only to injure himself to get the response he wants, the clothing put on. Here the self-injury has almost guaranteed certainty of reinforcement, as the danger of damage from the self-injury makes those caring for the person very reluctant to deny him the protective clothing – indeed usually they are only too eager to put him into it. (In one case, however, once it was realised that the restraints were reinforcing for a young man who self-injured, a highly successful pro-gramme was devised in which he was only allowed to have the restraints following increasing periods of time in which he had *not* injured himself (Foxx and Dufrense 1984).)

Restraints and protective clothing, then, may be helpful, especially if they give those caring for the person confidence that they can try out other programmes without constant anxiety that, in the meantime, the person may be badly hurt; but we need to be alert to their possible disadvantages.

Some people who injure themselves are seen also to restrain themselves: they will wind their hands up in their clothing, push them into pockets, wrap their legs intricately around furniture. This presents us with a con-tradictory picture of a person who will spontaneously and intentionally hurt himself, but at the same time does things that prevent him doing this. Although the self-restraint may provide those caring for the person with a few welcome moments of respite from anxiety for his safety, it is seldom completely effective – the person will, from time to time, break free of the restraints and inflict injury on himself – while they are also often extremely restrictive, so that the person is almost completely prevented from taking part in other activities such as feeding, dressing, toileting, let alone any activities that he might enjoy, such as riding or swimming. Medical treatment is often sought for people who self-injure, but with variable results. Sometimes it has a good effect, sometimes a good effect is seen early and then wears off.

Sometimes, when either a medical or behavioural treatment alone has not been effective, the two together may work well. Drugs may, in the future, be developed that will give significant help, but at present they cannot be seen as an infallible remedy.

Self-injury is perhaps the most distressing problem that those caring for people with learning disabilities have to cope with. The problems are often so complex, and potentially so dangerous, that it is in this area, above all, that it is worth asking urgently for outside help and advice. It is impossible here even to touch on all the variations and difficulties that may arise, and trying to cope alone with these is hard going. We think it very important that help from the Community Team, or from the local hospital, or psychology service, should be sought, especially where the problem is one of self-injury. We would not like to think of you struggling with this alone.*

Violence

Violent and aggressive behaviour, with self-injurious behaviour, probably represents the most difficult problem with which those caring for people with learning disabilities have to contend. It comes top of the list of behaviours that other people find hard to tolerate, and top of the list of behaviours shown by people who have to return to institutional living after a time in the community. From all points of view, we need to try to help the person to get rid of or to control violent behaviours.

Violence, like self-injury, while presenting major and distressing problems to those caring for people with learning disabilities, is a behaviour like other behaviours. It is governed by the same rules, and can be analysed in the same way, as other behaviours. Partly because it is so stressful for all concerned, it is particularly important that we should not jump headlong into a treatment programme, but should, as a first step, observe the behaviour, what goes before and what happens afterwards (the antecedents and the consequences) and that we should work out how these relate to each other. Once again, we need to look very carefully at the whole situation: at where, and when the person does these things, who he does

---

*   If you would like to know more about self-injury, both causes and treatments, see Murphy and Wilson 1985.

them to and whether there is anyone he does not do them to, whether there are any particular setting conditions or triggers that we can pinpoint. We need also to analyse why the person is doing these things; what he gets out of them. Sometimes, it may be that what he gets is some satisfaction from seeing other people suffer, or hearing them cry, but in some cases aggression, like self-injury, has brought the person attention, or has enabled him to escape from tasks or situations. Following this observation and analysis we draw up a treatment programme based on the analysis and, very important again, continue to keep records to show us whether our programme is or is not doing what we had hoped.

There is one approach, however, which does not so obviously require this preliminary analysis, and although it may not always be applicable it may be worth discussing it first. It concerns the amount of space that the person has. Some workers (Boe 1977) have found that, where people with learning disabilities were living together in rather crowded conditions, just giving them more space – throwing two rooms into one – resulted in some lessening of aggression, especially in some individuals. When the room was divided into two again, there was an increase in aggression, which dropped once more when the partition was again removed. So, although it may not always be possible to give extra space, this may be a strategy to bear in mind for those times when it is on the cards.

Another option that can be considered is that of giving the person more, and also more interesting, things to do and activities to occupy him. This would seem most obvious where the person is left alone, or unoccupied, for much of the time, when simply providing more tasks to engage him can reduce at least some of the violence shown. Because this is a structural and not a behavioural strategy, it is comparatively easy to bring about. It is less obviously appropriate in those cases where the person is already given plenty to do, and the violence occurs despite this; then other methods may be more effective.

All the methods discussed in Chapter 7 – DRO, extinction, time out, brief restraint, and restitution – are worth considering as ways of tackling violent behaviour. Whether any one will be tried with any particular person will depend on whether, from the initial observation and analysis, it seems likely to be useful. Janie (see Chapter 7 p.100–101) displayed many anti-social behaviours in her Centre, including both verbal and physical aggression. Her workshop instructor concentrated on a DRO programme, reinforcing her for every half-day period in which she had not shown any of these behaviours, and this programme resulted in a dramatic improvement in her behaviour.

Walter's violence, which consisted of hitting and head-butting people and throwing things from his wheelchair, was treated by a combination of DRO and time out. He was told he could earn extra money by being co-operative and doing little jobs around the hostel where he lived; while if he hit or butted or threw he was, first, given a calm warning and then, if the behaviour persisted, he was taken to a small ante-room for three to five minutes. This programme worked well, and the number of violent incidents went down. Then the hostel staff received a dictum from on high which said that they were not in any circumstances to use time out. Walter soon cottoned on to this, his violence increased, the staff felt they could no longer cope with him and he was expelled from the hostel and went into long-term hospital care. A sad ending to the story, especially when the original programme had seemed to open up a brighter future for him.

These, and other methods described in Chapter 7, may be considered and approaches worked out using the guidelines in the chapter. As these have already been quite fully described, we would like to go on now to discuss other methods.

Anger control and self-management methods

Self-management methods have been used to help many non-disabled people with problems of temper or anger, and are now beginning to be used for people with learning disabilities. Typically, the methods used include some of the following – relaxation, constructing hierarchies of frustrating situations and of the physical sensations accompanying anger, role play, self monitoring, and self-instruction (Cole, Gardner and Karan 1985; Fleming and Tosh 1982).

Malcolm lived in a hostel where he was learning the skills that would enable him to move into a flat of his own, but all this, and indeed his place in the hostel, was jeopardised by his temper and by repeated instances of explosive violence. Malcolm was quite aware of how shaky his position was, and asked for help. As a first step, he was taught to relax by asking him to clench his fists and then relax them, to stiffen his shoulders, thighs, toes, forehead and then to relax them and he was asked to notice the difference between his feeling of the two states. Then he was taught deep breathing exercises: 'Imagine a lift travelling up your spine as you breath in and arriving at the top of your head; then travelling down again as you breath out until it arrives at the base of your spine again'. Malcolm and his worker did this together, closing their eyes and first one and then the other announcing the arrival of the lift at the top and again at the bottom. He came to feel the relaxation and tranquillity that came with this slow, deep breathing and was able to some extent to use these when he felt tensions building up in real life, although the deep breathing seemed to be more like breath holding in his case.

Malcolm's worker tried to help him to draw up hierarchies of frustrating situations and of physical sensations he felt as his anger developed, with the aim that he would learn to recognise these stages and to stop himself at an early one. However, Malcolm was quite unable to do this; indeed, he could not, when he was calm, remember or imagine how it felt to be angry. So they were never able to go on as had been planned, to giving him a card to mark when he stopped at an early stage, nor to his taking his card to a helper for reinforcement for stopping and for discussion of the incident. Instead, they went straight on to role-play, he and his worker acting out situations which commonly led to his anger and violence . They alternated roles, so that sometimes Malcolm was himself and his worker provided the provocation, then the helper role-played Malcolm's part, while Malcolm provided the provocation. They varied, too, the response to the provocation; sometimes it was an explosive angry one, sometimes a calm rational one, and, especially at first, Malcolm was asked to label the response as either 'angry' or 'calm'. Later, real incidents that had recently occurred were acted out, as they took place and with alternative endings. So, for example, when Malcolm reported a recent incident in which he had been taunted by his girl-friend and had had to be restrained from striking her, the incident was rehearsed, both as it occurred and then as it might have done more benignly, with Malcolm using his deep breathing and relaxation techniques to take the heat out of the situation. At the same time, the urgency for Malcolm to learn to use these self-control methods was recognised: when asked what would have happened on this occasion if he had not been restrained and had hit and hurt his girl-friend, he was in no doubt. 'I'd have to leave here (the hostel) and I wouldn't be sent back to the hospital, I'd be down the nick.' This was discussed as a realistic possibility; Malcolm was clear as to what this would mean for him, and it helped him to participate fully in the self-management sessions.

Sometimes, this participation is less easy to obtain. Leila had an explosive temper and had frequently, with minimal provocation, attacked both her family and others. Anger control work was seen as the most positive approach available and sessions on it were set up, apparently with her agreement. However, she was difficult to work with, sometimes saying, when the psychologist arrived, that she hadn't time for the session, sometimes not turning up, and sometimes, when the session was in progress refusing to speak, putting her head down on her arms and to all appearances going to sleep. In the meantime, the violent episodes were continuing and the psychologist felt that the one real hope for Leila's safety and freedom lay in her participation in the self-management process to help her control her temper. It was impossible, by simple reasoning, to convey to Leila how important this was for her, so the psychologist used a token system. Leila was given a token for each role-play task that she participated in, five tokens to be exchanged for 50p. Leila was keenly aware of the value of money, and the immediacy of the monetary reward held more appeal for her than the long-range and, to her, rather shadowy benefit of staying out of prison. She became more interested in co-operating in the sessions and was able to make some progress.

To help the person resist provocation, he can be taught some phrase, which he is encouraged to say out loud in the role-plays, which will encourage him in this course. Often people are urged to ignore provocation, but this, although appropriate, is not always easy. So they may be taught to say 'I won't shout back, I'll ignore him'. In addition, this can be linked with some self-enhancing statement; many of these have been concerned with the maturity of someone who refuses to rise to taunts – 'I'm a good adult worker', 'I'm a mature person (so I won't respond)'. As the sessions proceed the person can be encouraged to repeat these phrases more and more quietly until he is saying them under his breath and finally saying them inaudibly or just thinking them.

These anger control methods have been used mainly with people with mild, and occasionally those with moderate learning disabilities. These are, of course, a significant group who, if they have problems with anger and aggression, may be in serious danger, partly because they are the more likely to be moving freely around ordinary environments and to be penalised if they offend against ordinary standards of behaviour. How far these methods can be extended to people with more severe disabilities is not known at present. For a person for whom they are appropriate, these methods are particularly attractive, because they offer him the chance to be in control of himself, to direct his own actions, without the usual reliance on external reinforcement and/or constraints.

Summary

1. *Masturbation*, although not harmful, is embarrassing and this can be dealt with by teaching the person to masturbate only in private.

2. *Stereotyped behaviours* interfere with more useful learning and make the person look strange.

3. Stereotypies may act as stimulation, to counteract boredom, in which case it may be helpful to give the person plenty to do: or they may act as a shield against excessive stimulation, in which case the person may be helped by being given an alternative way to screen out the stimuli, which later can be faded.

4. For somebody with a *phobia*, we will usually use desensitisation – drawing up a hierarchy from the least to the most frightening aspect of the feared thing; then working up through the hierarchy ensuring that the person is or becomes relaxed at each stage.

5. If desensitisation is not possible, we may use flooding – keeping the person in the presence of the feared (but harmless) thing until he loses his fear of it.

6. *Rituals* may be tackled by not allowing the person to carry out his ritual, either in whole or in part.

7. *Self-injurious behaviours* sometimes seem, like stereotypies, to be used as a form of self-stimulation; as a first step we provide plenty of occupation, if possible using the sort of stimulus the person prefers.

8. In other cases, the behaviours may have been learned as a way for the person to get or avoid things he wants or doesn't want.

9. Protective restraints or drugs are useful in some cases, especially in giving time in which other methods may be put into practice.

10. *Violence,* like self-injury, requires a specially careful preliminary period of observation and analysis of the behaviour and its antecedents and consequences.

11. Giving the person more space, and more to occupy him, may be helpful.

12. DRO, extinction, time out, brief restraint, and restitution are worth considering.

13. Anger control and self-management methods have been used to help people with mild learning disabilities to overcome violent behaviour.

14. This approach includes relaxation, construction of hierarchies, role-play and self-instruction.

Exercises

1. Can you think of a phobia, or irrational fear of your own, or of someone close to you? Draw up a hierarchy, starting at the first just-not-frightening aspect of it.

2. Could you treat it by flooding?

3. How would you tackle a problem of hair pulling, using the Least Restrictive Treatment Model?

CHAPTER 16

Persisting

You are almost at the end of this book. You may have read all the preceding chapters or just those that you thought would be most interesting or useful for you. You may have made use of some of the approaches described – taken observations of a particular person, worked out the reinforcers, set up a programme to help the person learn a skill or get over a difficult behaviour. The programme may have gone well, and you are pleased with the person's progress. Sometimes, though, programmes don't go well, progress slows down or stops, or things may actually get worse. What can we do then? This has happened to us quite often, and we have a few ideas which may help.

First of all though, how do we decide when a programme is not working? We have to give it a chance to succeed and we should not give up too easily. There are no hard and fast rules* as to how long we should go on with a programme before changing it, as this depends so much on the type of programme, the person it is for, and the person or people running it. We ourselves find it helpful to decide at the outset how long we will run a programme, this particular programme, before we review it. This might be a week, or ten sessions, or whatever seems appropriate in the particular case. At the end of that time, but not before unless something goes disastrously wrong, if we can see from our records that the behaviour has begun to change in the way we hoped it would, then the programme is probably continued. But if there is no change, or there is the wrong kind of change, we think again. Giving ourselves that kind of time limit helps both by ensuring we do not give up too soon and by reassuring us that an unfruitful programme will not go on indefinitely.

---

* We fear you may be sick of our saying 'There are no hard and fast rules' and long for some clear cut and invariable paths to follow. We would like them too!

Look at what is happening

The most useful thing we can do may be simply to stop and look at what is happening. When things are going wrong, we may be too close to them to be able to see what is going wrong. So we stand back; watch; write down what is happening. Often this helps us to see the problem more clearly, and that is the first step to seeing what we can do about it.

Talk it over

If standing back and watching shows you where the problem seems to be, but you still cannot see how to tackle it, find someone you can discuss it with. This might be a friend or a member of the family, or this might be the place to call in a professional – someone from your local Community Team, or your local hospital or school psychologist. Two people talking a problem over gives you more than twice what you would get if each thought about it on his or her own.

What to do

Check on what is being done

Perhaps one of the first things to ask, especially if the programme was to be carried out by more than one person, is; Is the programme being carried out properly? Are the different people involved carrying it out consistently? It is easy enough for small variations to creep in without anyone intending this to happen. In this case, we may all sit down together and talk about how each of us works with the person. We will try not to say, 'Well, I just carry out the programme, I do exactly what it says on the sheet'. Instead, we will say, 'First of all I...and then we...then he...'. At this point someone else may say 'But do you...?' and one or other may realise that something on the programme was being missed out, or something not on the programme was being included. If these discussions do not show up any obvious differences, it may be worthwhile to ask someone else, an outsider perhaps, to watch the various practitioners, to see whether there are any differences in what they do that might be important. Once we have spotted these inconsistencies, and the reasons for them, we will be better able to work out a programme that everyone can agree to, and to go over it and practise it until we are sure that everyone is carrying it out in the same way.

We have said that we try to work out a programme that everyone can agree to. Sometimes it happens that, however hard we try, there are one or two people who just cannot agree to a programme which everyone else thinks is the most useful one they can come up with. In this case, we have found it best to respect these people's feelings, not ask them to do things they disagree with, but to let them stand aside from and not take part in the programme. Sometimes this can cause a certain amount of hard feeling, especially if, as sometimes happens, the programme is an arduous one. The people opting out may be able to counter this by offering to take other tasks from their colleagues in exchange. Nevertheless, it is important that everyone understands that, however unfortunate it is that full agreement cannot be reached, it is very much better that any disagreements about programmes should be acknowledged, and that far greater harm can be done by expecting people to carry out programmes they disagree with, and which they may then, intentionally or not, sabotage.

If you feel that inconsistency is not the problem, there are a number of other areas in which snags can arise. We will look at each of these.

Reinforcement

This is crucial. Is the reinforcer we are using really reinforcing to the person? You will remember that the definition of a reinforcer is: **anything which, when it follows a behaviour, makes that behaviour happen more often.** If the behaviour is not increasing, we take a long hard look at what we are using as a reinforcer. We may simply have picked the wrong thing: we may have picked it more because it suited our own convenience than because we knew the person was enthusiastic about it. 'We always use praise as the reinforcer' and 'I don't believe in using foods' are phrases which arouse our suspicions as to the likely effectiveness of the reinforcers.

On the other hand, we may have picked a good reinforcer but may not be giving it in the best way. We may be giving too much, so that the person becomes bored with it. In this case we could try cutting down the amount (a tablespoonful of orange juice instead of half a glassful, ten seconds worth of music instead of a minute); or we could try interspersing it with another good reinforcer – sometimes a piece of crisp, sometimes a cold drink. Alternatively, although the amount we are giving seems reasonable, the person may be bored with the reinforcer because he gets a great deal of it at other times; so, if we are using food reinforcers, it will probably be better to have our teaching session before rather than after lunch. (Nevertheless, we should not be put off trying out a reinforcer just because it is freely available to the person. Vincent, who had stacks of records, was still eager to earn tokens towards another, and Patricia who had cups of tea at breakfast, elevenses, lunch, tea-time and after supper still worked briskly in order to get extra cups of tea).

Tokens are a special case amongst reinforcers: if we are using tokens, is the back-up reinforcer something the person really wants, or should we look for something else? If it is the right one, is the back-up reinforcer too far out of the person's reach – does he have to earn so many tokens before he can exchange them that he has no realistic expectation of doing so? If this is the case, we may need to draw up another programme, either making it easier to earn the tokens or requiring fewer tokens in exchange for the back-up reinforcer.

Other aspects of a programme

Perhaps we have looked carefully at the reinforcer we are using and can see nothing wrong with it. We may need, then, to look at other parts of the programme. If it is a teaching programme, are the steps in the programme small enough? Do we need more steps at one, perhaps specially difficult, point? Jane, a hostel worker, wanted to teach Helga to take off her coat. She broke down the task into small steps and, using backward chaining, began by teaching Helga to do the last step, to pull off the last, left, sleeve with her right hand. This proved unexpectedly difficult because Helga would fold her left hand over the cuff of the left sleeve, so that her right hand could not pull the sleeve off. We then extended the chaining scale so that Jane removed Helga's coat to the point where the left shoulder was pulled off to the elbow and the sleeve protruded well beyond Helga's left hand. Helga was then able to pull the sleeve right off. However, when Jane went on to the next step, with the cuff once again at Helga's wrist, she again folded her hand over the cuff. Jane then broke the task into several more small steps, so the end of the chain became:

(1) Left sleeve pulled beyond hand (this is the step Helga had mastered).

(2) Left sleeve pulled to just over finger tips.

(3) Left sleeve pulled to the point where finger tips are just visible.

(4) Left sleeve pulled to show one inch of middle finger.

(5) Left sleeve pulled to show two inches of middle finger.

And so on.

If, when the cuff is pulled just to Helga's palm, or to her wrist, she again folds her hand over the cuff, Jane plans to restrain the fingers gently; but already we have seen that inserting extra steps has lent a new lease of life to the programme.

So much for breaking down the steps in a teaching programme. Supposing it is a programme to reduce or get rid of a behaviour that is not working: what then? There are several areas we can look at. If we are using an extinction programme, is the person really *never* getting the reinforcer for the behaviour? Could it be that someone who is new, or doesn't know the programme well, is still giving the reinforcer? Especially, perhaps, if the reinforcer is attention, is the person getting it, not from those working with him but from other people – peers, visitors, members of the public? If we are using a time-out programme are we *quite sure* that what the person is being timed out from is something he or she is really interested in? If it is something that the person doesn't care about much, or only tolerates, a time out programme is doomed to failure and we had better think of something else.

Especially with these kinds of programmes designed to reduce behaviours, we need to ensure that there are plenty of good things in the person's life, and that he or she has plenty of opportunity to get reinforcers for positive, or even just OK, behaviours. If our programme only removes the chance of reinforcement (for an unwanted behaviour) without re-scheduling it for other, better, behaviours, it will have little hope of success. Fortunately, if we realise this is the case there are usually plenty of ways we can put this right.

There is the special case of the programme, of either kind, which works quite well at first, the behaviour changing in the way we hoped it would, and then, just as we thought we were home and dry, there is a relapse, skills fall off or unwanted behaviours increase. This may be where we need to stand back, as we suggested earlier, and look at what is happening but, once again, we think it may be worth checking on the reinforcement. Sometimes, when things are going well, those running the programme get careless about reinforcement (just as when we are well on the way to recovery from an infection we often find ourselves getting careless about taking the last few antibiotic tablets) as they feel the person is now perfectly well able to show the behaviour and ought to be able to do without reinforcement. For example, Derek had a programme to help him remember to wash and shave himself every day, and to wear clean clothes, and he was able to earn, to him, quite substantial sums for doing so. When Derek was regularly appearing clean and smart, the programme was stopped, and everyone was dismayed when Derek returned to his old slovenly behaviour. It was quite clear that the reinforcement had been stopped too abruptly, so the programme was reinstated, this time the reinforcement being faded much more gradually as suggested in Chapter 4, while Derek was also able to move on to earning reinforcement for other more advanced skills.

Conclusion

We have tried in this book to suggest ways in which people with learning disabilities can be helped to develop their skills to the fullest extent and to live the kinds of lives that they wish to. We have given many examples of methods that we have used to overcome certain problems, and we have to emphasise that, if we were successful, this does not mean that that method will always work with that problem. Always, what we need is a detailed look at the particular person and the particular problem, and a careful analysis of which kind of approach would be worth trying in this case. We offer here not so much a cook-book, with a recipe for this cake and for that cake: rather we offer an assembly of ingredients for your cupboard, from which you select those that you decide will be best to use at any one time. You may find there are gaps , and if you do, please write and tell us – we would always be glad to hear from you. But we hope you will have enough to enable you to achieve some useful results. We wish you every success.

The Exercises – Some Answers

Chapter 2. Observation

1. **Observations**

   He slapped me on the back.

   She drank her tea.

   He hit the cricket ball.

   Interpretations

   He is attention seeking.

   She needs to socialise more.

   Sally is not achieving her potential.

   He was upset at missing the party.

   He is careless about personal hygiene.

2. (a) We will be able to see if the person can do any part of the task we are aiming to teach him.

   (b) We will start with a detailed and factual description of what the person is doing.

   (c) Systematic observations can dispel misconceptions about the frequency and severity of a behaviour.

3. (a) It will be a permanent record, we will not have to depend on unreliable memory, and we can compare later records with earlier ones.

4. (a) Duration recording.

   (b) Event recording.

   (c) Weekly totals of the amount saved (this kind of record is sometimes called 'permanent product', the behaviour has a result which can be looked at, stored and collated). (a), (b) and (c) could also be recorded using either interval or time sampling, if this seemed more appropriate.

   (d) Duration recording.

5. (a) OK

   (b) Not acceptable.

   (c) Not acceptable.

   (d) OK.

   (a) and (d), Swearing and toileting accidents: we want to decrease them, so a rising baseline, showing that they are at present increasing, suggests the programme is sorely needed. However if (b), learning names of foods, and (c), dressing skills, are already increasing there may not be any need for a programme at all.

Chapter 3. Assessment and Goal Planning

(1) All goals need to specify when and where they will be worked on and by whom.

    (a) Peter needs to learn to dress himself. This sounds quite clear, but gives us no indication of which parts of the task Peter may already be able to do. It could include anything from tying his shoelaces to putting on a shirt. If after observing what Peter can already do it transpires that he can do many bits of the dressing process but requires supervision and prompting for most of it we might well pick on one of the last and easier garments to start with, eg, a jumper. The goal might well then be written as:

    Peter will put on his jumper, with physical prompting, every morning when his mother asks him to get dressed. He will then have his breakfast.

    At this stage his mother would still be doing a great deal of work throughout the dressing process. However, we would make sure she had a well documented plan of how she was going to withdraw her prompts in the case of the jumper and a good idea about how she would subsequently break down more of the dressing so that Peter could move towards independence in this area. The reinforcer in this instance is the breakfast.

    (b) Carmen should have a better social life. 'Social life' includes a vast variety of things. Here it might be 'Carmen will visit the skating rink every Tuesday evening with her friend, Trevor, and will visit MacDonald's afterwards'. This is, of course, not all the social life we envisage for Carmen – later it might include going to dances, cinemas clubs and all sorts of other activities – but this is the first, clearly specified, step we intend to help her to take.

    (c) Susan needs to learn to feed herself. In this case we narrowed feeding down to using a fork. Thus the goal could be: 'Susan, holding her fork in her right hand, will feed herself her already cut-up meal at lunch every day in her day centre. She will then spend some time with her friends in the Smokers' Lounge'.

(2) Task analysis

Every task analysis needs to be designed for the individual concerned so that the size of the steps suits that individual. We give here an example of an analysis of paying for your purchases at the checkout of a supermarket. (Task analyses of washing hands and putting on a jumper can be found in *Helping your handicapped child*, Janet Carr, Penguin.)

(1) Wheel trolley to checkout.

(2) Park with front edge of trolley against top edge of checkout counter.

(3) Put 'Next customer' sign at edge of previous customer's purchases.

(4) Pick out item from trolley.

(5) Place it on moving counter.

(6) Continue until available space is filled.

(7) When previous customer is finished go to other end of counter and open out three plastic bags.

(8) Go back to trolley end and place more items on now moving counter.

(9) Go to exit side of counter and start packing items in bags.

(10) Move back to trolley end of counter and place remaining items on it.

(11) Move back to exit side of counter and pack remaining items.

(12) Look at till display or listen to assistant giving total cost.

(13) Get out purse.

(14) Select notes and coins corresponding to total cost as closely as possible.

(15) Wait for change.

(16) Take change and put it in purse.

(17) Put purse away.

(18) Check that all items are packed.

(19) Pick up bags and leave shop.

Chapter 4. Giving Encouragement

1. A bribe is defined as: 'Money etc. offered to procure (often illegal or dishonest) action in favour of the giver' (Concise Oxford Dictionary). When we use reinforcement we are certainly not trying to procure any dishonest action: nor should we be trying to procure an action in our own favour. We use reinforcement to encourage (procure) action that will be of benefit to the person him or herself.

2. Ours include:

- warm houses with thick carpets
- chocolate
- approval from our friends
- a lie-in at the weekend

3. We thought of two things for us.

- One, walking over a 100 metre long, 30 metre high bridge over a river, only a metre wide and without guard rails. There is a bridge like this in the South of France which many people walk over every year – but we could not face it.
- The second is scuba-diving. Nothing would induce us to do it, even though we know that it would give us access to the immensely beautiful and interesting underwater world. In each case what we get out of not doing it is avoidance of paralysing terror. Aren't we pathetic?

Chapter 5. Points, Stars and Tokens

1. (i) We would consider this only if it would either

   (a) free the world of the threat of war

   (b) stop something awful happening to one of our children. Nothing less would be powerful enough to make us do it.

   (ii), (iii) and (iv) – We would probably do any of these if given enough money, say, upward of £5,000.

2. (i) Any secondary reinforcers like tokens, charts etc., which appealed to the man concerned would be applicable. His violence is beside the point.

   (ii) Anything which she could hold or touch; tokens in plastic, metal or other material. Points or star charts would probably be of little use for her as she could not see them and would be unlikely to understand or remember if she were told about them.

   (iii) Something which appeals to her. Her wish for attention has nothing to do with it, although earning and receiving tokens would in themselves give her the attention she likes.

(iv) Plastic counters, matchsticks, or any other small objects would not be a good idea here. Interesting charts might do the trick.

3. Make a 'Bank' into which she can put them, or buy or make her a special purse or pocket into which she can put the tokens. It must be made so that it is fastenable and she can keep it with her.

Giving her some fool-proof storage system like this would perhaps deal with the nagging doubt we would have as to whether the tokens were really reinforcing to her. Have we got the right back-up reinforcer for her? Is it too difficult for her to earn it? We could not avoid thoughts like these.

Chapter 6. Ways of Teaching

1. Because if a person cannot do the task, she will never receive the reinforcement. Prompting may give her this opportunity.

2. False. We often start by reinforcing an approximation to the task we are aiming for. We then gradually raise our criteria for success until the person is able to come closer and closer to performing the real task.

3. Partly true and partly false. When we first begin the teaching, when the person cannot carry out the task at all, our prompts are quite firm (although never so firm as to be painful). Later, as the person begins to learn what to do we fade our prompts, making them gradually lighter and lighter until eventually they fade away entirely.

4. Finger pointing.
   Head nodding and shaking.
   Eye pointing.
   The various signing systems. (Makaton is the most widely used in this country).

5. Deaf people who are blind, foreigners who can't understand the language, profoundly learning disabled people, people out of earshot. In short, anyone who can't hear or understand what we say.

6. True.

7. It depends entirely on the person involved. More able people can manage larger, fewer steps, less able people may need more and smaller ones. Detailed observation of what the person can do already suggests the number of steps we will need. If a person is not learning we may suspect that the steps are too big.

Chapter 7. Coping with Unwanted Behaviours

1. (a) Self injurious behaviour, for example, head banging.
   (b) Violent or aggressive behaviours.
   (c) Repetitive meaningless behaviours such as stereotypies.
   (d) Asocial behaviours – those which are not so serious as (a) or (b) but which may result in the person being avoided by other people, being dirty, smelly or noisy.

2. We would first look at the environment. Many people with learning disability have lived in impoverished institutional environments, in which it would be difficult for many a person to function. We have seen great changes in behaviour achieved solely by environment changes such as a move from a villa for 30 people into a small shared house for five.

3. We define punishment as 'Anything which, when it follows a behaviour, makes that behaviour less likely to occur in the future'. This is the opposite of our technical definition of reinforcement, which makes a behaviour more likely to occur. It is different from the more common usage of the word punishment which implies that something, to be punishing, must be unpleasant or painful. For us the crucial thing which defines punishment is that it should result in a lessening of the behaviour. Even something extremely unpleasant like taking an icy shower is not a punishment, in our terms, if it does not decrease the behaviour which precedes it.

4. We should always use the full title 'Time out from positive reinforcement' in order to remind ourselves that this sort of punishment involves, first, an analysis of exactly what is reinforcing about the situation which the person is in, and then the interruption of that reinforcing situation. Time out from positive reinforcement is not synonymous with removal from the room, nor with seclusion.

Chapter 8. Recording and Presenting Data

1. (a) Sellotaped to the side of the detergent pack.
   Inside the cupboard door.
   Under the sink.
   (b) In the notebook that we carry round with us (so that we can note it whenever it occurs).
   (c) In an address book or inside the telephone directory or message pad, which are inside the book of telephone numbers/messages kept by the telephone.
   (d) On a cupboard in the greenhouse.
   (e) Inside the linen cupboard. On K's bedside cabinet.
2. (a) Recording graded prompts for each step, and the steps achieved.
   (b) Event, or duration, recording. Or event recording within an hourly timetable – as in Figure 3 in this chapter. If the behaviour were frequent you might use either partial interval sampling – recording, say every five or 15 minutes whether the behaviour had occurred in the interval – or momentary time sampling – record every fifth or fifteenth minute whether the behaviour occurred at that moment.
   (c) Recording graded prompts.
   (d) Recording graded prompts and permanent product – the number of seedlings she plants.
   (e) Event recording – the number of times the bed is wet.

Chapter 9. Washing and Dressing

1. Hair washing.
   Some people wash their hair in the bath, some in the shower, some in a sink. The shower is probably the easiest but not everyone has one. A cheaply bought plastic shower attachment may enable hair to be washed more easily whilst sitting in the bath, or bending over the sink.
   We have decided to go for hair washing whilst sitting in a filled bath, using a shower attachment. A task analysis might look something like this.
   (1) Switch on cold tap.

(2) Switch on hot tap.

(3) Adjust cold tap until water feels warm to finger.

(4) Tip head back slightly.

(5) Hold shower attachment. Aim it at head and wet hair.

(6) Put shower head face down under water.

(7) Pick up shampoo bottle.

(8) Tip bottle so as to allow a little shampoo to run onto hand.

(9) Put down bottle.

(10) Rub shampoo into head with both hands.

(11) Massage shampoo around scalp making sure all hair is lathered.

(12) Pick up shower head making sure that it is kept pointing down.

(13) Tip head slightly back.

(14) Wash soap from hair starting at front and working backward.

(15) Keep rinsing until hair squeaks and no lather can be seen running from the hair.

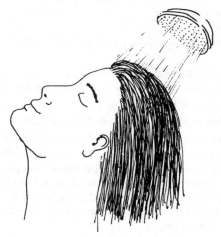

Start again from point 4 if required.

2. We think, getting the temperature right. Why? Because it involves making judgements, which are hard to teach.

3. We would start by observing exactly what Patrick is doing. This may involve a lengthy analysis of all steps taken when he gets up and dressed in the morning. What we would be looking for are the small skills which he may not be completing. These may be such details as not tucking his shirt in, not doing up buttons, not combing his hair, or having clothes on inside out. Even when we are clean and have clean clothes on, if these small details are not right we can look a mess.

4. Until recently, adult clothes were not available with any fastenings other than buttons or zips. Fashionable shoes with velcro fastenings, similarly, have not been obtainable. We have always felt that it is better to teach people to be able to fasten what is normally used – even if it takes some time – rather than stigmatize them by giving them clothes which make them look odd or unusual.

5. We would take a pair of dungarees and go through the process of getting them on and off ourselves, writing down the steps involved as we went along.

Chapter 10. Eating and Toileting

1. Food the person likes very much. We also make sure that it is easy to get onto the spoon or fork.
2. Behind the person.
3. Wrong. When the prompts have been faded we 'shadow' the person's hands with our hands until we are quite sure she can manage on her own.
4. We may need to insert an extra reinforcer for this part of the action, as it is furthest away from the natural reinforcer of the food or drink getting to the mouth. Otherwise we use the same prompting and fading method.
5. We would make sure we could prevent the snatch. We would then restart the timing (of how long the plate was removed).
6. The two methods used were, removing the plate for a short period – this was time out from the positive reinforcement of eating – and DRO (differential reinforcement of other behaviours) – chocolate marshmallows were given for eating nicely.
7. One thing we could try is to put a ping pong ball in the bowl – this can make correct aiming fun.
8. As many as it takes until the last piece is not soiled. Four pieces, doubled if necessary, is normally about right.

Chapter 11. Home Management

1. First, we would start by seeing what bits of the task the person understood and could do already. We would then do a detailed task analysis of window cleaning including:
Moving the furniture
Taking down the curtains
Filling the bucket, etc.
It would probably be best to start with low windows where cleaning could be physically prompted, going on to modelling and imitation with higher windows. Reinforcers would be chosen according to the individual's preferences. As the task is quite a large one, it might be advisable to reinforce the person after each small completed section.

e.g.   after window cleaner is applied.

after it is wiped off.

after each small pane is completed

– depending on how we have broken the task down.
2. Ashok will need to know:
(a) How to get to the post office.
(b) Where the counter is. Some post offices are in shops and the counter is not very obvious. Increasingly, in larger post offices there are roped-off areas where you are expected to queue.
(c) How to queue. In the small shop type of post office there may be more than one counter and more than one queue; in the larger kind with roped-off

queuing areas, he will have to learn to wait until he is in the front position and then look for the signal to go to the counter, usually either a light, or a clerk saying 'next please', or both.

(d) What money he needs to give for a book of either first or second class stamps. These are always changing, but at 1992 prices, given that we can probably depend on post office counter staff to give him the right change, he can be taught to give three one pound coins for a book of first class stamps and two for a book of second class.

(e) Take the stamps and the change and put them in a purse or wallet.

(f) Put the purse or wallet away in a safe pocket.

3. We think:

- Dealing with fire, including having and checking smoke alarms
- Electricity/gas – turning off and unplugging appliances
- Contacting emergency services
- Dealing with burns.

Chapter 12. Travel Skills

1. One example might be, crossing between parked cars. Any crossing between parked cars is likely to be dangerous, so the best course of action may be to teach the person always to walk to the next zebra or pelican crossing or the next traffic lights. Or, if there are none of these, to walk to a wide space between cars. After this, the teaching will follow the same lines as those on pp.189.

2. If the person being taught cottoned on to the fact that a stranger was following her it might be worrying. We could probably get over this by letting her know in advance that this was going to be done.

3. For us, the most tricky parts of a train journey are:

(a) Making sure the train is running.

(b) Ensuring that we go to the right platform.

(c) Making sure we don't fall asleep and get carried past our stop.

(d) Getting off at the right place – we have, on occasion, started up and got out of the train only to realise that we were on a platform we didn't mean to be on.

(e) Taking all our belongings off the train with us. We have left various things behind on trains, including a leather jacket, a violin, and a newly bought telephone answering machine. The violin was recovered; we weren't so lucky with the others.

Chapter 13. Going to Work

1. First, we need to describe what are the 'correct' clothes to wear when gardening and to check whether the prospective gardener actually has such clothes. For winter gardening, we thought that we would probably need:

Wellingtons
Dungarees or jeans
Short duffle coat or donkey jacket

Warm jumper
Warm shirt
Gloves

In the summer the list would be different. There is now some evidence to suggest that learning things first in a 'classroom' situation, even though it sometimes has to be learnt again in 'real life', results in better learning. So, starting with footwear, we would probably start by explaining what we were doing, and then presenting our prospective gardener with two sets of shoes – one, say, wellingtons and the other trainers. We would give lots of praise if, when asked the question, 'what would you wear for gardening', he pointed to the right pair, and would prompt him to the right answer if he seemed unsure. We would keep going with this until the gardener was getting it right four times out of five. Then we would go onto trousers, jackets, shirts etc.

Later, when he had been able to select the right clothing on several occasions (say, five times out of six) we would check him as he set out to go to his gardening job. We would praise him if he had on appropriate clothes and, if he had not, point this out to him and send him back to change.

2. Some of the skills involved in getting and keeping work seem to be:

- Being able to get up in the morning
- Travelling to work
- Good time keeping
- Being able to communicate basic needs
- Taking any necessary safety precautions
- Being able to do the job you are employed to do
- Getting on with your workmates and employer

Chapter 14. Social Competence

1. These are some of the things we thought of – you may come up with others.
   Advantages
   (a) People can learn from each other.
   (b) People in the group will have a variety of skills and deficits, so they can help each other.
   (c) The range of possible problems and solutions is wider with more people
   (d) Having more people makes it more fun.
   (e) People can learn to give positive feed back to others.
   Disadvantages
   (a) People's needs may be different and much of what goes on may be boring or irrelevant for any one person.
   (b) Each individual may have only a short time for his or her particular difficulties in any one session.
   (c) Some people may take more than their share of time. Others may not speak at all.
   (d) Not everybody is willing to participate in group work.
2. (a) Giving homework (tasks to be carried out outside the sessions) and making sure that these are done.

(b) Integrating social skills training into the curriculum of day centres.

(c) Encouraging staff and others in day centres or hostels, parents and friends to reinforce any instance of particular skills which they know are being worked on in the group sessions.

3. We found this one difficult – perhaps we needed assertiveness training ourselves. We started the sessions with a short discussion about the situation and people made various suggestions on how to deal with it.

The co-leaders then acted out one of the suggested solutions e.g. – 'go and knock on the door and ask him to turn it down' – and the group discussed this and other ways of handling it. We then went round the group with people in pairs, each pair trying different solutions or improved varieties of previous solutions. This was not a competitive exercise, we were genuinely looking for a good solution, and everyone was praised for the good suggestions that they made.

4. What you planned would depend on your assessment of the skills of your group members. We will assume that the people in the group are able to manage the skills necessary before they get to this point – i.e., they can walk in the street alone, have basic road sense, can understand some language, etc. You might then want to show a video of the sort of situation we are talking about, discuss it in the group, try role plays of the situation with different people taking turns to say 'No' and walk quickly away. Some people have run groups where the participants have actually practised saying 'NO' loudly and firmly over and over again. Others have integrated this sort of scenario among other issues which require self-assertion. These are judgements which only you could make when you know very clearly the needs of the individuals in your group.

Chapter 15. Disturbed and Problem Behaviours

1. Mine is a fear of heights. It only applies when I am unprotected by railings or glass or any other constraint. So I could approach this in one of two ways: either I could get myself onto places that were at first quite low, I think about six metres high, without any guard rail, and gradually making the places progressively higher; or, I might take myself up really high, 20 metres or so, and start with guard rails which reached above my head and gradually whittle them away until I could be at that height with no rail at all.

I have often thought of doing some programme of this sort, but I never seem to have got round to it. I wonder why?

2. In this case flooding would involve keeping me in the feared situation, high above the ground, without protection. If I was as frightened as I think I would be I might well fall off. So perhaps flooding would not be the treatment of choice.

3. We would begin by using environmental change, DRO, and DRI. For most activities we would keep the hair puller well away from other people (environmental change). Then we would warmly reinforce other things the person did (DRO) and we might bring in a dummy head with hair and give particular reinforcement to the person for touching and stroking, but not pulling, the hair (DRI).

Later, we would allow him to touch and stroke our hair, and reinforce him for this, and later still, to do the same with other people in his group.

All of these are positive approaches. Only if they failed would we consider more restrictive approaches such as time out or restraint.

Assessment Materials

This is a list of a range of currently available assessment checklists, rating scales and teaching manuals. It is by no means exhaustive.

1. **ABS Adaptive behaviour Scale**

    From: NFER Publishing Co
            Darville House
            2 Oxford Road East
            Windsor SL4 lDF

Applicable to all levels of learning disabilities and to any age over three years. Mainly devised for use in residential centres but also useful with parents.

   One section is concerned with adaptive behaviour in areas such as independent functioning, physical development, economic activity, numbers and time. The other section catalogues problem behaviour. This latter section we rarely use, since we usually have little difficulty in collecting descriptions of what the person is doing wrong.

   The scale can help identify broad areas of need which must then be investigated in more detail.

2. **PAC Progress Assessment Charts**

    From: SEFA (Publications) Ltd
          The Globe
          4 Great William Street
          Stratford upon Avon
          Warwickshire

A series of assessment charts covering skills ranging from profound learning disability right through to virtual independence. Special charts are available for use with children with Down's syndrome and for severely learning disabled adults. The items are carefully defined in manuals which should always be used when completing the chart.

   The charts include a visual representation of the data so that areas of deficit can be readily identified.

   This scale was used extensively in the 1980s.

3. **Portage Guide to Early Education**

    From: NFER Publishing (address above)

Consists of a checklist concerned with infant stimulation, socialisation, language, self-help, cognitive skills and motor skills.

These skills are listed in the order in which they are normally learned and range up to the six year level.

The guide is intended as an aid to educating learning disabled children and each item on the checklist is accompanied by a card which includes suggestions for teaching.

We have found it to be particularly useful with pre-school children.

4. The Kidderminster Curriculum for Children and Adults with Profound and Multiple Learning Difficulties

From: Lizanne Jones
        School of Psychology
        University of Brimingham
        Edgbaston
        Birmingham B15 2TT

Designed to meet the needs of people who are functioning at a very low developmental and/or intellectual level. It is a framework to assist in delivering effective education to the students setting clearly goals for them and giving guidelines for staff in deciding what to teach and how to teach it.

5. The Next Step on the Ladder

From: British Institute of Mental Handicap
        Wolverhampton Road
        Kidderminster
        Worcestershire

A manual outlining methods for assessing children with learning and physical disabilities who may also have sensory deficits. Once the child has been assessed, the manual provides advice and information on target setting and teaching methods. It utilises a developmental approach to working with disabled children.

6. Scale for Assessing Coping Skills

From: Copewell Publications
        29 Worcester Road
        Alkrington
        Middleton
        Manchester M24 1PA

and: Learning to Cope
        by E Whelan and B Speake
        Human Horizons Series

A checklist and book designed to be used together, by both professionals and parents with learning disabled adolescents and adults. The checklist covers the skills and knowledge which are of greatest importance for living in the community. It is a comprehensive assessment looking at all areas of skill development, self-help, domestic, academic, social and communication skills. The book provides advice on goal planning and teaching methods aimed at overcoming skill deficits identified by the checklist.

7. Work Skills Rating Scale

From: Copewell Publications (address above)

A scale containing 24 items all examining important features of an individual's performance in a working situation. Its primary aim is to assess performance, not ability or disability, and no allowances should be made for this when completing it. It is not aimed specifically at learning disabled people, but can be useful when assessing more able individuals' suitability for work placement or non-sheltered employment.

(8) The Berekweeke Skill Teaching System

From: NFER Publishing Co (address above)
        or courses on the system run by BIMH, see Appendix 3

A behavioural teaching system for use with severely and moderately learning disabled children and adults. The system includes an assessment checklist listing the major areas of everyday behaviour, writers' handbook providing information on how to write behavioural programmes, record forms for setting teaching targets and recording progress, and a system administration handbook giving guidelines on how to monitor the system. The whole package provides a good structure for identifying areas of skill deficiency and devising programmes to overcome them.

9. Individual Programme Plans

Information from: Mental Handicap in Wales,
                          Applied Research Unit,
                          55 Park Place
                          Cardiff
                          CF1 3AT
                          Tel: (0222) 226188

APPENDIX 3

Resources and Useful Addresses

Resources
Personal Relationships and Sexuality
Craft, M. and Craft, A. (1982) *Sexuality and the mentally handicapped.* Routledge and Kegan Paul.

Dixon, H. (1988) *Sexuality and Mental Handicap.* An Educators Resource Book. Wisbeach, Cambs: LDA.

Gunn, M.J. (1985) *Sex and the Law.* Family Planning Association.

Kempton, W. *Life Horizons, I and II.* James Stansfield and Company, PO Box Santa Monica, California, 90406. (Telephone (0101-800) 421 6534)

Set of slides and accompanying text looking at friendships, personal relationships and sexuality.

Teaching Language and Communication
Howlin, P. (1987) *Language and communication training.* In W. Yule and J. Carr, (eds)

Behaviour Modification for People with Mental Handicaps. London: Croom Helm.

Jeffree, D. and McKoney, R. (1976) *Let me speak.* Human Horizon Series. London: Souvenir Press.

Makaton: for information on the Makaton Vocabulary Development Project, contact Mrs M. Walker, 31, Firwood Drive, Camberley, Surrey, GU15 3QD (Telephone (1276) 61390)

Useful Addresses
AFASIC
Association of Speech Impaired Children
347 Central Markets, Smithfield, London EC1A 9NH
Telephone (071) 236 3623/6487
Offers advice, support and information to parents and professionals.

Association of Residential Communities for the Retarded (ARC)
Old Tithe Barn, Church Lane North, Old Whittington, Chesterfield, Derbyshire S41 9QY
Telephone (0246) 455881
Aims to ensure the quality of life, maintenance of standards and diversity of residential and day services. Runs a computerised information service matching residential needs and services (Caresearch, Tel: 0594 530220).

British Epilepsy Association

Anstey House, 40 Hanover Square, Leeds LS3 1BE
Telephone (0532) 439393
Provides care in the community for people with epilepsy and an advice and information service, local support groups and videos and literature on all aspects of epilepsy.

British Institute of Mental Handicap (BIMH)

(formerly British Institute of Subnormality)
Wolverhampton Road, Kidderminster, Worcester DY1O 3PP
Telephone (0562) 850251
Runs courses on many and varied topics; source of advice and literature.

Campaign for People with Mental Handicaps

Oxford House, Derbyshire Street, London E6
Telephone (071) 729 5436
Pressure group of parents and professionals, aiming especially for the integration of people with learning disabilities into the wider community.

Citizen Advocacy Alliance

26 Sutton Court Road, Sutton, Surrey SM1 4SL
Telephone (081) 643 7111
Recruits, trains and supports volunteers known as advocates who will act as both friends and independent spokespersons for people with a learning disability.

Contact-a-Family

16 Strutton Ground, London SW1P 2HP
Telephone (071) 222 2695
Provides links between families and between families and local or national self-help groups. Good source of information about other specialist groups.

Disabled Living Foundation

380–384 Harrow Road, London W9.
Telephone (071) 289 6111
Information service, especially regarding equipment for daily living needs.

Down's Syndrome Association

155 Mitcham Road, London SW17 9PG
Telephone (081) 682 4001
Help and support for people with Down's syndrome, their families, carers and professionals.

Family Planning Association

Education and Training Department, 27–35 Mortimer Street, London W1N 7RJ
Telephone (071) 636 7866
Offers a programme of courses and made-to-measure training, consultancy and supervision for staff in areas of sexual abuse and relationships.

Kings Fund Centre

126 Albert Street, London NW1 7NF
Telephone (071) 267 6111
A service development agency working with people in health and social services, in voluntary agencies and with carers and users of services. Encourages new developments and enables experiences to be shared through workshops, conferences, information services and publications.

Mencap

Royal Society for Mentally Handicapped Children and Adults
(Previously: National Association for Mentally Handicapped Children and Adults)
Mencap National Centre, 123 Golden Lane, London EC1Y ORT
Telephone (071) 454 0454
Provides homes and accommodation; leisure activities through a network of Gateway clubs; a network of specialist employment services (the Pathway Employment Scheme); and a range of other services on request, e.g. legal, welfare and benefit advice.

Mind

22 Harley Street, London W1N 2ED
Telephone (071) 637 0741
Pressure group on behalf of people with any form of mental disorder. Provides services, homes, publications, training, conferences.

Mobility Information Service

National Mobility Centre, Unit 2A, Atcham Industrial Estate, Upton Magna, Shrewsbury, SY4 4UG
Telephone (0743) 761889
Provides literature and advice on mobility, including wheelchairs and assessment for driving.

National Association of Family Based Respite Care

Norah Fry Research Centre, University of Bristol, 32 Tyndalls Park Road, Bristol BS8 1PY
Telephone (0272) 467230
An information-giving service for parents, carers and professionals involved in respite care. Carries out an annual survey and publishes a directory of family based respite care schemes in the UK.

National Autistic Society

276 Willesdon Lane, London NW2 5RB
Telephone (081) 451 1114
Runs schools and adult centres, offers a range of support, advice and information services. Supports the Centre for Social and Communication Disorders (Elliot House, 113 Masons Hill, Bromley, Kent BR2 9HT Tel: 081-466 0098) which offers diagnosis, assessment, professional training and research.

PHAB

Physically Handicapped and Able-Bodied
12–14 London Road, Croydon, Surrey CR0 2TA
Telephone (081) 667 9443
Works for the integration of physically disabled and able-bodied people on equal terms, through a network of 500 clubs throughout the UK.

Queen Elizabeth Foundation for the Disabled

Leatherhead Court, Leatherhead, Surrey KT22 0BN
Telephone (0372) 842204
Assessment and training for employment, work schemes, information and holidays. For people with disabilities over the age of 16.

Radar

Royal Association for Disability and Rehabilitation
25 Mortimer Street, London W1N 8AB
Telephone (071) 637 5400
A campaigning and information-giving organisation. Also produces many useful publications.

Rescare

The National Society for Mentally Handicapped People in Residential Care
Rayner House, 23 Higher Hillgate, Stockport, Cheshire SK1 3ER
Telephone (061) 474 7323
          (061) 439 1548
A voluntary organisation dedicated to seeking a range of care provisions which include sheltered village communities as one of the choices available.

Riding for the Disabled

Avenue 'R', National Agriculture Centre, Kenilworth, Warwickshire CV8 2LY
Telephone (0203) 696510
Offers the opportunity of horse riding to any disabled person who might benefit from it in their general health and well-being

Spastics Society

12 Park Crescent, London W1N 4EQ
Telephone (071) 636 5020
Services for people with cerebral palsy (including those with learning disabilities): schools, further education and residential care.

Sense (National Deaf-Blind and Rubella Association)

11–13 Clifton Terrace, London N4 3SR
Telephone (071) 278 1005
The national voluntary organisation which campaigns for the needs of deaf-blind children and young adults, providing advice, support, information and services for them, their families and professionals in the field.

S.P.O.D. (Sexual and Personal Relationships of People with a Disability)

286 Camden Road, London N7 0BJ
Telephone (071) 607 8851/2
Advises on sexual and personal relationships, collects and publishes information.

VOCAL (Voluntary Orgainsations Communication and Language)

336 Brixton, London SW9 7AA
Provides information and works for better services; aims to increase awareness of communication disabilities and co-ordinates the efforts of member organisations.

Bibliography

Azrin, N.H. Sneed, T.J. & Foxx, R.M. (1973) Dry bed: A rapid method of eliminating bedwetting (enuresis) of the retarded. *Behaviour Research & Therapy* 11, 427–434

Bertsch, G. Fox, C.J. & Kwiecinski, J. (1984) Teaching developmentally disabled persons how to react to fires. *Applied Research in Mental Retardation* 5, 483–497

Boe, R.B. (1977) Economical procedures for the reduction of aggression in a residential setting. *Mental Retardation* 15, (5), 25–28

Campaign for Mentally Handicapped People. (1983) *Leisure.* (Discussion paper)

Carr, J. (1980) *Helping your Handicapped Child.* Harmondsworth: Penguin.

Carr, J. (1987) Bedwetting: a new approach to treatment in a mentally handicapped boy. *Child: Care, Health and Development* 13, 239–245.

Cole, C.L. Gardner, W.I. & Karan, D.C. (1985) Self management training of mentally retarded adults presenting severe conduct difficulties. *Applied Research in Mental Retardation* 6, 337–347

Craft, A. (ed.) (1986) *Mental Handicap and Sexuality: Issues and Perspectives.* London: Costello.

Craft, M. & Craft, A. (eds.) (1983) *Sex and the Mentally Handicapped.* London: Routledge and Kegan Paul.

Cullen, C. & Partridge, K. (1981) The constructional approach – a way of using different data. *Apex, Journal of the British Institute of Mental Handicap* 8, (4), 135–136.

de Kock, U. Mansell, J. Felce, D. & Jenkins, J. (1984) Establishing appropriate mealtime behaviour of a severely disruptive mentally handicapped woman. *Behavioural Psychotherapy* 12 (2), 175–187.

Donnellan, A. Mirenda, P.L. Mesaros, R.A. & Fassbender, L.L. (1984) Analysing the communicative functions of aberrant behaviour. *Journal of the Association for Persons with Severe Handicaps* 9 (3), 201–212.

Dorsey, M.F. Iwata, B.A. Ong, P. & McSween, T.G. (1980) Treatment of self injurious behaviour using a water mist: Initial response suppression and generalisation. *Journal of Applied Behavior Analysis* 13, 343–354.

Fleming, I. & Tosh, M. (1984) Self control procedures. A useful means of helping people who are mentally handicapped to overcome problems of temper and aggression. *Mental Handicap* 12, 110–111.

Foxx, R.M. & Dufrense, D (1984) 'Harry': the use of physical restraints as a reinforcer, timeout from restraint, and fading restraint in treating a self-injurious man. *Analysis and Intervention in Developmental Disabilities* 4, 1–13.

Goldiamond, I. (1974) Towards a constructional approach to social problems. Ethical and constitutional issues raised by applied behavioural analysis. *Behaviourism, 2,* 1–84.

H.M.S.O. (1971) *Better Services for the Mentally Handicapped.*

Hartmann, D.D. (1977) Consideration in the choice of interobserver reliability estimates. *Journal of Applied Behavior Analysis* 10, 103–116.

Hegeler, S. (1957) Peter and Caroline. London: Tavistock Publications (translated from Danish).

Iwata, B.A., Pace, G.M., Kalsher, M.J., Cowdrey, G.E. and Cataldo, M.F. (1990) Experimental analysis and extinction of self-injurious escape behavior. *Journal of Applied Behavior Analysis*, 23, 11–27.

King's Fund (1980) *An Ordinary Life* Project Paper 24. London: Kings Fund.

King's Fund (1984) *An ordinary working life*. Project Paper 50. London: Kings Fund.

King's Fund (1985) *The employment of people with mental handicap*. Project Paper 55. London: Kings Fund.

LaVigna, G.W. & Donnellan, A.M. (1986) Alternatives to punishment: solving behavior problems with non-aversive strategies. New York. Irvington.

Lerup, L. Conrath, D. & Lui, J.K.C. (1980) Fires in nursing facilities. In Canter D. (ed) *Fires and Human Behaviour*. New York: John Wiley & Sons.

Lovaas, O.I. & Simmons, J. (1969) Manipulation of self-destruction in three retarded children. *Journal of Applied Behavior Analysis* 2 (3), 143–157.

Murphy, G.M. & Wilson, B. (eds) (1985) Self-injurious behaviour. Kidderminster: B.I.M.H. Publications.

National Development Group (1977) *Pamphlet No.5.*

Porterfield, J. & Blunden, R. (1978) Establishing an activity period and individual skill training within a day setting for profoundly mentally handicapped adults. *Journal of Practical Approaches to Developmental Handicap* 2 (3), 10–15.

Richardson, J.S. & Zaleski, W.A. (1983) Naloxone and self-mutilation. *Biological Psychiatry* 18 (1), 99–101 and in Murphy, G. & Wilson, B. (eds) (1985) *Self-Injurious Behaviour*.p.290. Kidderminster: B.I.M.H. Publications

Robson, I. (1988) Overcoming nocturnal enuresis in a 16 year old with mental handicap: an alternative to the dry bed approach. *Behavioural Psychotherapy* 16, 115–121.

Roos, P. (1977) Ethical use of behaviour modification techniques. In Mittler, P. (ed). *Research to practice in mental retardation. Vol.1 Care and Intervention* IASSMD.

Salend, S.J. & Kovalich, B. (1981) A group response cost system mediated by free tokens: An alternative to token reinforcement. *American Journal of Mental Deficiency* 86 (2), 184–187.

Smith, L. (1981) Training severely and profoundly mentally handicapped nocturnal enuretics. *Behaviour Research and Therapy* 19, 67–74.

Sowers, J. Rush, F.R. Connis, R.T. & Cummings, L.E. (1980) Teaching mentally retarded adults to time manage in a vocational setting. *Journal of Applied Behavior Analysis* 13, 119–128

Tyne, A. (1981) *The principle of normalisation – a foundation for effective services*. CMH London.

Whelan, E. & Speake, B. (1981) *Getting to work*. Human Horizons Series. London: Souvenir Press.

Williams, P. & Shoultz, B. (1982) Speaking for ourselves. London: Souvenir Press.

Subject Index

Author Index